DEVELOPMENT CENTR

COMPETITION, INNOVATION AND COMPETITIVENESS IN DEVELOPING COUNTRIES

By
Lynn Krieger Mytelka

DEVELOPMENT CENTRE
OF THE ORGANISATION FOR ECONOMIC CO-OPERATION AND DEVELOPMENT

ORGANISATION FOR ECONOMIC CO-OPERATION AND DEVELOPMENT

Pursuant to Article 1 of the Convention signed in Paris on 14th December 1960, and which came into force on 30th September 1961, the Organisation for Economic Co-operation and Development (OECD) shall promote policies designed:

- to achieve the highest sustainable economic growth and employment and a rising standard of living in Member countries, while maintaining financial stability, and thus to contribute to the development of the world economy;
- to contribute to sound economic expansion in Member as well as non-member countries in the process of economic development; and
- to contribute to the expansion of world trade on a multilateral, non-discriminatory basis in accordance with international obligations.

The original Member countries of the OECD are Austria, Belgium, Canada, Denmark, France, Germany, Greece, Iceland, Ireland, Italy, Luxembourg, the Netherlands, Norway, Portugal, Spain, Sweden, Switzerland, Turkey, the United Kingdom and the United States. The following countries became Members subsequently through accession at the dates indicated hereafter: Japan (28th April 1964), Finland (28th January 1969), Australia (7th June 1971), New Zealand (29th May 1973), Mexico (18th May 1994), the Czech Republic (21st December 1995), Hungary (7th May 1996), Poland (22nd November 1996) and Korea (12th December 1996). The Commission of the European Communities takes part in the work of the OECD (Article 13 of the OECD Convention).

The Development Centre of the Organisation for Economic Co-operation and Development was established by decision of the OECD Council on 23rd October 1962 and comprises twenty-three Member countries of the OECD: Austria, Belgium, Canada, the Czech Republic, Denmark, Finland, France, Germany, Greece, Iceland, Ireland, Italy, Japan, Korea, Luxembourg, Mexico, the Netherlands, Norway, Poland, Portugal, Spain, Sweden and Switzerland, as well as Argentina and Brazil from March 1994, and Chile since November 1998. The Commission of the European Communities also takes part in the Centre's Advisory Board.

The purpose of the Centre is to bring together the knowledge and experience available in Member countries of both economic development and the formulation and execution of general economic policies; to adapt such knowledge and experience to the actual needs of countries or regions in the process of development and to put the results at the disposal of the countries by appropriate means.

The Centre has a special and autonomous position within the OECD which enables it to enjoy scientific independence in the execution of its task. Nevertheless, the Centre can draw upon the experience and knowledge available in the OECD in the development field.

Publié en français sous le titre :

CONCURRENCE, INNOVATION ET COMPÉTITIVITÉ
DANS LES PAYS EN DÉVELOPPEMENT

*

* *

Foreword

This publication was undertaken in the context of the OECD Development Centre's research programme on Globalisation and Regionalisation. The programme seeks to assess the risks and benefits for both developing and OECD Member countries from international economic opening.

Table of Contents

Acknowledgements

The papers in this volume have benefited immeasurably from comments provided by Fabio Erber, Martin Fransman, Ulrich Hiemenz, Steffan Jacobsen, Charles Oman and Sandra Thomas, who participated in an OECD Development Centre Workshop held to discuss first drafts of these papers.

Preface

Vigorous inter–firm price competition on domestic markets is a necessary part of the foundation on which to build an economy's ability to compete in international markets. This view, long held by OECD countries, is increasingly shared by governments in the large number of non–OECD countries that have undertaken the sea change from highly inward-oriented to more outward-oriented, market-friendly growth strategies over the last decade. The question many countries in the latter group now face is: do trade liberalisation and domestic deregulation suffice as policies to ensure vigorous domestic inter-firm price competition, or are other policies also required to ensure that competition?

This question is particularly relevant for developing countries and the answer is not obvious for several reasons. First, the problem of concentrated power structures and uncompetitive domestic markets is often considerably more acute in developing countries than it is in developed countries. Second, at the same time, because of the relatively small size of firms in developing countries (compared to developed countries' powerful multinational corporations), these countries widely perceive a need to promote the concentration of capital in the hands of whatever local firms might be able to compete in global markets. The liberalisation of trade policy in developing countries and their attempt to compete in global markets has tended, if anything, to reinforce this perception in recent years.

The present study addresses this crucial policy issue by introducing another critical variable: innovation. Since competition in the current context of globalisation is increasingly innovation-based, it is particularly important for technological "latecomers" — a category to which most developing and newly industrialising countries belong — to ask how innovation fits into the relationship between competition and competitiveness. More precisely, how does competition affect innovation and how does innovation relate to competitiveness in developing countries?

By focusing on the concrete experiences of Brazil, Chinese Taipei, India and Korea in specific industries — machine tools, pharmaceuticals, telecommunications and biotechnology — the study seeks to answer this question. Both "success" and "failure" case studies illustrate that there are no simple answers. However, the study highlights the importance for latecomers of *continuous* innovation over time — in the way they produce as well as in what they produce — so that costs decline and quality improves constantly. Latecomers thus need policies to stimulate the development of appropriate management and organisational techniques as well as the development of a domestic science and technology base, however thin, that is closely linked to enterprises and production. The study also underlines the importance of avoiding policy vacillations that can easily undermine the stability that long–term deepening of industrial capabilities requires.

Written by a diverse group of distinguished specialists headed by Professor Lynn Mytelka, this study constitutes an important product of the Development Centre's research on Globalisation and Competition.

Jean Bonvin
President
OECD Development Centre

January 1999

Contributors

Rohini ACHARYA is Senior Research Fellow in International Economics at the Royal Institute of International Affairs, London, and former Programme Officer in biotechnology at the International Federation of Institutes for Advanced Study (IFIAS), Maastricht.

Hanumantha CHARYA is Corporate Economist with Hero Honda Motors Limited, New Delhi, and formerly Economist at the National Council of Applied Economic Research, New Delhi.

François CHESNAIS is Professor of Economics, Université Paris–XIII, Villetaneuse, and former principal administrator in the Directorate of Science, Technology and Industry at the OECD, Paris.

Ashok V. DESAI is Consultant Editor of the *Business Standard*, a financial newspaper published from Delhi and Calcutta, and former Chief Consultant to the Indian Ministry of Finance.

Hwan–Suk KIM is Assistant Professor, Department of Sociology, Kookmin University, Korea, and former Head, Industrial Innovation Research Division, Science and Technology Policy Institute (STEPI) of the Korea Institute of Science and Technology (KIST).

Marc LAUTIER is Assistant Professor in Economics at the Université Paris–VIII and former consultant in international development with the Association pour la Promotion et le Développement Industriel, working in Thailand and Korea.

Lynn Krieger MYTELKA, currently the Director of UNCTAD's Division on Investment, Enterprise Development and Technology, in Geneva, was previously Professor of Political Economy, Institute of Political Economy, Carleton University, Ottawa, and a research director at the Centre de Recherches sur les Entreprises Multinationales (CEREM), Université Paris–X, Nanterre.

Contributors

Executive Summary

"International competitiveness" has become a widely accepted objective — indeed, a priority — of economic policy in most developed and developing countries. In view of the increasingly important role played by international trade in the economies of most countries, this emphasis is not difficult to understand. But how should a country go about increasing its international competitiveness and, equally importantly, maintaining its competitiveness once it has been achieved?

There is one strand in the literature that gives an attractively straightforward answer to this question. To put it simply, it is argued that competition is both a necessary and a sufficient condition for the achievement of international competitiveness. The creation of competitive conditions, so the argument goes, will create both the pressures and the incentives to make firms internationally competitive. The policy imperative that follows from this argument is equally straightforward: create competitive conditions. This will be sufficient to facilitate the achievement of international competitiveness.

While the simplicity of this argument and its policy implications are undoubtedly attractive, a more careful examination shows, alas, that in the real world things are unlikely to be so simple. Several points will make this clear. To begin with, it is necessary to be more rigorous in analysing the mechanisms that allegedly will have the effect of producing international competitiveness once competitive conditions have been created (leaving aside the important question of what precisely is meant by "competitive conditions"and how we know in practice when they have been created).

The argument suggests not only that competitive conditions will create pressures and incentives for the improvement of efficiency (in terms of costs and/or quality), but that these pressures and incentives will be *sufficient* to generate international competitiveness — that is, competitiveness in cost and/or quality relative to the other international competitors in the market. The problem, of course, arises with the second part of the last sentence. The reason is that it is by no means intuitively, empirically, or theoretically obvious that competitive pressures and incentives will be sufficient to generate international competitiveness.

Moreover, looked at from the other side, it is clear that in some cases the creation of less–than–competitive situations has been accompanied by the emergence of international competitiveness. An example is the Japanese automobile industry, which began in the 1930s under conditions of heavy protection and government subsidy — conditions that were continued until the 1970s, although in modified form. While there were several competitors in Japan and while domestic competition is an important part of this Japanese success story, it is clear that in the early period international competition was severely limited and that Japanese firms were at first internationally inefficient, with the result that it would be wrong to suggest that "competitive conditions" existed in Japan during this period. While the evidence is not yet completely in, something similar appears to be happening in the Korean telecommunications industry and in the Indian pharmaceutical industry.

It must be concluded, therefore, that the relationship between "competition" and "competitiveness" is more complex than this strand of literature suggests. This raises the next question: How might the robustness of the arguments regarding the causes of competitiveness be improved?

The present study makes a contribution towards answering this question. We therefore need to make quite clear what our study does and, equally importantly, what it does not do. To begin with the latter, the study does not purport to provide a quantitative analysis of the causes of competitiveness. While such studies have their utility, we are also conscious of the significant difficulties that arise in attempting to get adequate measures of the "independent variables", variables that will capture the complex processes that lead to the achievement and maintenance of competitiveness.

Rather, the study draws conceptually on another strand in the literature which emphasizes the importance of the process of innovation. The argument, simply put, is that while competition may be necessary for the achievement of competitiveness, it is not sufficient. Nor is it sufficient, from a dynamic perspective, in maintaining competitiveness. What is also usually needed are innovative processes which will lead to the improvement of processes, products, management and organisational routines. Equally important, these innovative processes themselves have complex determinants that also need to be understood if the ultimate objective of increased competitiveness is to be achieved.

The study addresses the problem of competitiveness within the context of developing countries. It does this by examining the problem of competitiveness and its relationship with competition and innovation across four countries and four industries. The four countries are: Brazil, Chinese Taipei, India and Korea. The four industries are: machine tools, petrochemicals, pharmaceuticals and telecommunications equipment. Over 60 firms in these four industries were interviewed. The objective of the analysis was to examine more closely the interaction between changes in the set of policies that have shaped competition within these national markets over time and the behaviour of local firms with respect to innovation and competitiveness, and to do so within the context of changing global competitive requirements in these four industries.

While there are obvious methodological problems of extension in the use of a case study approach, this method is nonetheless important — indeed, perhaps necessary — to a better understanding of the complex processes that underlie the achievement of international competitiveness.

Both Brazil and Korea, for example, embarked upon a conscious process to develop the petrochemical industry in the 1960s and the telecommunications industry in the 1980s. For the most part this was done behind protective barriers and the state played an important role in reducing the risks of investment and in providing access to technology. Firms in both countries accumulated technological capabilities but in each case local enterprises, whether foreign subsidiaries, joint ventures or wholly locally owned firms, became highly complacent with respect to innovation. Costs remained relatively high, product ranges were limited, and few linkages were developed between in–house R&D and product development activities.

Initially the expansion of productive capacity and the development of technological capabilities in the two countries proceeded at a similar pace; then the trajectories diverged. That divergence was accelerated by changes in the requirements of international competition which rendered the sequencing and timing of policies to strengthen the competitiveness of local firms, as they faced increased competition, all the more critical. In the Korean petrochemical and telecommunications industries, domestic restructuring and deregulation prior to market opening pushed local firms to break with their traditional habits and practices and gave them a breathing space within which to do so. Tariff reductions were introduced very slowly and only after considerable domestic restructuring of industry had taken place. In fact, reforms in Korea were first aimed at transforming both the ownership structure and the regulatory environment of the telecommunications industry. The way privatisation took place also strengthened locally owned firms, and not until policy reforms had begun to stimulate these firms to look for new ways of competing was the market opened to foreign competition. In the telecommunications industry, where international competitiveness required the development of a vastly more elaborate marketing structure capable of working with a host of corporate and institutional users across a wide range of countries, sustained support in the form of public sector R&D and export marketing assistance was a major asset for Korean firms. Korean firms thus had both the time and the resources needed to adjust. The same cannot be said for Brazil, where radical deregulation coupled with rapid market opening sharply increased foreign competition on the local market, altering the preference of foreign firms for imports over domestic production and reducing the ability of smaller, independent firms to maintain their competitiveness through innovation.

The relationship between competition, innovation and competitiveness was also more complex in the Indian and Chinese Taipei machine tool and bio–pharmaceutical industries than anticipated. Macroeconomic policies were similar across both these industries in Chinese Taipei, yet the machine tool industry is noted for its innovativeness, and it exports a large percentage of output, while the pharmaceutical industry lags considerably behind. In contrast, not only is the Indian pharmaceutical industry more innovative and competitive than the Indian machine tool industry but pharmaceutical firms in India appear to have been more innovative than those in Chinese Taipei, despite a macroeconomic environment that is generally regarded as less favourable to competition, innovation and competitiveness. Here, too, the explanation lies not in a single factor but in a more thorough understanding of the way in which traditional habits and practices of local firms with respect to competition and innovation developed, and of the kinds of policies that might reshape or reinforce them. It is in this context that competition policies clearly have a role to play, but their impact is both temporally and contextually conditioned.

Much of the variance within and across countries, these studies suggest, can be explained, not by simple dichotomies such as open vs. closed markets or the market vs. the state, but by the interaction of many disparate factors, of which four stand out in particular. These are *i)* the type, timing and sequencing of market–opening policies; *ii)* the traditional habits and practices of firms with respect to competition and innovation, and hence the differing policy dynamics which result from the interaction between policies and the actors whose behaviour they are designed to influence; *iii)* the extent to which firms have access, either in–house or through local networks of innovation, to the critical complementary assets — technological capabilities and financing — needed to respond to the new policy environment; and *iv)* changes in technology and in the rules of competition which alter the set of opportunities and constraints for latecomer firms at different points in time.

From this disaggregated perspective emerges a number of guidelines for policy–makers in the design of policies to promote competitiveness and strengthen the national system of innovation. These have been left to the concluding chapter, but a few summary remarks can be made here. First, it is necessary to stress the overall conclusion that there are, unfortunately, no simple "quick fix" answers to what in effect is a highly complex problem. Second, the case studies show that opportunities for local firms to catch up and to maintain competitiveness over time in these four industries have been affected by the nature and pace of innovation in the global industry, by the industry's structure and by capital requirements at various stages in the production process. Monitoring changes in these global industries and adjusting policies on a continuous basis are needed in designing effective policies for technological catch–up. Third, the case studies provide empirical support for the position that policy dynamics — that is, the interaction between policies and the behaviour of actors they are designed to affect — are critical in shaping policy outcomes with respect to innovation and competitiveness. Complementary policies might thus be required to provide added support or stimulus when competition alone is not effective in promoting innovation and competitiveness. Lastly, from an innovation–based perspective, policy–makers need to pay greater attention to the type, timing and sequencing of market–opening policies, as these interact with the traditional habits and practices of firms across industries with significantly different characteristics.

I

Competition, Innovation and Competitiveness: A Framework for Analysis

Lynn Krieger Mytelka

Introduction

Much of the development literature on competition and competitiveness proceeds from the "market opening" perspective stressed by the World Bank and the IMF; it assumes there is a positive and direct relationship between these two variables[1]. In contrast, the literature on competition in advanced industrial countries focuses less on the competitiveness that trade liberalisation is assumed to stimulate, and considerably more on the welfare implications[2] of anti–trust policy. Neither of these approaches is wholly satisfactory today, in large part because of the increasingly important role that innovation plays in both advanced industrial countries and in developing countries in creating and sustaining competitiveness[3]. Following broadly the approach to innovation developed by those working within the evolutionary economics perspective[4], the framework for analysis presented here, therefore, assigns a critical linkage role to innovation in the relationship between competition and competitiveness.

This chapter begins by looking briefly at some of the paradoxes associated with traditional approaches to competitiveness. The second section disaggregates innovation strategies and elaborates upon the differing historical habits and practices of targeted actors that shape policy dynamics and thus affect policy outcomes with respect to innovation and competitiveness. The third moves on to examine the conditions under which innovation is stimulated, widening the perspective beyond competition policies and practices to include a variety of factors that create a demand for innovation or promote the use of new technologies. The final section presents the case studies to which this framework has been applied in subsequent chapters. These are the machine tool industry in Chinese Taipei and India, telecommunications and petrochemicals in Brazil and Korea, and the application of biotechnology in the pharmaceutical industries of India and Chinese Taipei.

The study is based on over 60 firm–level interviews within these four industrial sectors. Its objective, however, is not to engage in a broad econometric analysis of the relationship between competition and competitiveness at the aggregate level. Rather, it is to examine more closely the interaction between changes in the set of policies that have shaped competition within these national markets over time and the behaviour of local firms with respect to innovation and competitiveness and to do so within the context of changing competitive requirements in these four globalised industries. From this disaggregated perspective emerge a number of guidelines for policy–makers in developing countries in their attempt to evaluate the likely impact of policies designed to affect competition, on the innovation and competitiveness of domestic firms.

Creating and Sustaining Competitiveness

From a macroeconomic perspective, competitiveness has traditionally been seen as a question of prices, costs and exchange rates[5]. Its measurement is most often based on changes in market share. In the late 1970s, Nicholas Kaldor pointed to a number of curious paradoxes generated by the application of this conventional approach. Contrary to received theory, a fall in relative unit wage costs and in export prices, he demonstrated, was correlated with the loss of export market shares in manufacturing in the cases of the United States and the United Kingdom and conversely, a rise in relative unit wage costs and export prices took place alongside an increase in export shares for Germany and Japan (Kaldor, 1978, 1981). Later this would be shown to hold for the United States as well. Clearly there were intervening factors that these analyses did not capture. A more systematic analysis of the relationship between changes in costs and prices and export performance was thus needed.

Similar paradoxes emerged with regard to the assumed direct linkage between productivity growth and competitiveness. During the 1980s it became widely acknowledged that growth in non–material investment[6] contributes significantly to gains in productivity[7]. Nonetheless, the new growth models, designed to explore the relationship between productivity and growth, continued to resort to traditional calculations of productivity growth. Indeed, as Paul Romer recently wrote, "[m]y greatest regret is the shift I made...away from the emphasis on research and knowledge that characterised my 1986 paper and toward the emphasis on physical capital...Looking back, I suspect that I made this shift...partly in an attempt to conform to the norms of what constituted convincing empirical work in macroeconomics" (Romer, 1994, 20)[8]. As a result, such models have been unable to deal with empirical "anomalies" that show rising productivity levels going hand–in–hand with declining sectoral competitiveness[9] or the converse, dramatic export growth in countries like Chinese Taipei and Korea where "overall productivity growth in industry has not been spectacular...and can explain only a small part of total growth" (Rodrik, 1994, 15).

In search of an explanation for these "perverse' results Jan Fagerberg developed a model of international competitiveness that relates growth in market shares to technology, price and the ability to compete in delivery on the basis of sufficient prior investment. The result of his study shows that

> the main factors influencing differences in international competitiveness and growth across countries are technological competitiveness and the ability to compete on delivery. Regarding the latter, the findings point out the crucial role played by investment in creating new production capacity and exploiting the potential offered by diffusion processes and growth in national technological competitiveness. Cost–competitiveness does also affect competitiveness and growth to some extent, but less so than many seem to believe[10].

Cost competitiveness in export markets, moreover, may merely reflect conjunctural factors such as changes in exchange rates[11] which create temporary advantages or fluctuations in global demand which give rise to non–sustainable opportunities. Firms that are able to sell their products domestically in the absence of high levels of protection are also competitive, but the low–wage advantage or segmented markets[12] upon which they depend cannot survive in an increasingly globalised economy. To sustain their competitiveness such firms will also have to become more innovative.

Recent econometric work on the sustainability of export growth similarly shows that late industrialisers were able to maintain their export competitiveness by diversifying away from specialisations that involved products for which world demand was growing only slowly (Busson and Villa, 1994). Detailed case studies reveal that their ability to do so depended upon a conscious effort to deepen the industrialisation process and widen industry's linkage to the science and technology infrastructure[13], a point captured in the literature on "national systems of innovation" and "structural competitiveness" (Nelson and Rosenberg, 1993; Lundvall, 1992; Chesnais, 1986; OECD, 1992).

Underlying the "system of innovation' approach is a resurgence of interest in innovation and a reconceptualisation of the firm as a learning organisation embedded within a broader institutional context (Nelson, 1981; Nelson and Winter, 1982; Freeman, 1988; Freeman and Perez, 1988; Lundvall, 1988). From this perspective competitiveness can be seen as the outcome of a continuous process of innovation that enables firms to catch up and to keep up as technology and the mode of competition change. Understanding how competitiveness is created and sustained in developing countries thus requires a deeper analysis of the factors that motivate and support a process of innovation within firms in those countries. Yet much of the conventional literature associates innovation with the kind of activity undertaken by firms at the frontier.

Catching Up, Keeping Up and Getting Ahead

Following Ernst, Ganiatsos and Mytelka (1995), however, innovation can be defined more broadly "as the process by which firms master and implement the design and production of goods and services that are new to them, irrespective of whether or not they are new to their competitors — domestic or foreign". This approach enables us to include the catch–up strategies associated with latecomers, along with strategies to keep up and to get ahead[14]. In so doing we reject the position that "learners by definition do not innovate" (Amsden, 1989) and adopt the view that catching up is the period when the successful latecomer firm "learns to learn"[15], a skill which it can later apply to any product or process. Table 1.1 elaborates upon the characteristic forms of innovative behaviour that each of these strategies encompasses.

Catch–up strategies, for example, involve the building of problem–solving capabilities that enable the firm to improve its productivity, to imitate and to adapt product, process and organisational technologies already developed elsewhere. In newly industrialising economies, catching up critically depends upon deepening production capabilities, thereby ensuring that the clones, copies or OEM goods are, at the least, of similar quality and yet initially competitive because they are cheaper. By turning themselves into learning institutions, firms which "learn to learn" during the catch–up phase are in a position to sustain their competitiveness over the longer term, a point which emerges clearly in the case of the Chinese Taipei machine tool industry and to a lesser extent in that of the application of biotechnology by firms in the Indian pharmaceutical industry.

Catch–up strategies are most likely to succeed when *i)* the target is clear — a product or process whose characteristics are widely known or obtainable through such means as reverse engineering and licensing, *ii)* the technology is incremental, thereby permitting enough time to build technological capabilities by starting with an earlier generation, and *iii)* the components and skill inputs are easily identified and relatively freely available, through purchase, hire or local development. The classic post–war example of a successfully pursued catch–up strategy was the Japanese VLSI project (Levy and Samuels, 1990; Fransman, 1990; Kodama, 1991). A similar catch–up strategy was pursued in the development of digital telecommunications switches in Korea.

Keeping up is more difficult than catching up because the target is much closer, the technology still in flux and there is less time to put the package of components and skills together. It thus requires a more substantial science and technology infrastructure on which it can draw rapidly for new inputs, a strong production base to move down the cost curve quickly, and the design and development capabilities to go beyond imitation to the introduction of variety. As one recent OECD document pointed out, moreover, innovative behaviour is not simply an attribute of individual firms. Rather, to a large extent, it results from "national or local environments where organisational and institutional developments have produced conditions conducive to the growth of interactive mechanisms on which innovation and the diffusion of technology are based" (OECD, 1992)[16]. Nowhere is this more evident than in supporting quick follower strategies. Since keeping up is a continuous process, moreover, it is predicated upon having sufficient financial resources to move products to the market early enough in the product cycle so as to capture market share and generate the revenue needed for investment in successive product generations.

If catching up and keeping up are difficult processes, they are still more predictable than getting ahead. Front runners, for example, have no firm targets to guide their choices. Unlike quick followers, they derive few learning benefits from the failures of their predecessors (Freeman, 1974). Uncertainty affects decisions such as which combination of generic technologies might produce a product acceptable to consumers or which new frontiers will yield the greatest benefits. Whether hot pursuit, a rupture in the technological trajectory or a change in standards will deprive them of the rents that make such races rewarding cannot be predicted with much certainty. To hedge against the high costs, risks and uncertainties involved in competing at the frontier, would–be front runners have increasingly complemented in–house research and development with a wide array of R&D, production and marketing partnerships[17].

Not all firms, however, pursue innovation strategies, whether of the catch–up, keep–up or get–ahead variety. Much depends upon the set of habits and practices they have developed to deal with the challenges of change and competition. When these historical habits, practices and routines are generalised across many firms and achieve some measure of longevity, they become important elements in determining policy dynamics and hence policy outcomes. Only by understanding the historical habits and practices of targeted actors can policies be devised to strengthen and/or change them. A few examples will illustrate this point.

Small industrialists who are risk–adverse, for example, may not be as responsive to a credit–based stimulus for investment in new machinery and equipment as they would to a risk–spreading inducement to innovate. It was precisely this kind of reasoning that lay behind the Japanese government's decision to create the Japan Robot Leasing Corporation as a means to diffuse robot technology more rapidly to small and medium–sized enterprises. To take another example, a small firm whose management has traditionally used retained earnings to finance its investments might be reluctant to incur debts in order to innovate. In France, where this was typical of small tradition–bound textile manufacturers in the early 1970s, tax credits intended to stimulate innovation were used instead to reduce the firm's debt burden. By adopting a short–term perspective on the need for change, such firms failed to adjust in an incremental fashion as competitive pressures increased. Ultimately, many of them went into receivership.

Policy dynamics consist principally of the interaction between policies and the actors whose behaviour they are designed to influence. But each of these elements is embedded in other structures and systems. Innovation policy, for example, is part of a larger set of sometimes complementary, sometimes contradictory policies whose interaction will affect policy dynamics by shaping the parameters within which firms make decisions. Firms, moreover, are embedded in a variety of national and international structures involving social regularities that govern behaviour. These rules, norms and expectations[18] differ in different spatial and temporal contexts.

Table 1.1 **Innovation Strategies and Their Characteristics**

Innovation Strategy	Catch–Up Strategies (latecomer)	Keep–Up Strategies (quick follower)	Get–Ahead Strategies (front runner)
Capabilities	*i)* problem solving innovation - attention to "know-why" - learning to learn *ii)* improvements in productivity and machinery maintenance *iii)* imitation *iv)* adaptation	*i)* introduction of variety *ii)* improvement in quality *iii)* reduction in costs *iv)* incremental change	*i)* new combinations of generic technologies *ii)* pushing back the frontiers of knowledge
Critical Knowledge Inputs	Engineering and management capabilities: feedback from the production process, product scanning and adaptation capabilities.	Engineering, testing, design and marketing: linking design and production within the firm.	Scientific research and scaling up of laboratory models. Linking of R&D and marketing within the firm.
Policy Objectives	Technology transfer, diffusion, demonstration, training	Technology development, R&D networking	In-house research, technology development; R&D networking
Useful Partnership Linkages	To apprenticeship programmes, productivity centres, clients, equipment suppliers and intermediaries	To university engineering faculties, consultancy firms, design centres, technology institutes, users	Windowing through a broad array of long–term R&D collaborative projects with research institutions, users & materials suppliers

Competition and Innovation: Evidence for a Link?

Stressing the importance of innovation to competitiveness does not negate a role for competition as a stimulus to innovation. Thus Michael Porter's research suggests that "vigorous domestic rivalry" is a critical factor in stimulating firms "to innovate in ways that upgrade the[ir] competitive advantages" (Porter, 1990). But as Nathan Rosenberg (1976) points out, competition is only one such stimulus. Moreover, there are paradoxes here, too, as the work of Alfred Chandler, Jr. (1990) shows by documenting the waves of mergers and acquisitions at the end of the 19th century in the United States that took place in precisely those industries undergoing technological change.

As production becomes more knowledge–intensive in all industries and as competition globalises, institutional support for research and development and for innovation more broadly has also emerged as an important factor in the competitiveness of firms and of industrial sectors. A number of scholars have used these new developments to support arguments for government policies to promote large firms (Teece, 1989; Amsden, 1992). Yet the market power exercised by large firms might reduce the incentive to innovate. While considerable work has been undertaken with respect to innovation and competition policies in the advanced industrial countries, as Sanjaya Lall (1990) points out, "[t]his whole area of policy making is under–researched ... as far as developing countries are concerned."

In what follows we take a closer look at the spectrum of policies and practices that might stimulate innovation and thus competitiveness. Although policies and practices interact with each other and may thus set up both counterproductive cross pressures and positive reinforcement, for analytical purposes, Table 1.2 divides the pressures for innovation into those emanating from various forms of competition and those which are pulled by demand or pushed by supply.

Table 1.2. **Factors Stimulating Innovation**

Competitive pressures emanating from	Demand pull or supply push generated by
Characteristics of the industrial structure	Production problems within the firm
Emulation of the practices of others	Requirements of suppliers or clients
Imports	Developments in other sectors
Government policies	Government policies

Among the former are the classic pressures to reduce prices or improve products that result from the introduction of competition into domestic markets through imports or through changes in the industrial structure, for example, by encouraging new entrants, breaking up monopolies or otherwise affecting the market power of firms. Under certain circumstances, however, each of these policies has the potential to generate quite different policy dynamics and hence outcomes. In the case of imports, for example:

> where foreign suppliers have market power, domestic prices will not be reduced to the full extent of a tariff cut. Indeed, in any circumstance where the supply of imports is not perfectly elastic, a reduction in tariffs is unlikely to be fully matched by a reduction in the domestic price. The impact of freer international trade on domestic prices can also be diluted by the strategic responses of domestic oligopolists. A tariff reduction can even lead to an increase in domestic prices if competition among domestic suppliers is imperfect and the tariff reduction makes import deterrence through low pricing unfeasible. Such findings as these imply that trade liberalisation and globalisation should not, in general, be viewed as satisfactory substitutes for an effective competition policy in constraining the exercise of market power domestically (Anderson and Dev Khosla, 1995).

From an innovation perspective, firms which do not have a habit of competing may not be able to adjust with sufficient rapidity to rising imports. A lack of supporting mechanisms such as export credits and R&D financing may also limit a firm's capacity to respond to imports that cut too quickly into the firm's market share. The introduction of competition through radical trade liberalisation, for example, had negative consequences for innovation and competitiveness in a number of Latin American countries. In the absence of policies to facilitate their adjustment, many competitive forms went bankrupt in Argentina under Videla (Chudnovsky, López and Porta, 1994), sank or switched from production to importing under the Pinochet regime in Chile (Pietrobelli, 1994)[19], or, as in Mexico at the end of the 1980s, cut back on technological activities, substituting licensing for innovation in order to respond rapidly to the new competitive pressures (Unger, 1992). Savage competition of this sort thus did not contribute to the gales of creative destruction that Schumpeter advocated.

Radical trade liberalisation, however, is not the only means to stimulate the kind of competitive pressures that lead to innovation and competitiveness. Government policies that are not directly targeted at changing the pattern of domestic competition might, under certain conditions, be more effective in promoting the kind of competitive pressure that leads to innovation. In exchange for credit facilities and procurement contracts, for example, pressures derived from the imposition of performance criteria, especially those related to exporting, have been shown to stimulate the catch–up process in several Asian countries (Amsden, 1989; Rodrik, 1994; Wade, 1990). Once again, however, the need to consider the historical habits and practices of firms when designing policies to stimulate innovation and competitiveness is critical. Thus, while performance criteria have led some firms consciously to adopt best practice and innovate in products, processes, or management routines, they have led others to rely too heavily on sub–

contracting or OEM relationships that are sustainable only as long as the firm remains a least–cost supplier. As wages rise, the failure to innovate results in an erosion of competitiveness[20].

Similarly, pressures emanating from the need or desire to emulate the practices of others may give rise to contradictory outcomes with respect to innovation and competitiveness. Consider the pressure of emulation that contributed to the development of a culture of innovation in Silicon Valley (Saxenian, 1995) and produced the kind of inter–firm rivalry which, despite the oligopolistic structure of Japan's electronics and automobile industries, stimulated innovation there (Porter, 1990; Womack, Jones and Roos, 1990). In contrast, emulation was a negative factor for innovation in Korea where the nature of competition among that country's chaebols involved an imitative pattern of continuous diversification with, until recently, little of the technological deepening required to sustain competitiveness in the long term (Mytelka and Ernst, 1995). In Argentina, the presence of large foreign pharmaceutical firms created emulative practices with both positive and negative effects for competitiveness. Unable to compete on the technological frontier, Argentinean–owned firms were induced to compete through product differentiation, investing primarily in minor modifications to existing products and expending considerable sums on advertising to develop the brand loyalty that builds market share. While this had some positive effects for the maintenance and development of R&D capabilities in the Argentinean pharmaceutical industry, it raised drug prices overall because of the higher advertising costs that oligopolistic market competition involves and the therapeutic benefits that resulted from the differentiated products marketed by local firms were questionable (Chudnovsky, 1979).

In addition to the dynamics generated by trade and competition policies, the literature is replete with examples of how innovative behaviour has been pulled by the requirements of suppliers or clients (Lundvall, 1988; Ernst, Ganiatsos and Mytelka, 1995), pushed by the need to expand output or resolve internal bottlenecks (Rosenberg, 1976; Rosenberg and Frischtak, 1985; Katz, 1987; Fransman and King, 1984) and pulled by developments in other sectors, notably defence industries (Chesnais, 1990). Which policies work best and under which conditions, however, requires further research. So, too, does the way differing policy dynamics are generated by the interaction of policies and the behaviour of targeted actors.

The Case Studies

The case studies presented in the following chapters examine the relationship between competition, innovation and competitiveness in four industries: machine tools, telecommunications, petrochemicals, and biotechnology. These industries represent, in the words of François Perroux, *industries industrialisantes* — that is industries whose successful development has ramifications for other industrial sectors and indeed for development more broadly. They are either fundamental to a broad "technological revolution" as in telecommunications and biotechnology, or produce basic capital and intermediate goods entering into a wide spectrum of other industrial activities such as petrochemicals and machine tools. In each of these industries, moreover, innovation is particularly important for competitiveness. This makes it possible to focus less on the link between innovation and competitiveness and more on the way in which competition is or is not needed to stimulate innovation.

By taking a sectoral approach and applying it cross–nationally to four countries, Brazil, India, Korea and Chinese Taipei, the studies in this volume have been able to match windows of opportunity for the entry of latecomers within these industries to a variety of national policy initiatives and to assess the impact of these policies on the habits and practices of local firms with respect to innovation and competitiveness. The research design for this study was also consciously constructed so as to permit both within–country comparisons in which the policy environment could be held constant across sectors and same–sector, cross–country comparisons in which differences in policies and their impact on firm–level innovation and competitiveness could be analysed. As the case studies look at the evolution of policies from the 1970s into the 1990s, inter–temporal comparisons further widened the base of possible observations.

From an orthodox perspective, these comparisons produced a number of counter–intuitive outcomes that required explanation. Consider the development of the machine tool and pharmaceutical industries in Chinese Taipei. During the 1970s and 1980s entry into these two industries was relatively easy either because investment costs were low, in the former, or because licensing from abroad provided opportunities for local firms, in the latter. Throughout this period the domestic market could be characterized as competitive and publicly funded R&D became available to support innovation in both industries. One might have expected that the two industries would thus evolve in a similar fashion. Yet over time firms in the machine tool and pharmaceutical industries diverged markedly in their innovativeness and their ability to export. Clearly the policy environment alone was not determinant. Nor were differences in industry characteristics a critical factor, when the evolution of the machine tool and pharmaceutical industries in Chinese Taipei and India are compared.

Anomalies also appeared in cross–national comparisons. During the 1980s, for example, Brazil and Korea embarked upon a conscious process to develop their telecommunications equipment industry. For the most part this was done behind protective barriers and the state played an important role in reducing the risks of investment and in providing access to technology[21]. As might be expected, in both cases local enterprises[22] became highly complacent. Their costs were well above international best practice and they did not export. Yet a scant five years later, firms in Korea had re–engineered their products, substantially cut costs and were exporting, while those in Brazil floundered. How might we account for this radical divergence in what initially appeared to be similar trajectories? In the four chapters which follow, we seek to explain these anomalies by looking more closely at changes in the sequencing and the set of policies that shape competition in the domestic market and support innovation in local firms, focusing in particular on the interaction between these policies and the behaviour of actors whose habits and practices with respect to innovation they were designed to affect.

Notes

1. See, for example, Balassa *et al.* (1982). For an alternative view see Westphal (1982). A good survey is contained in Sachwald (1993).

2. Notably in terms of lower prices and rents and a more efficient allocation of resources throughout an economy (Scherer, 1980).

3. For a more complete discussion of this point see Mytelka (1991) and (1994).

4. This perspective traces its roots to the work of Joseph Schumpeter (1939) and more recently that of Nelson and Winter (1982), Freeman (1982) and Lundvall (1988) among others.

5. The conventional position with respect to Korea, for example, is taken in Rhee, Ross–Larson and Pursell (1984), while Amsden (1989) argues for "getting prices wrong". Along similar lines, Rodrik in a more recent article suggests that high growth rates in Korea and Chinese Taipei were triggered by government policies that increased the profitability of activities associated with investment in export–oriented manufacturing (Rodrik, 1994).

6. This is understood to include research and development as well as design, engineering, marketing and management capabilities (Mytelka, 1987*a* and 1987*b*; OECD, 1992, 48–58 and 113–35; Commission, 1994, 49).

7. A well documented case is the Japanese automobile industry. See Womack, Jones and Roos (1990).

8. See also Fagerberg's (1994) observation that growth models which proceed from very different assumptions tend to be reductionist in much the same way and fall back upon a similar set of proxy variables.

9. Thus productivity levels in the United States and France have frequently exceeded those of Japan in industrial sectors where the latter is clearly more competitive when measured by export success and market shares. Over the period 1973 to 1990, for example, the contribution of total factor productivity to GDP growth was identical in France and Japan (CEPII, 1992, 27) and average growth in total factor productivity in France and the United Kingdom was superior to that in Japan in both the 1979–85 and 1985–89 periods (CEPII, 1992, 49). In the manufacturing sector, the growth in the productivity of capital over the period 1985–89 was eight times higher in the United States than in Japan (CEPII, 1992, 54).

10. Fagerberg (1987). See also his "Why Growth Rates Differ" where his econometric model of economic growth leads him to conclude that there is "a close relation between economic growth and growth of national technological activities...to catch up with the developed countries, the results obtained here suggest that semi–industrialised countries cannot rely only on a combination of technology import and investments, but have to increase their national technological activities as well" (Fagerberg, 1988, 451).

11. This applies to both that country's exchange rate and also to relative differences in the yen/dollar rate.

12. As we will see in Chapter 2, for several decades, a large number of small Indian machine tool manufacturers survived by producing low quality machine tools for a segment of the Indian market that produced goods for local consumption and neither required nor could afford better quality machine tools.

13. See, for example, the work on Korea, Chinese Taipei and Malaysia by Amsden (1989, 1992); Ernst, Ganiatsos and Mytelka (1995); Evans (1995); Lall (1990); Rasiah (1995) and Wade (1990).

14. These categories were inspired by Abramovitz (1986) although he developed them in a rather different context, that of the convergence of productivity levels across countries. They can be found again in the work of Ernst and O'Connor (1989) and Amsden (1989, 1994) in connection with strategies adopted by Asian newly industrialised economies.

15. The concept is borrowed from Stiglitz (1987).

16. See also the work of Christopher Freeman and two recent collections: Lundvall (1992) and Nelson and Rosenberg (1993).

17. For a longer discussion of the reasons behind the growth of strategic partnerships in the 1980s see Mytelka (1991), Chapter 1.

18. The concept "institutions" covers what elsewhere in the literature might be referred to as "regimes" (Boyer, 1988) or "conventions", that is "rules of thumb, based on precedent, that establish specific, context–bound expectations in actors, enabling them to proceed under conditions of uncertainty in ways that are consistent with, and therefore likely to be met by appropriate forms of reaction", (Storper, 1995, manuscript page 14).

19. "The reduction in protection was drastic and the average tariff fell from 94 per cent in 1973 to 10.1 per cent in 1980" (Pietrobelli, 1994, 434). All non–tariff barriers were eliminated by the end of 1976. Among the consequences, were a "drop in gross manufacturing production...a high number of bankruptcies, and the shrinking number of productive establishments" (Pietrobelli, 1994, 442).

20. The case of textiles in Korea illustrates this problem (Mytelka and Ernst, 1995).

21. In petrochemicals this involved the state in negotiations with foreign partners for licences. In telecommunications, public research institutions were created to develop digital switching technology and transfer it to local private sector firms.

22. In Brazil, the well known triple alliance of state–local private and foreign capital characterised joint ventures in the petrochemical industry. In telecommunications, most firms were joint ventures involving foreign and domestic private capital only and a few of the smaller firms were wholly owned by local entrepreneurs. In Korea, major actors in the petrochemical and telecommunications equipment industries were wholly nationally owned private firms and most were parts of the large Korean conglomerates known as chaebols.

Bibliography

AMABLE, B. AND R. BOYER (1993), « L'Europe est–elle en retard d'un modèle technologique ? », *Economie Internationale*, 36.

AMSDEN, A. (1977), "The Division of Labor Is Limited by the Type of Market: The Taiwanese Machine Tool Industry", *World Development*, 5(3).

AMSDEN, A. (1989), *Asia's Next Giant: South Korea and Late Industrialization*, Oxford, New York.

AMSDEN, A. (1992), "A Theory of Government Intervention in Late Industrialization", in L. PUTTERMAN AND D. RUESCHEMEYER, (eds.), *State and Market in Development: Synergy or Rivalry?,* Lynne Rienner Publishers, Boulder, Colorado.

ANDERSON, R.D. AND S. DEV KHOSLA (1995*), Competition Policy as a Dimension of Economic Policy: A Comparative Perspective*, Bureau of Competition Policy, Industry Canada, Ottawa, Occasional Paper No. 7, May.

BALASSA, B. AND ASSOCIATES (1982*), Development Strategies in Semi–Industrial Economies*, Johns Hopkins, Baltimore.

BUSSON, F. AND P. VILLA (1994), *Croissance et spécialisation*, CEPII, Paris, Document de Travail, No. 94–12, November.

CHANDLER, A.D. JR. (1990), *Scale and Scope: The Dynamics of Industrial Capitalism*, The Belknap Press of Harvard University Press, Cambridge, MA.

CHESNAIS, F. (ed.) (1990), *Compétitivité internationale et dépenses militaires*, Economica, Paris.

CHESNAIS, F. (1986), « Science, technologie et compétitivité », *STI Revue*, OECD, Autumn.

CHUDNOVSKY, D. (1979), "The Challenge by Domestic Enterprises to the Transnational Corporations' Domination: A Case Study of the Argentine Pharmaceutical Industry", *World Development*, Vol. 7.

CHUDNOVSKY, D., A. LÓPEZ AND F. PORTA (1994), "The Petrochemical and Machine Tool Industries: Business Strategies", *Cepal Review*, No. 52, April.

ENOS, J. AND W.H. PARK (1988*), The Adoption and Diffusion of Imported Technology: The Case of Korea,* Croom Helm, London.

ERNST, D., T. GANIATSOS AND L.K. MYTELKA, (eds.) (1995), *Technological Capabilities and Export Success: Cases from Asia*, UNCTAD, Geneva.

EVANS, P. (1995), *Embedded Autonomy: States and Industrial Transformation*, Princeton University Press, Princeton.

FAGERBERG, J. (1987), "International Competitiveness", *The Economic Journal*, Vol. 98, No. 391.

FAGERBERG, J. (1988), "Why Growth Rates Differ", in G. DOSI, C. FREEMAN, R. NELSON, G. SILVERBERG AND L. SOETE (eds.), *Technical Change and Economic Theory*, Pinter Publishers, UK.

FRANSMAN, M. AND K. KING, (eds.) (1984), *Technological Capability in the Third World*, Macmillan, London.

FREEMAN, C. (1982), "Innovation as an Engine of Economic Growth", in H. GIERSCH (ed.), *Emerging Technologies: Consequences for Economic Growth, Structural Change and Employment*, J.C.B. Bohr, Tübingen.

GÖRANSSON, B. (1993), *Catching Up in Technology — A Comparative Case Study of the Telecommunications Equipment Industry in Brazil, India and the Republic of Korea*, Taylor Graham, London.

HOBDAY, M. (1990), *Telecommunications in Developing Countries — The Challenge from Brazil*, Routledge, London.

JACOBSSON, S. (1984), "Industrial Policy for the Machine Tool Industries of South Korea and Taiwan", *IDS Bulletin*, Vol. 15, No. 2.

KALDOR, N. (1978), "The Effect of Devaluations on Trade in Manufactures", in *Further Essays on Applied Economics*, Duckworth, London.

KALDOR, N. (1981), "The Role of Increasing Returns, Technical Progress and Cumulative Causation in the Theory of International Trade and Economic Growth", *Economie Appliquée, Cahiers de l'ISMEA*, Vol. 34, No. 4.

KATZ, J. (1987), *Technology Generation in Latin American Manufacturing Industries*, Macmillan, London.

LALL, S. (1990), *Building Industrial Competitiveness in Developing Countries*, OECD Development Centre, Paris.

LUNDVALL, B.–A., (ed.) (1992), *National Systems of Innovation: Towards a Theory of Innovation and Interactive Learning*, Pinter Publishers, UK.

LUNDVALL, B.–A. (1988), "Innovation as an Interactive Process: From User–Producer Interaction to the National System of Innovation", in G. DOSI, C. FREEMAN, R. NELSON, G. SILVERBERG AND L. SOETE, (eds.), *Technical Change and Economic Theory*, Pinter Publishers, UK.

MYTELKA, L.K. (1991), "Global Shifts in the Textile and Clothing Industries", *Studies in Political Economy*, No. 36, Autumn.

MYTELKA, L.K. (1994), "Regional Co–operation and the New Logic of International Competition", in L.K. MYTELKA, (ed.), *South–South Co–operation in a Global Perspective*, OECD Development Centre, Paris.

MYTELKA, L.K. AND D. ERNST (1995), "Catching Up, Keeping Up and Getting Ahead: The Korean Model under Pressure", in D. ERNST, T. GANIATSOS AND L. MYTELKA (eds.), *Technological Capabilities and Export Success: Cases from Asia*, UNCTAD, Geneva.

NELSON, R. AND S. WINTER (1982), *An Evolutionary Theory of Economic Change*, Harvard University Press, Cambridge, MA.

OECD (1992), *Technology and the Economy: The Key Relationships*, OECD, Paris.

PIETROBELLI, C. (1994) "Trade Liberalization and Industrial Response: The Case of Chile (1974–87)", *Banca Nazionale del Lavoro Quarterly Review*, No. 191 [December].

PORTER, M. (1990), *The Competitive Advantage of Nations*, Free Press, New York.

RASIAH, R. (1995), *Foreign Capital and Industrialization in Malaysia*, St. Martin's Press, London.

RHEE, Y.W., B. ROSS–LARSON AND G. PURSELL (1984), *Korea's Competitive Edge: Managing the Entry into World Markets*, published for the World Bank by the Johns Hopkins University Press, Baltimore.

RODRIK, D. (1994), "Getting Interventions Right: How South Korea and Taiwan Grew Rich", NBER Working Paper No. 4964.

ROMER, P.M. (1994), "The Origins of Endogenous Growth", *Journal of Economic Perspectives*, Vol. 8, No. 1, Winter.

ROSENBERG, N. (1976), "The Direction of Technological Change: Inducement Mechanisms and Focusing Devices", in N. ROSENBERG, *Perspectives on Technology*, Cambridge University Press, Cambridge.

ROSENBERG, N. AND C. FRISCHTAK (eds.) (1985), *International Technology Transfer*, Praeger, New York.

SACHWALD, F. (1993), "Competitiveness and Competition: Which Theory of the Firm?" in F. SACHWALD (ed.), *European Integration and Competitiveness*, Edward Elgar, UK.

SAXENIAN, A.L. (1994), *Regional Advantage, Culture and Competition in Silicon Valley and Route 128*, Harvard University Press, Cambridge, MA.

SCHERER, F.M. (1980), *Industrial Market Structure and Economic Performance*, Houghton Mifflin, Boston (2nd edition).

SCHUMPETER, J. (1939), *Business Cycles: A Theoretical, Historical and Statistical Analysis of the Capitalist Process*, McGraw–Hill, New York.

TEECE, D. (1989), "Economic Welfare and the Allocation of (Private) Resources to Innovation", Walter A. Haas School of Business, Berkeley (mimeo).

UNGER, K., L.C. SALDAÑA, J. JASSO AND G. DURAND (1992), *Ajuste estructural y estrategias empresariales en las industrias petroquímica y máquinas herramientas de México*, Mexico City, Mexico (mimeo).

WADE, R. (1990), *Governing the Market: Economic Theory and the Role of Government in East Asian Industrialization*, Princeton University Press, Princeton.

WESTPHAL, L. (1982), "Fostering Technological Mastery by Means of Selective Infant–Industry Protection", in M. SYRQUIN AND S. TEITEL, (eds.) *Trade, Stability, Technology and Equity in Latin America*, Academic Press, New York.

WOMACK, J.P., D.T. JONES AND D. ROOS (1990), *The Machine That Changed the World: The Story of Lean Production*, Harper–Collins, New York.

II

Machine Tool Industries in India and Chinese Taipei: A Comparison

Ashok V. Desai, Marc Lautier and Hanumantha Charya

The World Machine Tool Industry

The essence of all engineering is construction: a mechanical device is assembled out of parts. The parts may fit into a one–off design or be made for a small number of machines. This was common across engineering products in the early days of the industry. It is less so now. In fact, cars, which are also machines, are manufactured on such a large scale that their manufacturing technology has become a prototype for mass manufacture. But engineering goods are expensive and infrequently purchased. Hence buyers are particular about their design, and matching the design to their requirements is an important selling point. Product differentiation is thus endemic, and all product differentiation reduces scale.

Fragmentation of production can be reduced to some extent by assembling a product out of standard parts and components. But product differentiation even at the cost of scale is a frequent and often successful strategy in engineering, and every engineering industry is a mixture of firms that make specially designed products on a small scale and those that make standard products on a large scale. At one end are firms that put together expensive equipment such as draglines for quarrying or platforms for deep–sea drilling almost entirely on a custom basis; at the other end are firms which produce a standard product such a car or a refrigerator in thousands. Even in the car industry, however, models will be introduced periodically to incorporate innovations and respond to changes in costs and in customer preferences. There are also firms which produce a special product on a small scale, such as the Lotus car, of which only 300 are produced a year.

Once mass manufacture was introduced in the automobile industry, it was applied to other forms of transport equipment, such as heavy vehicles and tractors, and consumer durables such as refrigerators, washing machines and television sets. But there are many engineering products in which this development is still not so far advanced. Machine tools, or machines for cutting and forming metals, for example, still retain the characteristics of a classical engineering industry. It is a small industry whose total world sales in 1993 were barely $30 billion (Table 2.1), down from a peak of $45 billion in 1990. In comparison, the sales of motor vehicles exceeded $400 billion.

World output currently stands at about $30 billion of which a quarter is produced in Japan, and almost three–quarters in seven countries — Japan, Germany, the United States, Italy, China, Switzerland and Chinese Taipei. All the countries except China exported over 30 per cent of their output, and all except Japan imported over 30 per cent of their domestic offtake. This openness is characteristic of the industry in all countries except some ex–communist countries and it arises from the high level of product differentiation. Firms tend to specialise, and to seek international markets for their specialities. India, one of the minor producers, had a low export ratio but imported 57 per cent of its domestic offtake.

The number of firms in the industry is very large (Table 2.2). Average firm size is small. Averages can be misleading; for instance in Japan, the 15 largest Japanese firms accounted for 79 per cent of production in 1991 (*American Machinist*, 1991–92, various issues). Somewhat older figures show 85 per cent of United States production being accounted for by 12 firms in 1982. The typical pattern is a small number of large firms producing a broad range of machines and a large number of small firms specialised in simpler products or special machine tools or components. Nevertheless, the industry is less concentrated than other engineering industries. For instance, the three leading producers accounted for 76 per cent of United States car output, and the five leading producers for 85 per cent of Japanese car output in 1992. The share of Amada (Japan), the largest firm, in world machine tool production in 1991 was 3.2 per cent, whereas General Motors accounted for 9 per cent of world car output, and IBM 28 per cent of world computer output (Flamm, 1990).

The industry is skill–intensive. Innovation and adaptation of machines to the technical requirements of the market call for competent engineers; leading firms employ a high proportion of their manpower in research and development. Also, much craftsmanship goes into the machines, whose quality depends on workers' skills. The industry is not labour–intensive; the value of output per employee is not lower than in mass engineering industries. But this is because of the high skill requirements of labour; the labour used is highly trained and hence expensive. Manpower is the key to success in this industry.

Such are the longstanding characteristics of the industry in the countries that were the original home of the industry. In the past three decades, however, the industry has been profoundly affected by two related events — the entry of Japan, and the introduction of electronic controls.

Table 2.1. **Machine Tool Production and Trade of Major Countries, 1993**

	Production			Trade		Consumption	Share in			
							Production			Consumption
	Total $m	Cutting $m	Forming $m	Exports $m	Imports $m	$m	Cutting %	Forming %	Exports %	Imports %
Japan	7 154	5 579	1 575	3 644	378	3 887	78.0	22.0	50.9	9.7
Germany	5 145	3 345	1 801	3 229	1 150	3 066	65.0	35.0	62.8	37.5
United States	3 275	2 225	1 050	1 010	2 500	4 765	67.9	32.1	30.8	52.5
Italy	2 366	1 586	780	1 391	637	1 612	67.0	33.0	58.8	39.5
China	1 753	1 319	435	200	1 522	3 075	75.2	24.8	11.4	49.5
Switzerland	1 354	1 016	339		203	372	75.0	25.0	87.5	54.6
Chinese Taipei	1 074	716	358	688	441	827	66.7	33.3	64.1	53.3
United Kingdom	953	620	333	489	543	1 005	65.1	34.9	51.3	54.0
Korea	623	523	98	110	700	1 213	83.9	16.1	17.7	57.7
France	618	459	159	300	636	954	74.3	25.7	48.5	66.7
Russia	615	490	125	15	40	640	79.7	10.3	2.4	6.3
Ukraine	518	420	98	12	58	564	81.8	18.9	2.3	10.3
Spain	401	268	134	241	189	348	66.8	22.3	60.1	53.4
Canada	340	201	139	218	511	633	59.1	40.9	64.1	80.7
Brazil	326	262	64	196	91	221	80.3	19.7	60.1	41.1
Austria	288	189	99	12	58	334	65.6	34.4	4.2	17.4
Belgium	172	17	154	309	213	76	9.9	90.1	179.7	280.2
Sweden	167	85	82	184	141	124	50.9	49.1	110.2	113.7
Czech Rep.	165	150	15	123	74	116	90.9	9.1	74.5	63.8
India	156	143	13	17	185	324	91.7	8.3	10.9	57.1
Singapore	152	93	59	189	335	297	61.2	38.8	124.9	112.8
Poland	149	97	52	42	92	200	65.1	34.9	28.2	46.5
Yugoslavia	105	79	26	0	0	105	75.2	24.8	0.0	0.0
Netherlands	70	24	46	102	222	190	34.3	65.7	145.7	116.8
Finland	47	3	44	42	34	39	7.0	93.0	89.4	87.2

Note: m = millions

Source: *American Machinist*, March 1994, p. 44.

Table 2.2. **Number of Firms and Employment, 1987**

	Number of firms	Employment	Workers per firm
Germany	390	93 500	240
United States	455	62 300	130
France	148	10 025	68
Italy	430	30 500	71
Japan	1 600	32 700	20
Chinese Taipei[a]	250	20 177	81
India[b]	365	51 604	141

a. 1993.
b. Excludes small firms, estimated at 2 500–3 000.
Sources: UNIDO, 1989. TAMI. IMTMA Industry profiles, 1994.

Japanese electronics firms took an early interest in the development and use of semiconductors. The major semiconductor innovations, which were made in the United States in the 1950s and 1960s, were closely followed by Japanese firms. More important, the Japanese firms were often quicker at commercialisation of the innovations and mass production of their products than their US counterparts. This is also true of the application of semiconductor–based controls to the machine tool industry. Early research on the application of numerical controls was done in the Servomechanisms Laboratory of the Massachusetts Institute of Technology, which demonstrated a prototype in 1952. Almost immediately thereafter, pilot projects were started by the Tokyo Institute of Technology and by the Mechanical Engineering Laboratory of the Ministry of International Trade and Industry. Commercialisation was taken up by Fanuc, a subsidiary of Fujitsu, which was a leader in electronics. Soon Fanuc became the major Japanese producer of electronic controls. Between 1961 and 1964, 29 technology import agreements were signed by machine tool makers, some relating to numerical controls (Fransman, 1986). In the years that followed, Fanuc began to design numerical and computer–numerical controls for machine tools based on a close study of user requirements. The controls were standardised, low–cost, and reliable. It thereby scored a lead over US and European manufacturers of electronic controls, which adapted their products less quickly to the requirements of machine tools (Sciberras and Payne, 1985). The combination of standardisation and market adaptation has remained the strength of Fanuc and has given it a market share of 60 per cent even now.

Together with cheap and simple electronic controls went a number of process innovations in the Japanese machine tool industry. The most important was that instead of making custom–built machines to meet the requirements of users, Japanese firms translated the user requirements into the most sought–after characteristics and designed standardised machines with these characteristics. In this way they cut down product diversification and could achieve long production runs for a small number of machines. The Japanese firms also tried to simplify the machines and to cut down the number of parts in them. The result was considerable labour saving. Japanese output per employee in dollar terms almost tripled between 1975 and 1980; in 1980 it was roughly twice the level in the United States, Germany and Italy and four times the British level (Sciberras and Payne, 1985). The pronounced edge in CNC and low costs gave Japanese firms a strong competitive advantage, and led to a rapid rise in their world market share after the mid–1970s (Table 2.4).

Table 2.3. **Share of Major Types in Selected Countries' Output of Metal–Cutting Tools, 1992**

(per cent)

	Numerical Controls (NC)					Non–NC
	Lathes	Milling Machines	Machining Centres	Other	Total	Total
Japan	18.6	2.9	24.2	26.8	72.5	27.5
Germany[a]	15.5	8.6	17.4	28.5	70.0	30.0
United States	8.6	9.0	18.9	21.2	57.6	42.4
Korea	31.7	2.9	23.4	15.2	55.2	44.8
United Kingdom	8.0	4.6	20.4	19.0	52.0	48.0
Chinese Taipei	19.4	2.1	22.8	1.6	45.9	54.1
India	13.6	1.5	15.2	10.5	40.8	59.2

a. West Germany only.

Sources: CECIMO statistics.

The emergence of Japan in a market that for at least 50 years was dominated by Germany, the United States and the United Kingdom marks a technological threshold — a transition from mechanical to electronic controls, from craft–driven to market–driven design, from batch production to mass production. With these innovations, Japanese firms lowered costs and developed a market amongst smaller firms and firms in developing countries; from this base they went on to develop more sophisticated models. The first hardwired NC machines yielded to programmable machines; these led to machining centres which could work on a number of axes with inter–changeable tools; automatic tool changing was combined with automatic handling of the workpiece in flexible manufacturing cells (FMCs); and finally, machining centres and FMCs were linked by conveyor belts and moving palettes to move the workpiece through a series of operations in flexible manufacturing systems (FMSs). Japan has retained leadership in this technological trajectory.

The trajectory is not linear, however; improvements have continued in older types of machines. Despite the rise of electronic controls, conventional and special machine tools have remained important; and intermediate forms of electronification, involving simpler and less versatile controls in cheap machines, have also emerged. Japan's technological lead has been followed by Chinese Taipei and Korea; and import competition from the East Asian countries has led to the restructuring of the older industries, notably in the United States. The resulting competitive pressure has been communicated to most major markets and opened them up, as is shown by the rising ratio of exports to world production (Table 2.8). The rise in the world export ratio owes much to the rising export share in Japanese output and import share in United

States consumption; but increasing specialisation and consequently rising import ratios are characteristic of the industry everywhere. Machine tool manufacture has spread to more countries since World War II; firms are generally small, and the characteristics of national markets differ. Foreign direct investment is insignificant in the industry. High firm specialisation leads to a high level of international trade.

Table 2.4. **World Export Shares of Major Machine Tool Producing Countries, Selected Years, 1913–93**

	1913	1937	1965	1970	1978	1980	1985	1990	1993
Japan	-	-	3	5	13	11	23	19	25
Germany[a]	48	48	31	34	26	22	20	24	23
United States	33	35	22	16	7	6	5	5	7
Italy	-	-	7	10	7	6	7	8	10
Switzerland	-	5	9	10	8	7	9	12	8
United Kingdom	12	7	13	11	5	6	4	4	3
France	-	-	6	6	5	4	2	2	2
Chinese Taipei	-	-	-	-	1.2	1.6	2.1	3.0	4.7
Korea	-	-	-	-	-	0.2	0.2	0.4	0.8
India	-	-	-	-	0.3	0.2	0.2	0.1	0.1
NB: World export ratio	-	-	-	-	-	43	44	47	57

a. Federal Republic only from 1965 till 1985.
Sources: 1913–70: OECD, 1982. 1978–93: *American Machinist*, various issues.

Although NC machine tools have seized an increasing share of the market, non–NC tools are by no means on the way out. Numerical controls are expensive: they constitute around 40 per cent of the costs of NC tools, which are themselves far more expensive than ordinary machine tools (96 times more expensive per unit in Chinese Taipei and 6.5 times in India — see Table 2.5 below). Hence the commonest use of numerical controls is in fast, accurate turning and milling operations (Table 2.3). NC lathes and machining centres are primarily used for precision shaping of complex components required on a large scale in mass engineering industries such as automobiles. This still leaves a large market for non–NC tools in simple operations, operations where the scale is not large enough or work flow is uneven, operations peculiar to individual industries for which dedicated machine tools are designed, or countries where labour is relatively cheap. Electronification has spread furthest in Japan; as Table 2.3 shows, the proportion of NC machines other than lathes, milling machines and machining centres is very high there. In other countries with a smaller proportion of NC tools, the weight of NC tools in these three categories is relatively higher. Thus electronification has made more progress in some countries and in some tools than in others. The entry of numerical controls has profoundly affected the economics of the industry; the changing patterns of specialisation reflect this.

Performance of the Indian and Chinese Taipei Industries

Until the late 1960s, the Chinese Taipei machine tool industry, like the Indian industry, largely served the domestic market. Although it had begun to export by the 1970s, Amsden had doubts when she studied it in 1974 that it could break out of its low price–low quality syndrome to win substantial markets abroad. Table 2.4, however, shows the rise of Chinese Taipei exports from the late 1970s onwards, whereas India continues to be an insignificant exporter.

In Table 2.1 we saw that machine tool output in Chinese Taipei was about seven times as large as in India. Table 2.5 compares output and Table 2.6 exports of the two industries as given by national statistics. Too much should not be read into these figures since the unit values of Chinese Taipei's output and exports of most non–NC machine tools are identical, suggesting that both are assumed, estimated benchmark prices. The Indian figures need not be any less approximate. Nonetheless, the differences displayed by the two sets of figures are so gross that they can support a few simple conclusions.

The most striking feature of the table is the unit values, which are lower for all Chinese Taipei machines except boring machines. Indian NC machine tools are about three times as expensive, non–NC cutting tools are about 42 times as costly and non–NC forming tools are roughly six times the cost of Chinese Taipei tools. The difference in most cases is so large that it must be suspected that the machines are not comparable; but if so, it would appear that Chinese Taipei has specialised in the production of smaller and cheaper machines. As Chinese Taipei machine tool manufacturers have targeted the price–sensitive customer, they have developed machine tools using smaller motors and less sophisticated materials and heat treatment. Wherever thereby they have achieved large volumes they have been able to produce at dramatically lower costs. (The sole exception is boring machines where the volume was the same in Chinese Taipei; in this case, the Indian unit value was lower than that of Chinese Taipei.) The intensely competitive environment has channelled innovation into cost saving and miniaturisation (Lautier, 1994). On display in the Indian Machine Tool Exhibition in Delhi, in January 1995, was one of the world's smallest NC lathes, no bigger than a sewing machine, made in Chinese Taipei — a striking contrast to the heavy Indian products.

The export unit values of Chinese Taipei, as noted earlier, are identical to those of domestic output except for three NC tools — lathes, milling machines and grinding machines — whose domestic unit values are considerably lower. The export unit values calculable from Tables 2.5 and 2.6 are broadly comparable to those available from other international sources, for instance those of CECIMO, which also suggest that Chinese Taipei export unit values for most machines are 50 per cent or less of those of machines from Germany and Japan. In other words, the bulk of Chinese Taipei's output of conventional machine tools is exported, and in their case, there is little difference between domestic and export prices. In some types of NC machine tools where a high proportion of domestic output is retained at home, exports are sold at a higher price than domestic sales.

Table 2.5. **Machine Tool Output, Chinese Taipei and India, 1993**

	Units		Value ($m)		Value (%)		Unit value ($000)	
	Chinese Taipei	India	Chinese Taipei	India	Chinese Taipei	India	Chinese Taipei	India
NC machines	**6 567**	**291**	**323.6**	**40.9**	**29.5**	**30.6**	**49.3**	**140.5**
Lathes	2 486	122	134.1	9.8	12.2	7.3	54.0	80.3
Drilling machines	36	10	1.3	1.0	0.1	0.8	35.0	80.3
Milling machines	1 010	9	12.0	1.4	1.1	1.0	11.8	149.5
Grinding machines	93	14	5.0	4.4	0.5	3.3	54.4	315.0
Machining centres	2 702	101	165.8	22.3	15.1	16.7	61.4	221.0
EDM machines	240	35	5.4	2.0	0.5	1.5	22.6	56.9
Non–NC metal–cutting machines	**745 724**	**3 015**	**384.8**	**64.7**	**35.1**	**45.9**	**0.5**	**21.5**
Lathes	16 556	945	67.3	12.7	6.1	9.5	4.1	13.5
Drilling machines	568 627	581	73.1	5.0	6.7	3.7	0.1	8.6
Milling machines	19 262	1 048	77.4	13.8	7.1	9.6	4.0	12.2
Grinding machines	8 578	374	46.3	6.7	4.2	4.9	5.4	17.8
Sawing machines	120 677	50	41.4	0.4	3.8	0.3	0.3	7.4
Shapers/planers	1 300	8	3.8	0.2	0.3	0.2	3.0	28.4
Boring machines	25	25	4.0	2.8	0.4	2.1	159.4	112.0
Gear–cutting machines	270	61	1.0	3.4	0.1	2.5	3.7	55.0
Screw–cutting machines	1 123		53		0.5		4.7	
EDM machines	2 684	157	38.7	2.4	3.5	1.8	14.4	14.9
Special purpose machines	150	126	7.5	17.3	0.7	12.9	50.1	137.1
Other	6 472		19.0		1.7		2.9	
Metal–forming machines	**58 986**	**322**	**389.3**	**12.0**	**35.5**	**9.0**	**6.6**	**37.3**
Presses and shears	30 591	322	194.9	12.0	17.8	9.0	6.4	37.3
Other	28 395		194.9		17.7		6.8	
Other machines		**650**		**17.8**		**13.3**		**27.3**
Total	**811 117**	**4 638**	**1 097.7**	**135.4**	**100.0**	**100.0**	**1.4**	**28.9**

Sources: Chinese Taipei – TAMI; India – IMTMA *Bulletin*, May 1994.

Table 2.6. **Machine Tool Exports, Chinese Taipei and India, 1993**

	Units		Value ($m)		Export ratio (%)		Unit value ratio (%)	
	Chinese Taipei	India	Chinese Taipei	India	Chinese Taipei	India	Chinese Taipei	India
NC machines	**2 788**	**8**	**158.5**	**0.4**	**42.5**	**2.7**	**1.13**	**0.54**
Lathes	800	8	48.5	0.4	32.2	6.6	1.12	0.4
Milling machines	382		11.3		37.8		2.48	
Grinding machines	5		0.5		5.4		1.89	
Machining centres	1 601		98.2		59.3		1.00	
Non–NC metal–cutting machines	**686 684**	**153**	**334.0**	**1.2**	**92.1**	**5.1**	**1.00**	**0.83**
Lathes	14 901	122	60.5	0.9	90.0	12.9	1.00	0.57
Drilling machines	540 196	7	69.5		95.0	1.2	1.00	0.63
Milling machines	17 336	2	69.7		90.0	0.2	1.00	1.32
Grinding machines	7 292	20	39.4	0.2	85.0	5.3	1.00	0.60
Sawing machines	96 542		33.1		80.0		1.00	
Shapers/planers	653		1.9		50.0		1.00	
Boring machines	5		0.8		20.0		1.00	
Gear–cutting machines	135		0.5		50.0		1.00	
Screw–cutting machines	730		3.4		65.0		1.00	
EDM machines	4 363	2	41.9		162.6	1.3	1.07	0.97
Other metal–cutting machines	4 531		13.3		0.9		1.00	
Metal–forming machines	**38 451**	**59**	**253.1**	**3.5**	**65.2**		**1.00**	
Presses and shears	21 414	7	136.5	0.2	70.0	2.2	1.00	0.77
Other	17 037	52	116.6	3.1	60.0		1.00	
Total	**727 923**	**220**	**745.6**	**4.9**	**89.7**	**4.7**	**1.02**	**0.77**

Note: Export ratios are ratios of units exported to those produced. Unit value ratios are ratios of export unit values to output unit values.

Sources: Chinese Taipei – TAMI. India – IMTMA (1994).

The Indian case is just the reverse. The proportion of output exported is low or zero in the case of all machine tools, and the machines that are exported are sold at prices far below the domestic prices. As Table 2.5 shows, Indian domestic unit values are between 3 and 6 times higher than those in Chinese Taipei, and hence implicitly comparable to or higher than German or Japanese ones. So it is not surprising that Indian machines can be exported only at prices much below domestic prices. This does not necessarily mean that they are exported at a loss, for the price difference may be accounted for by duty drawbacks. But our impression is that duty drawbacks do not amount to the high discounts suggested by Table 2.6. It is thus very likely that exports are significantly less profitable than domestic sales. Indian machine tool exports are negligible because Indian machine tools are uncompetitive in terms of prices; and this uncompetitiveness must be based on domestic costs.

It should be added that Indian machine tools are uncompetitive in terms of not only price but also product design. Controls on technology imports combined with a lack of domestic competition delayed the diffusion of international trends in tool design, with the result that Indian machine tools were left far behind in terms of design and quality. This is graphically illustrated by the experience of Ace Designers, a Bangalore firm which makes CNC lathes and hydraulic multi–slide auto lathes of its own design.

> When Ace started examining closely their CNC products with regard to their exportability, they noticed that they were neither price–competitive, nor did their machines compare well in looks and finish with competing machines abroad. In fact, when they did show their machines in the EMO fair at Paris, many critics commented on the way they brought a machine which was not looking so good. One British visitor even commented, "Do you want me to believe the machine functions better than it looks?" After these disheartening remarks, Ace realised that for a real export effort one has to look inwards at the design, appearance of the machine, price, and of course, basic quality aspects. Ace took the machine back to the drawing boards and set out to produce a machine which they would be ultimately proud of (S.G. Shirgurkar, Managing Director; interview 7 December 1995).

Ace Designers is a firm founded in 1979 by three engineers from the Central Machine Tool Institute to capitalise on their own technological capability. Their standards are high: 70 of their 180 employees are qualified engineers. If their designs were so outdated by world standards, the position of the rest of the industry is considerably worse. Briefly, the Indian machine tool industry has not only been outpriced, but a good deal of its product range is obsolete by international standards. The obsolescence may be partly material and partly cosmetic, but it is significant enough to make the industry uncompetitive even if it were able to match international prices. We shall endeavour in the rest of the paper to explain how this came about.

Explaining Chinese Taipei's Success

Unitary explanations of such broad developments as the performance of the Chinese Taipei machine tool industry are always hazardous. Important here are the initial conditions, the organisation of the industry, and its strategic orientation.

Origins and Structure

Only limited material is available on the origins of the Chinese Taipei machine tool industry. However, it tells a consistent story. When the Kuomintang (KMT) moved to Chinese Taipei in 1949 after being defeated by the communists in China, it was accompanied by some of its supporters from among the Shanghai and Shantung business communities. Favoured by the KMT government in the early years, these businessmen eventually founded great industrial empires. Hsu Yu–Hsiang, for example, started his Far Eastern Textile Company with substantial government help in the 1950s and later diversified into cement and department stores where his Far Eastern Textile Company continues to wield major influence. His business group is currently the third largest in Chinese Taipei. The seventh largest group, Yue Loong, has a similar history. Apart from the mainland Chinese, many Chinese Taipei businessmen were also co–opted by the KMT and founded industrial empires (Bello and Rosenfeld, 1990). Alliances between the ruling party and big business, however, were not the driving force in the machine tool industry where most firms started small, and new, relatively obscure entrepreneurs played the leading role in building up the industry.

The government in Taipei also operated an industrial licensing system which regulated entry. In some industries entry was banned for specific periods or conditions for entry such as export requirements or minimum import substitution were imposed (Hsiang, 1971). But industrial licensing was never directly applied to machine tools. Apart from access to imports which is discussed later, there were thus no barriers to entry and exit in machine tools, both of which were frequent.

Entrepreneurs in the machine tool industry thus typically originated in small workshops that either repaired machinery or custom–made some for local industry, particularly textiles, sewing machines, bicycles, cars, agricultural machinery etc. Both Amsden (1977) and Tsai (1992) are clear about the craft origins. They most likely shared the characteristics of Chinese Taipei entrepreneurs outlined, for instance, by Gold (1986): family men who wanted to leave an enterprise for each son; individualists who did not co–operate easily. Distrustful of government, they tried not to attract its attention. They relied on profits for investment, and when profits were not enough, they turned to close groups of kin and friends for funds. There were thus no branches or licensees of foreign manufacturers, no government enterprises and no large enterprises endowed with significant financial or technological resources. In this the machine tool industry in Chinese Taipei differed markedly from the pharmaceutical industry discussed in Chapter 3.

Small entrepreneurs bred more small entrepreneurs; and workers aspired to start their own enterprises. Galenson (1992) attributes this to restrictive labour legislation. Until 1975, there was only the Chinese Federation of Labour, a branch of the KMT, and it was moribund. In that year, new legislation legalised enterprise and district unions, but half the members of a union came from the KMT, and unions were forbidden to strike. Strikes were legalised in 1989 if approved by two–thirds of the membership, but were often brutally suppressed. Thus during most of the period in which the machine tool industry grew rapidly, organised labour did not exist. It is difficult to assess how significant this repression was for the growth of the machine tool industry. It is possible that the role of restraints on trade union activity was not as great as Galenson believes. From the end of the 1960s onwards Chinese Taipei experienced full employment and a labour shortage; in the circumstances, real wages rose rapidly anyway. Even in countries where trade unions are active and unfettered, competition in product markets constrains their ability to raise or protect wages — as it has begun to do in India. More than keeping wages low and limiting labour unrest in the form of strikes, absenteeism or unwillingness to work, the absence of collective bargaining gave entrepreneurs flexibility in the use of labour, and was instrumental in facilitating the rapid change of production patterns that is characteristic of the Chinese Taipei machine tool industry. And there is no doubt that there was an abundant supply of new entrepreneurs willing to compete aggressively in the domestic market, which was the main market for this industry until the 1960s. These fiercely competing small enterprises (Amsden, 1977) were extremely price–sensitive, and the emphasis in the machine tool industry was on price competition.

Technology

Formal arrangements for technology import, such as licensing agreements, joint ventures and foreign subsidiaries, were not uncommon in Chinese Taipei industry. Like the Korean cases discussed in Chapters 4 and 5, these licences were subject to approval by the government, which often took the lead in bringing a technology into Chinese Taipei and actively participated in the bargain that was driven (Wade, 1990). However, licensing of technology, which was so important in India, was uncommon in the Chinese Taipei machine tool industry.

To attract a licensor, a licensee must be able to offer a stable market over the medium to long term thus assuring the licensor of significant income from the production of licensed models. In the case of Chinese Taipei, while the national market could be secured for potential licensees by means of import restrictions, which were as stringent in Chinese Taipei as in India, cut–throat competition in the domestic market limited the extent to which a stable or rising market share for the licensor could be guaranteed. Market structure was thus the main reason why technology licensing and foreign investment were so unimportant in the Chinese Taipei machine tool industry[1]. By the 1990s it was easier for successful local firms to obtain licences, but the proportion of Chinese Taipei machine tool output produced under licence remained low. In the fast–changing market for machine tools, demand for the licensed models did not justify the allocation of an assembly line, and one Chinese Taipei firm that licensed production for an NC lathe from a German company in 1990 terminated the licence in 1994 when income from the licensed models proved insignificant (Lautier, 1994). Flexibility and rapidity of model changes, which were of the essence in the success of the Chinese Taipei industry, were thus incompatible with licensing.

Technology in the Chinese Taipei machine tool industry thus came almost entirely from reverse engineering which, in turn, was facilitated by the availability of unrestricted imports. Throughout, Japan has been the major source of machine tool imports, 63 per cent in 1993, and hence of reverse–engineered technology. It should be noted, however, that reverse engineering is not peculiar to the Chinese Taipei machine tool industry but has always been common in the machine tool industry throughout the world. It prevailed just as much in India where the entire small–scale machine tool industry, which steadily encroached on the market of large firms, was built up by copying the latter's machines.

During the 1970s and 1980s, Chinese Taipei production was based primarily on the firms' own designs and brands. But once Chinese Taipei manufacturers established a reputation for making cheap and reliable machines, another source of technology, OEM production, opened up for them as manufacturers from high–cost countries offered to license their own branded machines to Chinese Taipei enterprises for manufacture and buy–back. Especially in the 1980s, when the dollar became overvalued and foreign competition in the United States market intensified, sometimes from the very same Chinese Taipei producers, a number of United States manufacturers began to source their own machines from Chinese Taipei or to sell Chinese Taipei machines under their own name. The switch to OEM manufacture became more pronounced in the 1990s. Of the 12 firms interviewed, only one used OEM manufacture as an important export channel in the 1980s, against three in 1994; another three had OEM contracts of low or unknown significance in 1994 (Lautier, 1994).

By the 1990s, most firms had R&D departments which concentrated mainly on design. In particular, the R&D capacity is used to monitor technological developments at the frontier, undertake reverse engineering, and extend the range of models. With the introduction of numerical controls the process of product differentiation accelerated, since a wide variety of machines could be built around controls of varying cost and capabilities. Whereas in the mid–1980s Chinese Taipei firms were producing from one to three models (Jacobsson, 1986), by 1993 most of the firms interviewed were producing more than five types of machining centres in addition to other machine tools.

Employment of foreign scientists and engineers was relatively rare in Chinese Taipei, but recruitment of Chinese Taipei nationals trained abroad, mainly in the United States and to a lesser extent in Japan and Germany, became a significant source of technology, not only for firms but also for technology support departments and institutes. Some 20 per cent of Chinese Taipei graduates in science and technology go abroad for further education but only 20 per cent of these returned in the period 1976–86 (Wade, 1990). Despite this drain, Chinese Taipei scientists and engineers educated in the United States have become more common now in industry as well as government.

Apart from in–house R&D, Chinese Taipei firms have also received extensive support from technical institutes, of which two were particularly important — the Metal Industries Research Laboratories (MIRL) and the Centre for Machine

Development (CMD), later renamed the Precision Machinery Research and Development Centre (PMC) (Lautier, 1994). MIRL is one of six research institutes under the aegis of the government's Industrial Technology Research Institute, which was set up in 1973 and had a staff of 4 500 and a budget of $215 million in 1987 (Wade, 1990). MIRL is itself a large organisation of 1 000 people dealing with a wide range of machinery; about 50 are engaged in research on machine tools. In the early 1980s, MIRL designed a number of NC lathes and machining centres and transferred them on a non–exclusive basis to local manufacturers. MIRL provides access to information and technology, supplements firms' R&D teams, and takes on research contracts. Its employees have also often left to start their own firms or to join existing firms, taking their experience with them.

The Centre for Machinery Development was set up by 14 of the largest machine tool manufacturers in 1983 with an official subsidy. With a small group of 15 employees, CMD developed a product evaluation and assessment system based on Japanese standards and in co–operation with the Japanese Machinery and Metals Inspection Institute. It created a CMD mark which aimed at becoming a product quality standard. The Centre for Machinery Development has now been merged into a larger institute, the Precision Machinery Research and Development Centre (PMC), with 66 employees, jointly funded by the government and the Taiwan Association of Machine Tool Industry (TAMI). PMC continues to confer the CMD mark, but in addition it helps local firms to meet foreign standards and to create documentation for that purpose. PMC provides services related to product improvement including facilities for testing and quality control, whilst MIRL concentrates on product development.

Export Orientation

As Table 2.7 indicates, the machine tool industry was an insignificant exporter until the mid–1970s. Its share in Chinese Taipei's exports amounted to less than 0.2 per cent and even its share of metal and machinery exports in 1966 was less than 2 per cent. The machine tool industry was a late starter in Chinese Taipei, and its explosive growth was tied to the growth of exports which started after the oil crisis in 1973.

The timing of its growth was also related to changes in the policy environment. By the mid–1960s, restrictions on industrial investment had been largely phased out. Direct allocation of foreign exchange and multiple exchange rates were also discontinued in the early 1960s. Maximum import content restrictions continued until the 1980s, but did not apply to machine tools (Scott, 1979). The most important trade–related policies for the machine tool industry were tariffs, import controls and tax concessions.

Chinese Taipei tariffs at the end of the 1960s were high; in 1965, half the tariffs were over 30 per cent, and a quarter over 50 per cent (Hsiang, 1971; see also Scott, 1979). The average collection rate was much lower — 23 per cent in the late 1960s

Table 2.7. **Direction of Chinese Taipei's Machine Tool Exports, Selected Years, 1966–93**

	Exports	Developed countries				Developing countries		
	Total	Total	United States + Canada	Japan	W. Europe	Total	Hong Kong	SE Asia
	$m	%	%	%	%	%	%	%
1966	1.3	0.5				99.5		
1970	2.1	6.7				93.3		
1973	8.0	28.2				71.8		
1981	178.0	77.2	52.6			22.8		
1982	125.0	77.4	52.4	4.0	12.1	22.6		11.6
1988	504.0	59.8	31.0	3.8	21.2	40.2	7.8	10.0
1990	640.0	60.0	21.9	5.9	30.5	40.0	8.0	18.4
1991	644.0	52.8	18.9	5.6	26.8	47.2	12.2	20.3
1992	660.0	42.7	18.8	3.3	19.3	57.3	24.9	18.7
1993	688.0	35.2	19.8	4.1	10.0	64.8	35.6	17.5

Sources: Amsden (1977); Jacobsson (1986); TAMI.

and early 1970s (Scott, 1979)[2]. The actual tax burden was much higher because all imports paid a surcharge and a harbour charge which raised their cost by 51 per cent in 1968, and because the import duty was levied on the cost including these charges (Lin, 1973). The tariff system was buttressed by a system of import licensing which ensured that nothing that was produced in the country could be imported unless the prospective importer proved that the domestic price exceeded the import price by more than a specified percentage. This percentage was brought down from 25 to 10 in 1968. In other words, if the tariff plus the various surcharges raised the import cost by 100 per cent, the product could still not be imported as long as a domestic manufacturer supplied it at less than 120 per cent above import cost (Lin, 1973).

Exporters were also subject to these quantitative import restrictions, but had to satisfy much less stringent conditions. They were allowed to import if the domestic supplier's price exceeded the c.i.f. import cost excluding duties and surcharges by more than 10 per cent. Further, exporters got full rebates not only on import duties and surcharges, but also on business tax, stamp tax, and domestic commodity taxes on inputs. Thus although the gross customs revenue came to 23 per cent of imports in 1968–69, only 17 per cent was collected; the rest was rebated to exporters (Scott, 1979). By the 1970s, the proportion being rebated had risen to nearly half (Wade, 1990). Not only could an exporter get duty rebated on his imports but a domestic supplier to an exporter could receive a rebate equivalent to the duties the exporter would have saved had the input been imported instead (Little, 1979). The import entitlements were based on physical input–output ratios for major inputs, and a value–

based percentage was added to cover minor inputs. The entitlements were generous and transferable. Exporters could import more than they needed and sell surplus entitlements to producers for the domestic market; in 1968 at any rate, the premia on such transfers were no more than 1–4 per cent, suggesting that despite high tariffs, domestic prices of the importable inputs were not much higher than duty–free import costs. Small exporters often sold off their duty–free import entitlements to big importers (Wade, 1990). Apart from duty rebates, exporters could import duty–free against a bank guarantee which was vacated as long as they exported within a year of the import of materials. Even larger amounts were rebated on direct taxes (Lin, 1973). Thus the rigours of import control were used to make exports attractive. Between 1970 and 1974, the proportion of controlled items fell from 41 per cent to 2 per cent (though restrictions on who could import and authorisation requirements remained important — see Wade, 1990); with this, the discrimination in favour of exporters declined. But imports became more generally available and import–based export production became easier for everyone.

It is likely that even in the heyday of protection, the machine tool industry was less protected than the rest. In 1966, the nominal import duty on lathes and drilling machines was 11.34 per cent — the lowest except for duties on a few products like cement and fertilisers. The rate of effective protection was low — 0.85 per cent on lathes and 3.26 per cent on drilling machines. The import bias was negligible. In general, the metal and machinery industries bore the lowest tariffs (Hsiang, 1971; Lin, 1973). Thus machine tools were probably internationally competitive even in the early period when many other goods were not; in the 1970s and 1980s when the exchange rate came to be heavily undervalued, they were favourably placed to exploit the emerging export opportunities.

Initially, Chinese Taipei machine tools found markets in neighbouring countries. The outward orientation coincided with the height of the Vietnam war which created a boom in the neighbouring countries that created a demand for machine tools. This was met by Chinese Taipei firms. In 1968, Thailand took 36 per cent of the exports, Vietnam 21 per cent and the Philippines 20 per cent (Jacobsson, 1986). Chinese communities in these countries spearheaded the exports. By the early 1970s, the boom created by the Vietnam war had led to widespread shortages of machinery, opening new opportunities for exports to the United States, Japan, Australia and New Zealand (Amsden, 1977). During the 1970s, Chinese Taipei firms which did not export complete machines began to take sourcing and sub–contracting orders from exporters. The rapid rise in exports thus led to vertical disintegration and increased specialisation in the domestic industry. Even now a distinction can be found between older, more integrated producers that sell 50–80 per cent of their output within the country and newer exporter–assemblers that export 70–80 per cent of their output and buy a larger proportion of their inputs (Lautier, 1994).

The United States emerged as the major market for Chinese Taipei's machine tool exports in the late 1970s; by 1981, more than half the exports were going to the United States (Table 2.7). The buyers, as in Chinese Taipei, were mostly small engineering enterprises. The selling points were low prices and quick delivery. The rising share of Chinese Taipei machine tools in the United States market drew the ire of domestic machine tool manufacturers. Under their pressure, the United States and Chinese Taipei entered into a voluntary export restraint (VER) agreement in 1986 restricting Chinese Taipei's market share in the United States market to 5 per cent and preventing any growth. In consequence, Chinese Taipei firms increased their exports to Western Europe — first to Britain, and later to Holland, Italy, Germany, France and Belgium. By 1990, almost a third of the exports were going to Western Europe. When Western Europe entered into a recession in the early 1990s, Chinese Taipei found a market in China. Thus Chinese Taipei rapidly shifted between markets, and its share of the world market was maintained despite the decline first of the United States and then of the Western European market.

As the Chinese Taipei machine tool industry increased its exports, its perception of opportunities in world markets changed and it began to compare itself with the international industry. This led to a change in product strategy. Chinese Taipei's policy of restricting imports of goods competing with domestically produced goods, we saw earlier, had encouraged the copying of foreign machines but there seems to have been no concentration on particular products or on standardisation. By the 1970s, however, manufacturers were modelling their machines on particular foreign machines with a broad international market. The Bridgeport milling machine was amongst the popular brands, and imitations were good enough for their parts to be interchangeable with the original. The degree of imitation probably did not change much in this period but there was a notable improvement in the quality of engineering and heightened sensitivity to international design. This was certainly true by the late 1970s and early 1980s when Fransman (1986) surveyed Chinese Taipei firms. All designs except one in his sample were originally copies of Japanese machines. While Japan continued to be the major source of machine tools and, implicitly, of designs for Chinese Taipei firms, Fransman's firms also learnt much by watching one another, and from customers at home and abroad. Product adaptation for the international market was learnt at this stage.

Competition and Innovation

Thus as exports grew, the sources of learning for Chinese Taipei firms changed: the market demanded broader learning, which was available in the immensely varied range of machine tools in the world market. But Chinese Taipei manufacturers continued to rely on Japanese machines which were imported in large numbers. This may have been because Japanese machines were easier to copy than European machines, which embodied more process technology. Japanese designs, however, were also part of a highly successful marketing approach which since the 1960s had consisted in the creation of new international markets by cheapening and simplifying machine tools. Chinese Taipei exploited this trajectory through product innovation. Following the Japanese lead was made easier for Chinese Taipei producers by the close links between the two countries[3]. As we observed above, this early mastery of the Japanese model of innovation, based on close economic and social ties, was a key element in the Chinese Taipei (and Korean) lead over India and other newcomers.

Advance along the trajectory of improving conventional tools became easier once Japanese firms secured a decisive lead in NC tools and began to concentrate on them thus opening a market niche in conventional tools which Chinese Taipei exploited. As Table 2.6 shows, 80 per cent of Chinese Taipei machine tool exports by value were of non–NC tools even in 1993. The same process is seen to be at work, however, in NC tools themselves: Chinese Taipei has thus concentrated on the workhorses — NC lathes and machining centres — whilst Japan has moved on to more complex and heavier machines. The technological edge of Japanese firms is acknowledged by all Chinese Taipei manufacturers interviewed.

From this brief survey it is clear that a number of factors differentiate the growth and innovation trajectories of Indian and Chinese Taipei machine tool manufacturers. First, there is a crucial difference between the conventional tools made in Chinese Taipei and in India — namely, Chinese Taipei tools appear to be more standardised and more reliable. This is closely related to the difference in export performance between the two sets of producers. In the 1970s, Chinese Taipei firms produced cheap and simple machines for export to neighbouring developing countries. Once Chinese Taipei graduated to exports to the United States and Europe, however, machine tool manufacturers were obliged to upgrade product design and performance standards to meet the requirements of those markets. Feedback from distributors, especially those in the United States, yielded useful information on competing machines and suggestions on improvements.

Second, the shift to larger and more demanding export markets had an impact on the organisation of production in the Chinese Taipei machine tool industry. During the 1970s, Amsden (1977) noted the tendency of Chinese Taipei manufacturers to make a high proportion of components in–house — a characteristic of early manufacturing history that persisted in India to the 1990s. The poor quality of bought–out components and consequently the need for in–house manufacture to ensure quality control and the fear that sub–contracting components would lead to a loss of technological secrets were major reasons behind the vertical integration practised by Chinese Taipei machine tool manufacturers initially. However, the buy–out ratio began to increase when exports rose in the 1970s. The new export markets created opportunities for large–scale production which favoured specialisation both in components and in final products; and once product design was dominated by the fast–changing requirements of the export market, design capabilities had to be built up, and the scarcity value of in–house designs declined. As the pace of product innovation accelerated, the shelf life of technological secrets declined drastically; and with increasing scales of production, the cost of out–sourced components fell relative to that of those manufactured in–house, particularly when the size of orders to components manufacturers rose. The extensive sub–contractor networks subsequently generated further economies of scale, created specialist skills within firms, relieved capacity bottlenecks, and led to rapid diffusion of technological knowledge. These advantages outweighed the tendency of firms to produce in–house for protection of technological secrets[4]. Sub–contracting is certainly very common now, but a difference in buy–out ratios persists between old and new firms. As Tsai (1992) notes, older manufacturers are more integrated, whereas Leadwell, which came up in 1980 and rapidly grew into Chinese Taipei's largest machine tool manufacturer, consistently followed a strategy of minimising in–house manufacture. Leadwell reflects a trend discernible throughout the Chinese Taipei machine tool industry towards vertical disintegration.

Third, although OEM production rose considerably over the 1980s, it still constitutes only a small part of Chinese Taipei's total output. More importantly, OEM manufacture has not meant the replacement of local by foreign designs. Instead, foreign firms have often adopted and placed their own brandnames on Chinese Taipei products. This is the greatest difference with India: Chinese Taipei industry is no longer selling only machine tools, it is selling engineering and manufacturing expertise — the ability to reproduce machines accurately, at low cost and with minimum outside technological inputs.

Fourth, the spatial clustering of machine tool manufacturers in Chinese Taipei marks yet another difference with the Indian experience. Networks of competitors and suppliers in Chinese Taipei are located quite close together. The Taichung industrial estate, for example, displays the greatest concentration of machine tool and related manufacturers. Black Hand Road in particular is well known for the number of machine tool makers situated along it. Perhaps because of its size, geographical concentration came more easily to Chinese Taipei than to India where the industry is much more dispersed. Until quite recently, moreover, there was little interaction between the four geographical clusters that make up the Indian industry. Only two of these clusters, Bangalore and Ludhiana, have grown sufficiently large to support sub–contracting networks. Poona still does not support a significant network and Rajkot is in a nascent stage. This insulation of Indian clusters contrasts strongly with the closeness of competitors and sub–contractors in Chinese Taipei. Thanks to proximity, everything — people, ideas, information, goods — moved faster from one firm to another in Chinese Taipei. The intensity of these tacit as well as explicit material and non–material exchanges reduced entry costs and facilitated the creation of new firms, which is the determining factor in Chinese Taipei's industrial dynamism. Abundance of sub–contractors, skilled workers, information and imported inputs thus combined to create a highly competitive environment in the Chinese Taipei machine tool industry[5].

The Sequence in India

To a certain extent, the Indian story is more complex than that of Chinese Taipei. India is a larger and less integrated country than Chinese Taipei, and there are a number of independent but interacting regional developments proceeding simultaneously. The origins of industrial enterprise in India, moreover, are diverse and machine tools are only a small part of India's entrepreneurial history. Government policies have been just as interventionist and complex in India as in Chinese Taipei. This tendency has undoubtedly been reinforced by an entrepreneurial class which asked for and profited from government intervention. The interplay of these varied factors makes it more difficult to give a unified interpretation of the failure of the Indian machine tool industry to grow and establish a world presence in the context of policies which were intended, however misguidedly, to help it do precisely that.

Structure

Compared to Chinese Taipei, the machine tool industry was not only more geographically dispersed in India, but its structure was also more segmented. Three segments can be distinguished. The first is composed of Hindustan Machine Tools (HMT), a company set up in 1953 by the Government of India with the help of Oerlikon and located in Bangalore. It soon broke with Oerlikon, captured a large share of government orders, obtained licences on the strength of this captive market, diversified rapidly and dominated the market. Even now it holds a 33 per cent share of the official market (i.e. excluding the small manufacturers).

Second, there are the relatively large firms in and around Bombay, Poona and Bangalore. Bombay, as the largest port and industrial city, has been home to machinery and tool manufacturers since the 19th century. Poona, 120 miles south–east of Bombay, is the headquarters of the Western Command of the Indian army. It emerged as an industrial centre as a result of ordnance factories sited there during World War II. Since then it has grown owing to its proximity to Bombay. Bangalore, 300 miles south–east of Bombay, also had ordnance factories and repair workshops as the headquarters of the Southern Command. Recently, the growth of electronics, computers and software businesses in the area has increased its attractiveness for machine tool manufacturers.

With the exception of Cooper Engineering, set up in Poona in 1937 as a licensee of Alfred Herbert, the British machine tool maker, and of Mysore Kirloskar, started in 1941 in Mysore near Bangalore when imports were cut off by the war and there was a severe shortage of machine tools, all large firms were established in 1951–66, the period in which severe import restrictions made imports difficult and domestic production was given complete protection. The result was that a number of industrialists set up machine tool production as subsidiaries or licensed affiliates of foreign manufacturers. Several had previously been import agents of foreign companies. Voltas, Batliboi, Machine Tools India, Empire Machine Tools, Allen–Bradley India, Advani–Oerlikon and Traub India, for example, all began as import agents, while Bharat Fritz Werner (BFW) was a subsidiary of Fritz Werner set up by the brother of F. Matulla, who headed Hindustan Machine Tools during its initial years.

In the 1960s when importing was difficult, domestic manufacturers had full order books and low technological capacity, and were not very good at servicing customers. Hence a number of large user firms set up divisions or subsidiaries whose chief job was maintenance, setting up jigs and fixtures, making dies, and working out specifications and costs of machine tools to be purchased. Some of them also made machine tools. Amongst them are Tata Engineering and Locomotive Company (TELCO), the largest truck manufacturer, which bought up Investa Machine Tools in the late 1960s and turned it into a captive machine tool maker, and Mico–Bosch, which is mainly a manufacturer of fuel injection equipment. None of these user firms became a major supplier of machine tools to the market. However, Cooper Engineering, which was taken over by Premier Automobiles in 1987[6], continues to sell machine tools in the market.

Finally, there are hundreds of small firms which produce a large and probably growing share of the total output. Early information on small machine tool manufacturers is sparse; but it appears that they originated mainly in West Punjab, which became part of Pakistan in 1947. This heavily irrigated, highly prosperous agricultural area supported many blacksmiths and tool–makers; the metal–working skills resided in a Sikh sect called the Ramgarhias[7]. With partition they migrated to East Punjab in India and set up shop. In the late 1950s, the massive Bhakra–Nangal dam became operational and irrigation began to spread over Indian Punjab. The prosperity it brought from the mid–1960s onwards led to the emergence of a number of new engineering industries to make and repair sewing machines, electric fans, bicycles and diesel and electric irrigation pumps. The green revolution got a sudden boost with the arrival of high–yielding seeds from 1966 onwards; the resulting surge in agricultural output also stimulated the machine tool industry amongst others. It was concentrated in two centres, Ludhiana and Batala. Apart from Punjab, small machine tool manufacturers also emerged near other centres of small–scale industry: for instance, in Rajkot, Surendranagar and Surat in Gujarat[8] on the west coast, and in Coimbatore and Madras in the south.

The Slump of 1966

The period 1951–66 was the golden age of import substitution. The government not only banned imports of machine tools that were produced at home; it also encouraged new manufacturers to produce machines that were not being produced within the country, and discouraged them from producing machine tools similar to those that were already in production. So the field of machine tools got mapped out, and competition was minimised in each segment — a system of product monopolies was set up. Production grew very rapidly — the constant–price index of output constructed by Jethanandani (1985) rose more than tenfold between 1956–57 and 1966–67. Demand was buoyant and competition was constrained both at home and from abroad. So machine tools were produced and sold regardless of cost. Production was highly concentrated: in 1964, HMT produced 44 per cent of official output, Mysore

Kirloskar 17 per cent, Cooper and BFW 4 per cent each, and Investa Machine Tools 3 per cent. Thus five firms produced 72 per cent of output. The large firms were highly integrated. Indian industry was little developed then, and it was difficult to find component manufacturers. The few that existed were reluctant to take on production of the machine tool manufacturers' small requirements, and their quality was poor. Quality castings in particular were difficult to procure. Hence the buy–out ratio of the early manufacturers was low.

The boom came to an end in 1966–68, and official output fell by 40 per cent. There is reason to believe that this fall was not entirely real, but that demand shifted from HMT and the large firms to small firms which were not members of the Indian Machine Tool Manufacturers' Association and whose output did not enter official statistics. This third sector of the industry is still not included in official statistics and is largely ignored in studies of the Indian machine tool industry. Jethanandani (1985), the only researcher who has paid it some attention, estimates its share of output at 17 per cent in 1963, 27 per cent in 1970 and 34 per cent in 1972. But he assumes the price difference between machines manufactured by large and by small firms to be over 13:1. This could be too high. If it were, say, half as much, the small firms' share of output would be 29 per cent in 1963, 43 per cent in 1970 and 51 per cent in 1972. Further, the censuses of machine tools which are used as a basis for estimates are apt to make gross underestimates of machines in small firms and workshops, which are also generally produced by other small firms. Whilst it is impossible to make any accurate estimate, it is clear that the small–scale sector was and is very significant, and that it has been eating into the large firms' market, more rapidly after 1966 than before.

The sudden shift in market share from large to small firms in the late 1960s was due to two factors: a shift in the market from government to private purchases, and the end of the seller's market in inputs. First, the economy–wide recession in 1966–68 led to a collapse of government investment: real government revenue fell, and investment was more adversely affected than government consumption. As a result, the nexus between the purchasing government departments — principally the defence industries, railways and heavy engineering — and big machine tool makers — principally HMT — broke down. Earlier, government departments spotted the new machine tools they wanted, the government banned their imports, and on the strength of the ban, HMT obtained a licence to make them. Other firms played the same game with other imported machines. This game continued after 1966. Large firms continued to target imports and replace them after 1966; the share of imports in official apparent consumption fell from 67 per cent in 1967 to 30 per cent in 1970. But the drastic import substitution only slowed the decline in demand; it could not sustain the growth of the industry.

The green revolution, which was equally unexpected, led to a quick surge in the demand for engineering services to agriculture, especially in Punjab. This brought sudden prosperity to the small machine tool manufacturers, which began to manufacture a wide variety of machine tools. Relying entirely on reverse engineering, the small firms produced crude machine tools which were called *addas*. These were modelled

Table 2.8. **Machine Tool Export Performance of Selected Countries, 1973–80**

	1973	1974	1975	1976	1977	1978	1979	1980
				($ million)				
WORLD OUTPUT	10 604	12 671	13 644	13 543	15 127	19 068	22 920	26 748
Chinese Taipei	18	22	21	35	58	126	198	245
India	55	71	93	96	90	112	127	165
Korea				10	57	95	163	135
Brazil	55	111	137	223	283	255	387	315
WORLD EXPORTS	3 891	4 940	5 897	6 500	8 071	9 661	11 439	10 360
Chinese Taipei	6	15	15	30	50	94	144	178
India	4	9	10	11	21	24	20	25
Korea					2	5	14	27
Brazil	5	6	14	11	11	20	28	71
				(percentage)				
WORLD EXPORT RATIO	37	39	43	43	43	42	42	43
Chinese Taipei	38	67	81	86	85	75	73	73
India	6	13	11	12	23	22	16	15
Korea					4	5	9	20
Brazil	9	5	10	5	4	8	7	22

Source: Jethanandani (1985).

on the brands of larger firms, but were poorly made and used non–standard components. The Kirloskar lathe was particularly popular amongst them, but they tried their hand at many machine tools and turned out passable copies. Their machines were so cheap that they found a market even among large buyers of machine tools. Soon buyers were coming from far and wide, wandering around the alleys of Millergunj in Ludhiana, and shopping around for copies of machines they fancied. Eicher Tractors, for instance, equipped an entire factory in the late 1960s with *addas*, and jigged them up for precision work, thereby keeping down capital costs. With this cheap factory, Eicher went on to become a major manufacturer of tractors. In this instance, the upgrading of the *addas* was done by Eicher itself. But later, the example of machines produced by large firms and, as in the Chinese Taipei case, the demands of buyers led small firms to improve their products. Today, although their products are distinguished by poorer external finish and painting, their accuracy has improved over time, much assisted by the advent of electronic controls.

The shift in market share from large to small producers was reinforced by a change in the market for inputs. From 1955 to 1966 there was a continual shortage of pig iron and steel. Both were allocated by the government, and large firms with an industrial licence had privileged access. Small firms were also given a small quota; but this was channelled through industry departments of state governments, and its allocation was riddled with corruption. Small firms thus tended to buy steel in a limited and unreliable black market at high prices. In the 1966 slump, the demand for steel declined, the shortage suddenly disappeared, and with it went a binding constraint on the growth of small firms. The choice of sections available also improved. Till 1966, the sections that were mainly available in the black market were those used in building — bars, angles and channels. After 1966, a greater variety of sections became available in the open market. Thus developments on the demand and supply sides coincided to create new opportunities for small firms to raise their market share.

As their markets ceased to expand, large firms now found it difficult to get licences from foreign firms. The number of new licences fell from an average of 16 a year in 1961–67 to less than six a year over the next 15 years. It was not until 1983 that collaborations again rose to double digits. The fall in licensing was also due to government efforts to stimulate import substitution in technology and to force foreign firms to disinvest their share in their Indian subsidiaries. The ties between foreign companies and their subsidiaries were loosened by the Foreign Exchange Regulation Act of 1973, which forced the parent companies to reduce their shareholding to less than 40 per cent. With this, the foreign firms often lost management control. Hermann Traub, for instance, sold out to its Indian partner, and Traub (India) became Perfect Machine Tools (PMT). Even where the parent retained control, it was often difficult for it to confine the subsidiary to the parent's products when profits depended on diversification; so subsidiaries (for example, Bharat Fritz Werner) had more freedom to diversify and were even allowed to take licences from firms other than their parent companies. The forced divestment of foreign controlling shares combined with the long slump to make the industry unattractive to licensors from 1966 until the late 1970s. In consequence, over the 1970s the large firms extended their product range by reverse engineering, giving rise to much boasting about "successful development" of various machine tools.

The reverse engineering was nowhere as extensive or creative as in Chinese Taipei, however. The late 1960s and 1970s were the period in which the Chinese Taipei machine tool industry became outward oriented. The Japanese industry moved into NC tools, the Chinese Taipei industry moved into the niche so vacated, and both deeply penetrated the markets, first in Asia and then in the United States. Thus reverse engineering in Chinese Taipei was oriented towards world markets; internationally best- known machines were targeted. In India, the industry served mainly the domestic market; and it had poor access to imports of foreign tools and components. It therefore extended the range of its existing machine tools by marginal variations within a more limited product range. Whereas the Chinese Taipei product range approached the internationally available range, the Indian product range obsolesced and moved away from world trends.

The Aftermath of the Oil Crisis

The oil crisis created instability which different countries dealt with in different ways. The United States dealt with it by running massive fiscal and payments deficits and keeping the dollar overvalued; the payments deficit could be financed out of foreign capital inflows, including inflows from those oil–producing countries which earned a bonanza thanks to the oil price increase. Overvaluation of the dollar and buoyant demand in the United States attracted imports; imports deeply penetrated the United States market in many goods in the 1970s, including machine tools. Apart from the United States, the oil–producing countries also offered expanding markets. Both Japan and Chinese Taipei made good use of the opportunity to achieve rapid export growth. As Table 2.8 showed, Chinese Taipei's output of machine tools in 1973 was a third of India's. India tripled its value of output by 1980; but by then Chinese Taipei's output was 50 per cent more than India's. More remarkably, Chinese Taipei's exports in 1980 exceeded India's output.

Thus the 1970s saw the machine tool industries of all the countries in Table 2.8 becoming more export–oriented, but Chinese Taipei led, whilst India lagged. After 1980, however, even the modest surge in Indian exports petered out in all markets except Eastern Europe, where they could be sold because special payment arrangements created a sheltered market (Table 2.9).

Table 2.9. **Direction of Indian Machine Tool Exports, Selected Years, 1975–83**

	1975	1978	1981	1983
Total exports (Rs million)	82	210	233	266
of which (per cent) to:				
SE Asia	15	25	14	5
Australia–New Zealand	13	7	3	1
W. Europe	26	17	19	10
United States	18	9	12	3
W. Asia	8	9	4	5
All the above	80	67	52	24
E. Europe	3	10	7	58
Other	17	21	41	18

Source: IMTMA Annual Reports.

Protection and the Loss of Competitiveness

Why did Indian machine tools so rapidly lose the markets won in the 1970s? Wogart *et al.* (1993) attribute the loss of competitiveness to the rise in domestic steel prices. Steel, like other industrial products, was protected by quantitative restrictions; most of it was produced by the Steel Authority of India (SAIL), a government corporation. Between 1980 and 1985 the terms of trade of machinery against metals worsened by 24 per cent. In 1985, Indian steel prices were 80–100 per cent above world prices, while special steels were almost 200 per cent more expensive. Thus Indian machine tools were priced out of the world market because of the protection of upstream industries. An ICICI study shows how, from being more profitable than domestic sales in the late 1970s, exports of machine tools became unremunerative from 1980 onwards (ICICI, 1985). In this way, irrational patterns of protection caused a serious setback to machine tool production in the 1980s. This irrationality has persisted to this day, although it is much less pronounced now: machine tools are subject to a duty of 25 per cent, while steel and metals bear a duty of 40–50 per cent. The high level of protection has also attracted competition and reduced the market share of the two large, integrated producers, SAIL and Tata Iron and Steel company (TISCO). Smaller producers have emerged using either scrap or sponge iron. Since 1991, imports have been opened up and import duties reduced. But steel still bears a higher duty than engineering goods, and domestic steel remains more expensive than imported steel.

The adverse impact of protection on exports can be avoided by a system of duty drawbacks and exemptions. India set up such a system in the 1960s, at about the same time as Chinese Taipei, and continues to operate it, but differently. The incentive to export that it gave was always insufficient. Import entitlements are finely calculated and leave no surplus to sell in the domestic market; sale of duty–free imports or entitlements in the domestic market is illegal, and customs authorities pursue suspected offenders and punish them. This means that manufacturers whose import requirements are small or irregular find it difficult and expensive to import, and find the procedures too cumbersome. It often takes 5–6 months to claim a duty drawback. Meanwhile, the investment made in paying duty is locked up, and interest costs are high. Especially in the late 1980s when duties of 80 per cent and more were common, the capital required and its interest costs made importing on duty drawback unviable. Thus the drawback system has worked against small producers and producers of differentiated goods, including machine tool manufacturers.

As drawbacks fell into desuetude, exporters pressed the government to allow duty–free imports against orders for exports. These advance licences remain the mainstay of import replenishment for exports to this day. They are not always given in advance; often bureaucratic delays lead to their being issued weeks after exports are made. But they are more expeditious than duty drawbacks, and do not require investment in paying import duty. Nonetheless, the lags in importing were also very long. In the early 1980s, the average lead time for inputs under import licensing was 48 weeks. As a result, Indian manufacturers could not offer delivery as fast as their competitors abroad. Their inventory costs were also significantly higher. The red tape involved in getting advance licences continued to discourage potential exporters.

Structural Changes in the 1980s

In the 1980s, the leading machine tool industries of the world moved into numerical controls. The Indian industry moved very slowly. The reason appears to be twofold. One was a perverse change in trade policy. In 1979 the government decided to move away from quantitative import restrictions to tariffs. In pursuit of this policy, an increasing number of machine tools were placed on Open General Licence (OGL) (i.e. did not require an import licence); the number increased from 24 in 1972–82 to 128 in 1982–85 and 300 in 1985–88 (Wogart *et al.,* 1993). Generally speaking, advanced–technology products, including NC machine tools, were placed on OGL. But, those so placed bore higher tariffs; and tariff differentials were raised throughout the 1980s. In 1972–82 there were two tariff bands for machine tools — 25 per cent and 48 per cent. In 1986–89 there were four bands — 35 per cent, 55 per cent, 95 per cent and 115 per cent. The idea was to give more protection to more advanced products. For instance in 1985, effective protection on ordinary lathes was 9 per cent, whilst on CNC lathes it was 83 per cent (BICP, 1988). The effect was, however, the opposite. The demand for new machines tends in any case to be initially small and the high margins of protection increased their domestic price, thus reducing demand even further. The lower the sales of domestic manufacturers, moreover, the less experience they acquire in production, the less feedback they receive from servicing machine tools and the less reliable are their products. Sophisticated buyers in India thus preferred to import advanced–technology products despite their higher price. Over time, the small domestic scales of production kept costs high and made domestically produced tools uncompetitive.

As Table 2.10 illustrates, the share of imports in consumption went up sharply in the 1980s. While it is likely that much of the increase was accounted for by the rise in the relative prices of imported machine tools with the increase in tariffs, it also reflects the fact that an increasing proportion of imports represented NC tools. For instance, the Maruti car factory, set up in the early 1980s as a joint venture between the central government and Suzuki, entirely imported its machinery; this was also true of the new consumer durables and equipment producers who set up production in the 1980s. Thus in the 1986 machine tool census, 1 046 imported NC tools were counted, against 136 domestically produced ones (CMTI, 1989). Of the latter, the oldest Indian–made NC machines were five lathes that were at least 16 years old and must therefore have been produced in the late 1960s. But production of more than one lathe a year was not reached until 1975–80 and only 58 were produced in 1980–85. The first machining centres were a pair produced in 1975–80; but the first machining centre to be offered off the shelf was a horizontal machine HMT designed after importing the design of a vertical one from Kearney, Trecker and Marvin in 1983. Then there was a flurry of technology imports; 15 collaborations were signed in 1983 and 1984 (Jacobsson and Alam, 1992). In 1981 HMT bought technology for numeric controls from Siemens and began to produce a series of them. Because of the high import duties, they found ready sales amongst the local NC tool manufacturers, and captured most of the market. But the high monopoly price also limited the market for NC machine tools and slowed down technological change. It was only after 1991, when quantitative import restrictions were removed and tariffs were scaled down, that HMT's controls faced competition and prices came down. But the share of imports in consumption continued to rise.

Table 2.10. **India's Machine Tool Export and Import Ratios, Selected Years, 1975–93**
(in per cent)

	Exports/ Production	Imports/ Consumption
1975	7.9	31.5
1978	16.9	28.5
1981	9.9	38.8
1984	7.0	41.8

Sources: DGTD, Annual Reports; IMTMA, Annual Reports; Ministry of Finance, Economic Surveys.

The second major policy change took place in 1983. Broad–banding, as it was called, meant that machine tool manufacturers no longer had to obtain industrial licences in order to produce new models within their licensed capacity. In other words, they could diversify without government permission. Tariffs were also being raised in this period leading Staffan Jacobsson to predict that this combination of domestic liberalisation and import restriction would stimulate a proliferation of producers as a growing number of them sought to capture the rent created by tariffs. The domestic contribution to technology development, however, would fall (Jacobsson, 1991).

It is difficult to say whether the number of firms increased since the total number of small firms is not known. The membership of the Indian Machine Tool Manufacturers Association (IMTMA) did increase. But some small firms are always growing and becoming members of IMTMA, so the growth does not necessarily represent new firms. But it is clear that while there was a surge in technology imports, almost all the licences were taken by established firms[9]. Technology suppliers obviously preferred firms that already had production and marketing facilities. Thus the connection Jacobsson postulated between the restrictive trade regime, liberalisation of technology imports and proliferation of new firms using the liberalisation to import new technology has not been borne out.

The 1980s saw the emergence of some new firms, but of those known to us, only one (Machines and Machine Tools Limited) imported technology; none of the rest formally obtained any technology from outside. All were set up by technocrats who left either HMT or the Central Machine Tool Institute (CMTI), a public research institute. These new entrepreneurs went into one of two lines of business. One group developed relationships with large users and designed machine tools specially for them. For instance, there is the Hyderabad–based group, Machine Tool Aids and Reconditioning (MTAR). It consists of three firms — Marc, Montage, and Metal Treatment Systems. It specialises in high–technology products. MTAR specially designed and made precision machine tools for the space programme. There are similar informal tie–ups between machine tool firms and the major vehicle manufacturers. The second group designs and makes standardised machine tools. Its speciality is to achieve high standards while buying in a high proportion of its parts. Thus the vertical disintegration which was seen in the newer firms in Chinese Taipei is also noticeable in India. To this group belong Parisudh Yantra Sadhan, Ace Designers, Pragati Engineering Works, A.K. Hitech Machines, and Precihole Machine Tools. They manufacture a mutually complementary set of machine tools and components, share a brand name — Micromatic — and have a common marketing and servicing organisation. Together they offer product diversity, high quality and good servicing. As a result, these firms are amongst the most successful. They were less affected than others by the recession of 1990–92 and they have been exporting. Again, in contrast to Jacobsson's earlier prediction, the policy changes did not reduce the domestic contribution to technology development and may actually have stimulated new firms to innovate in products and in the organisation of production, marketing and service.

What is curious, however, is that these changes are not reflected in official output figures which show almost no rise in the number of machine tools produced during the 1980s, and a substantial fall in the 1990s. The import ratio also rose substantially in the 1980s (Table 2.10), but much of this rise was due to the rise in import duties; hence imports do not explain the stagnation of recorded output. There are two other possibilities. One is that the productivity of NC machine tools is much higher and so fewer machines are needed. The impact of NC machine tools can be seen in the factories of HMT, TELCO and Godrej and Boyce, where entire bays have emptied with the installation of NC machine tools. The other possibility is that small firms have continued to eat into the market of large firms. This is very likely. The growth of small firms is reflected in the growth of IMTMA membership. Their growing sophistication is also evident. Their product quality has improved, and they have become more accurate and reliable. In effect, large firms have vacated certain simple product groups — for instance, horizontal non–NC lathes — and small firms have captured them. As evidenced in the 1994 Indian Machine Tool Exhibition, small firms have also captured a substantial market share of automats. The advent of electronic and numeric controls has favoured small firms: they can buy in the controls and thereby achieve high levels of accuracy without in–house investment.

In addition, the firms in Punjab suffered a setback in 1985–90 because of terrorism: credit became unavailable, and outstation buyers stopped coming. This was particularly true of firms in Batala, which is close to the Pakistan border; less true of Ludhiana firms. But their troubles did not stop the growth of small firms; they simply began to grow in other centres. Their lower wage costs, together with other privileges such as cheap, reserved credit and lower taxes, gave them a decisive advantage. The troubles of Punjab small industry contributed to the growth of small firms in Rajkot and Coimbatore.

Policy Reforms of the 1990s

The early 1990s saw a major shakedown in the industry. First, the Soviet market collapsed in 1990. Second, the government delicensed the machine tool industry in 1991. With this, official restrictions on domestic competition disappeared. Third, it abolished import licensing in machine tools and industrial inputs and abandoned forced import substitution in the form of phased manufacturing programmes in 1992. Finally, it began to bring down import duties. From 170 per cent in 1992 the maximum rate came down to 90 per cent in 1993, 65 per cent in 1994, and 50 per cent in 1995. The fall was particularly sharp for NC controls. It was partly mitigated by a 50 per cent devaluation in 1991–92; but there was still a fall in the rupee costs of imports.

The abolition of import licensing has greatly cut down the difficulties of importing, and reduced import lead times and hence inventories of imported inputs. As a result, imports rose from $110 million in 1990 to $150 million in 1993. The official value of domestic output changed little: it was Rs 7 billion in 1990 and Rs 6.4 billion in 1993. But prices came down considerably. For instance, a machining centre which cost Rs 7.2 million now costs Rs 2.4 million; the price of an NC lathe has come down from Rs 2.2 million to Rs 1.4 million. So real output is likely to have increased substantially.

Compounding the need to restructure in the face of increased competition from abroad, was the recession of 1990–93. Although only one major firm — X–Cello — went bankrupt in this period almost all made losses, and were therefore under additional pressure to restructure. The new firms set up by technocrats, which have low overheads and low labour costs, were the least affected. Small firms also suffered little and, by improving their product technology with the help of numeric and electronic controls, began to compete directly with large firms. Older and larger firms were harder hit. The most affected were those large firms, like HMT, which were dependent on government orders — on defence and the railways.

In response to these changes, these firms have taken a number of steps. First, they have reduced their product range; the over–diversification that was the consequence of blanket import substitution is declining. At the same time they have begun to look for outside products to market in order to spread overheads. Second, they have concentrated production to reduce overheads. Some have closed down factories or production lines; others have shifted production to a smaller number of factories. Third, they have been vertically disintegrating, phasing out the production of components and sourcing more from outside. Finally, they have begun to think about process technology and to look outside for ideas. The tendency to innovate independently of and outside technology import agreements, which first emerged in the 1980s, has been strengthened. For instance, firms which had hitherto followed the practices of their European partners have begun to look to Japan and its practices such as just–in–time production, product simplification, standardisation and production in series.

When the government began to dismantle controls in 1991, restructuring of industry was expected to founder on labour resistance. Indian labour laws make it illegal for enterprises with 100 workers or more to close an establishment or retrench labour without the permission of state governments, which was almost never given (although some state governments have become more flexible in the past two years). The central government made some moves to amend labour laws, and worked out amendments in 1992, but gave up in the face of trade union resistance. However, interviews with firms suggest that considerable restructuring has taken place despite the labour laws, particularly as the emergence of competition changes workers' attitudes. For instance, Electronica, a firm in Poona, reported an increase in workers' commitment as competition increased. Previously, they used to agitate to make casual workers permanent so that worker strength would go up. Now they no longer press the case of casual workers, and are more intent on increasing their own productivity. In general they are more sensitive to the performance of the company.

Another change is a stronger tendency to build networks. Firms no longer seek to produce components in–house and have instead been looking for sub–contractors to reduce costs. Sub–contractors are most commonly found in the Bangalore area and this has served to attract more of the industry there. Thus clusters of competitors and suppliers, like the Chinese Taipei ones, show signs of emerging. Manufacturers are also grouping together for common marketing and after–sales service, as we saw above.

While the industry was thus adapting itself to the stresses of recession, a boom suddenly struck it in 1994. The vehicle industries experienced a surge in demand, and their expansion led to orders for machine tools, especially NC machine tools. In 1993 the offtake of NC machine tools was 425, down from 689 in 1991; in 1994 it was estimated to be 700. The boom has also changed the large manufacturers' attitude towards import liberalisation. Till 1993 IMTMA was hostile. In 1994, however, its member firms were able to react much faster to the surge in domestic demand because they could import inputs quickly. Now IMTMA no longer wants tariffs to be increased, and is prepared to accept further decreases in import duties provided duties on its inputs come down simultaneously. It has pressed for particularly large reductions in duties on imported inputs into NC tools — controllers, servomotors, spindle motors and drives. Partly under its pressure, tariffs on electronic intermediate products were cut in the budget of February 1995.

The quickening of pulse has attracted the interest of Fanuc. Fanuc manufactures 6 000–8 000 controls a month in Japan; India's market for 500–600 controls a year, largely dominated by HMT's Hinumeric system, did not attract it initially. But following import liberalisation in 1991, imports of numeric controls gained a foothold in the market. Control prices fell, the demand for numerical controls expanded, and Fanuc gained a sufficient market share to consider domestic manufacture. It set up a joint venture with Voltas in 1992; Fanuc has a 50 per cent share in the equity, Voltas 25 per cent, and the Indian affiliate of General Electric Controls, which is Fanuc's United States subsidiary, has a 10 per cent share. In 1994 Fanuc expected to sell about 250 controls out of national sales of 700. It is also working with Ace Designers and other firms to design simple NC controls for the Indian market which would cost less and thus lead to faster entry of NC tools into the production of small firms. Having built up considerable technological capacity over the 1980s and altered their traditional habits and practices during the early 1990s, HMT and Kirloskar Electric were able to react quickly to Fanuc's competition by bringing out a range of cheaper controls.

Conclusions

Judging by exports and market shares, Japan has been the most competitive producer of machine tools; its competitive strength has been based on the edge in technology and marketing which it has maintained for 20 years. Germany, which 20 years ago had similar competitive strength based on technology, has held on to it. Chinese Taipei is the producer which has most improved its competitiveness. Low production costs are an important part of the explanation for Chinese Taipei's success; its machine tools sell internationally at a half to a third of the price of machine tools of the same description (though obviously not the same quality) from Japan or Germany. But low costs were not all; the Chinese Taipei firms also developed a product innovation strategy, first applied to conventional machine tools and later pursued in NC machine tools.

By contrast, India has been internationally uncompetitive, and its lack of competitiveness extends to both cost and design. We have tried in this chapter to probe the causes of this uncompetitiveness. The question therefore arises: why did not the Indian firms break out into the international market and acquire competitiveness like the Chinese Taipei firms? The answer must be given at a number of levels: external influences, macroeconomic policies, and industrial structure.

External Factors

To begin with, it is worth noting certain factors external to the machine tool industry. The first is the level and quality of education. Simple indicators of education such as literacy or the proportion of the eligible population receiving secondary or tertiary education place Chinese Taipei far ahead of India. But these output indicators may not be very relevant since the number of India's primary, secondary and tertiary graduates is quite adequate for its requirements. But there appears to be a significant difference in the quality and orientation of education. Only a quarter of the applicants are admitted to Chinese Taipei's universities. A fifth of Chinese Taipei's graduates go abroad for further study. India's elite institutions — for instance, the Indian Institutes of Technology — graduate an even larger number; but of India's vast output of university graduates, only a very small proportion go abroad or would qualify for admission in the universities of industrial countries. The high proportion of graduates Chinese Taipei sends out suggests a considerably higher quality of tertiary education than in India. Chinese Taipei's educational system is also far more vocationally oriented than India's; the ratio of enrolments in vocational to those in academic institutions in Chinese Taipei rose from 40:60 in 1963 to 69:31 in 1986 (Wade, 1990). In view of the high skill intensity of the machine tool industry, it is likely that it is better served by the manpower supply in Chinese Taipei than in India.

Parallel to this difference in the quality of manpower inputs is a difference in material inputs. Throughout the post–war period, a very high proportion of Chinese Taipei's imports came from just two industrial countries — the United States and Japan. The proportion has been over 70 per cent in most years; till the 1970s it was over 80 per cent. This high proportion of imports must have conformed to the quality standards prevalent in those two countries. Between a third and a half of Chinese Taipei's exports are marketed by Japanese trading companies; they too constitute a ready source of information about the standards in the industrial country markets to which they sell. Till the early 1980s Chinese Taipei operated a system of export quality inspection which was closely modelled on Japan's. Since then it has oriented the inspection system towards quality standards in the domestic market. In this way, imports, exports and domestic production in Chinese Taipei have been closely linked to industrial country standards. India, on the other hand, is characterised by the absence of standards both in the domestic market and in imports. For most of the period, the two domestic integrated steel producers supplied most of the steel, and their standards were nowhere near international standards; the quality of products of smaller plants was even more variable. The same was true of the domestic producers of non–ferrous metals, lubricants or any other input required by machine tool manufacturers. The sources of imports were equally varied; amongst them, the Soviet Union, whose standards were low, accounted for a fifth to a quarter of total imports. Thus the effort required of Indian machine tool manufacturers to reach international standards of quality and reliability was much greater than in Chinese Taipei; in effect, they had to set up a separate, high–cost production line to supply buyers abroad or at home whose quality requirements were high and this undoubtedly affected their export potential in an industry where product reliability is a key factor in client–supplier relations.

Policies

Robert Wade has comprehensively demolished the view that Chinese Taipei's policies were liberal or non–interventionist. In fact, almost all the interventionist policies for which India is known — planning, industrial licensing, import controls, local content regulations, or other more minor forms of intervention — can be found to have been followed in Chinese Taipei at one point or another. Hence it is impossible to attribute the difference in the performance of the two countries, whether in the machine tool industry or in others, to a difference in the degree of intervention. The difference must be looked for in the content or quality of intervention, the sequencing and complementarity of policies and the way in which policies interacted with the habits and practices of the actors whose behaviour they were designed to influence, a point we address further below.

Although the range of interventionist policies in both countries tried out over a period of 45 years was similar, the relative importance of various forms of intervention was very different. Chinese Taipei did operate a system of industrial licensing in the 1950s and 1960s. But it applied to only a few industries. The range of industries to which it applied shrank progressively and by the end of the 1960s it only amounted to obligations on a few industries to export or to reduce import content (Hsiang, 1971; Scott, 1979). Chinese Taipei has throughout kept the steel, metal and energy industries under government ownership or control, and through the price and quality of these domestic inputs influenced the development of other downstream industries. Chinese Taipei has also had controls on technology imports which amount to controls on entry, expansion and exit in industries which require advanced technology or technology which has few suppliers. But this had little direct impact on machine tools. Nor were they ever subject to industrial licensing or formal import content restrictions. Although individual enterprises may have been subjected to restrictions as part of bilateral bargaining with the government, there is no information on such constraints. And formal technology imports in the form of licensing, for example, were rare in the machine tool industry.

This is very different from the Indian machine tool industry. The largest Indian firm — Hindustan Machine Tools — was owned by the government; it had privileged access to the public sector market. The industry was subject to industrial licensing, which was used to create and maintain a network of product monopolies. These monopolies were buttressed by control of technology imports, on which large Indian firms relied. Small firms were not subject to industrial licensing; but they were exempt only as long as they remained small, thus creating a strong disincentive to growth. This restriction of domestic competition is where India is most strongly distinguished from Chinese Taipei.

The two countries had very similar mechanisms of import regulation. Chinese Taipei's tariffs on metals and machinery were always low; India's were higher, but not much higher till the 1970s. Import licensing operated similarly in both countries; and it was driven by the same aim of minimising imports. Machine tools were equally subject to import control in both countries, and controls were used to ensure that machine tools that were produced domestically were not imported. Besides, upstream import substitution, actively pursued in both countries, was of great consequence for machine tools. As we saw earlier, a rise in the cost of domestic steel destroyed the competitiveness of the Indian machine tool industry in the international market in the 1980s. That nothing similar happened in Chinese Taipei reflects less on the machinery of import control, and more on the objective towards which it was driven.

A domestic producer can supply three markets with progressively higher realisation: direct exports, supplies to exporters, and the domestic market. Direct exports realise the price in the country of destination less shipping costs and tariffs. Supplies to domestic exporters can earn a price equal to the offer price of a foreign supplier plus shipping costs if exporters are given complete exemption from domestic taxes. Supplies to the domestic market may earn the import price including shipping costs and tariff. Competition in the domestic market may bring the price below these ceilings. A perfect system of tax rebates would equalise the realisation to the domestic producer from supplies to exporters and to the domestic market. If it did so, the three markets would be reduced to two: domestic sales and exports. While import control authorities in both countries strove to minimise imports, the Chinese Taipei authorities used an additional criterion of maximum price of domestic supplies. If a domestic supplier charged a price more than 10 per cent above the cost of imports including tariffs and other border taxes, a domestic buyer could import instead; similarly, if a domestic supplier charged a price more than 10 per cent above the import price excluding tariffs and other taxes, an exporter could import his inputs. Either way the domestic producer's margin over the import price was 10 per cent, but the base from which the margin was calculated was higher for domestic sales than for exports.

If this were the only rule, everyone would try to import something and sell it to someone else for a 10 per cent commission. No one would manufacture, there would be excess demand for import licences, and whoever got them would earn a rent. This can be prevented in one of two ways. Either there should be no import licensing, and everyone should be allowed to import after paying a 10 per cent tariff; or a condition of manufacture and value addition should be attached to the granting of an import licence. Chinese Taipei did the latter. Preference was given to manufacturers in granting import licences. This was only one of the concessions given to domestic manufacturers; in addition they were given bank loans which were cheaper than black market loans, as well as rebates on business tax and stamp tax.

Thus in effect, a producer faced a demand curve with three steps. He got a price for sales in the domestic market which exceeded the import price by 10 per cent of the tariff–inclusive import price, a price for sales to exporters which exceeded the import price by 10 per cent of the tariff–exclusive import price, and a price for exports which would be below the international price — which may be taken to be the same as the import price — minus the shipping costs to the nearest market. Domestic competition could drive down these margins and unify the markets, and thereby remove the discrimination against exports.

The import controls did not work as well as this ideal system assumes. There was much friction in their working, and it is possible that the margins were not kept down to 10 per cent. Wade (1990) gives examples of the frictions between domestic suppliers and exporters and how they were mediated by officials. There were enormous variations in effective protection across commodities in 1966, though less in metals and machinery (Hsiang, 1971). But liberalisation took the controls closer to the system we have described (Lin, 1973). By 1969 both the average effective protection and its dispersion had come down considerably (Lee and Liang, 1982). Of the 587 products surveyed by Lee and Liang, the domestic price of 230 was lower than the world price. For another 264 it was lower than the tariff–inclusive import price. It was exceptional for any industry in Chinese Taipei to take full benefit of import duties; the prices of most were driven far below the level permitted by duties, and those of many below the import price excluding duties.

Thus the machine tool industry, which began its rapid growth in 1970s, did so under a regime which approximated closely to the system we have described. The controls did not so much locate the manufacture of particular goods in Chinese Taipei; rather, they located particular manufacturing processes, based indiscriminately on imported or domestically produced inputs, provided the processing costs were internationally competitive or close to being so. The machine tool industry is a case in point: it was based not on producing particular machine tools, but on the application of certain engineering and manufacturing skills to any machine tools that could be economically produced in Chinese Taipei.

Indian authorities operated import controls and local content regulations in the same way as the Taipei Chinese; but a cost criterion was missing. The result was that processes set up in important industries such as steel and metals had such high costs that they could not bear even the limited competition that arose from the leakage into the domestic market of exporters' replenishment imports; the customs authorities zealously pursued such exporters and prevented such competition. Besides, not everything that was costly at home could be imported: sometimes it was not on the replenishment lists, sometimes the quantities were too small to import, sometimes the lead times of imports were too long. Thus firms that planned to export had to rely on the domestic market for supplies whose costs made exports internationally uncompetitive.

Another respect in which Chinese Taipei policy differed from India's was in stability of the exchange rate. Till the mid–1960s India's exchange rate was extremely stable. But since then it has been characterised by periods of stiffening import restrictions interspersed with maxi–devaluations every few years. Chinese Taipei, with its low inflation and strong balance of payments, could follow a policy of stable exchange rates well into the 1980s, although it has appreciated its currency in recent years as its payments surplus grew too large. The stable exchange rate provided Chinese Taipei exporters with a benchmark: they could aim to equal or better the prices of their foreign competitors without windfall gains or losses arising from exchange rate policy. The exchange rate was also undervalued in the 1970s and 1980s, which contributed to making exports profitable (Wade, 1990).

Finally, we would stress the policies of the Chinese Taipei government designed to enhance the skills resident in firms, and to provide them with useful information. We earlier described the official and semi–official technological institutes — the Machine Industry Research Laboratory and the Precision Machinery Research and Development Centre; both are aimed at raising the technological sights of firms. India has an equivalent in the Central Machinery Development Institute. But it has not been as close to the industry as the Chinese Taipei institutes. And because it pays government salaries, it cannot attract or retain high–quality staff. The more adventurous of its engineers leave and start their own firms or join other big firms. The experience of Chinese Taipei R&D organisations is not entirely dissimilar. They too found it difficult to sell their services to firms and were largely financed by the government; they too found insufficient interest in potential client firms; they too found their star engineers leaving and starting new firms (Wade, 1990). Despite these difficulties, the government has expanded and strengthened R&D services to industry including the machine tool industry[10].

Chinese Taipei gives financial incentives to research and development. India has also given them off and on, though on a smaller scale. Incentives to R&D by itself are poorly targeted since it is the fruits of R&D that matter, not the inputs. The Chinese Taipei government tries to target them better by making them conditional on a minimum level of R&D activity. India tries to achieve the same result by a process of certification of R&D departments. But there is no selectivity about certification; official statistics suggest that the expenditure of many certified R&D departments is too modest to make any difference. Further, Indian R&D departments were stretched into worthless activities by the import substitution policy; a high proportion of R&D resources went into finding import substitutes, helping supplier firms with low technological capacity, and adapting products to indigenously available inputs — all activities that would have been unnecessary if the imposed import substitution had been less severe or had been subject to price and quality benchmarks as it was in Chinese Taipei.

Industrial Structure

The structure of the Indian machine tool industry is characterised by dualism: a small number of large, technologically more advanced firms co–exist with a large number of small, backward firms. This structure was created by the industrial licensing regime, which minimised competition amongst large firms and allowed small firms to evade industrial regulation on the condition that they remained small. Yet there was nothing to prevent the proliferation of small firms, nor to prevent them from competing with large firms.

As we saw, the Indian small firms were similar in many respects to the vastly more successful Chinese Taipei firms. They were run by patriarchs in the interest of families. They were highly profitable and ploughed back a high proportion of their profits. They were active in reverse engineering. They had low wage costs and overheads. With these advantages, Indian small firms steadily increased their market share.

The question therefore needs to be asked: why did the Indian industrial structure not change and become closer to the Taipei Chinese? Why did not the Indian small firms wipe out large firms and create a Chinese Taipei type of highly competitive industrial structure? After all dualism is not peculiar to the machine tool industry; it is present in many Indian industries. In the textile industry, small firms finally completely swamped large ones, so that today only a handful of textile mills are left, and the bulk of the production has passed to small units, each owning a few power looms. The emergence of the textile industry as the largest foreign exchange earner is based on this restructuring into a large number of small, competitive firms. The same process in automobile components had created a large number of manufacturers making cheap copies of OEM designs. This structure was given a peculiar twist when Suzuki, in partnership with the Indian government, set up the Maruti car factory in the early 1980s. Maruti gave systematic technological assistance to selected component manufacturers, helped them import technology from Suzuki's component suppliers in Japan, and raised their quality to international levels. Today those component manufacturers are spearheading an export boom. Thus there is a promise of competitiveness in a dual industrial structure which was fulfilled in textiles and automobile components, but not in machine tools. Why not?

The answer must be sought in three features of the Indian situation. First, there was a section of the market for machine tools which was oligopolistic, sensitive to technology and insensitive to price. Government agencies — especially the armed services and the railways — were an important part of it; it was their custom which helped Hindustan Machine Tools, a government firm, to dominate the market for 40 years. The automotive industries were also highly concentrated. For instance, there are only two major commercial vehicle manufacturers, Telco and Ashok Leyland; Telco commands over 60 per cent of the market. Japanese manufacturers challenged this structure in the early 1980s by supplying technology for smaller commercial vehicles to three Indian companies; but Telco, with its strong technological base, ground all three into bankruptcy. There are only three major car manufacturers, of which Maruti has 80 per cent of the market. There were many entrants into the market for scooters and motor cycles in the 1980s; but today, Bajaj dominates the market for scooters, and Hero Honda for motor cycles. Thus the industries which buy precision machine tools are highly concentrated; they have provided a market in which a foreign brand name and the implied quality matter. The large machine tool manufacturers have hung on to this market. The average foreign buyer who bought from Chinese Taipei was a technologically well informed but price–sensitive buyer; even when he was not technologically sophisticated, he could compare competing machine tools from all over the world, or was served by a distributor who could do so. For him there has been no equivalent in India.

Second, technology matters in machine tools, especially technology embodied in manpower. Topical ingenuity, trouble–shooting, and informal innovation pay in machine tools; they require good engineers. Engineers are normally highly mobile; they are the carriers and diffusers of technology across firms. But the small firms of Ludhiana and Batala were never able to attract engineers. Engineers look for secure jobs, and did not feel comfortable in small north Indian firms. This problem persists. This is perhaps the greatest damage done by policies favouring small firms — product reservations, exemption from industrial licensing, priority credit, lower taxes etc. All these were available to firms provided they remained small — too small to build up the technological concentration required to capture the oligopolistic markets served by large firms.

Finally, the growth rate of the Indian machine tool industry was too low to force structural change. When demand is growing rapidly, bottlenecks crumble. Firms become less possessive of technology and more prepared to buy from outside. Sticky inputs such as engineers can be moved by large price differentials. The lure of growth induces workers to accept changes in jobs and work practices. Growth forces flexibility on an industry. The Indian machine tool industry grew too slowly to be forced to change.

Reorientations

Over the past four years this set of conditions began to break down as changes in economic policies — industrial delicensing, import delicensing, devaluation, tariff reduction and liberalisation of the capital market — accelerated and the industry was hit first by recession and then a boom in demand as vehicle industries recovered. While one cannot predict with certainty how these changes will affect the structure of the machine tool industry, its innovativeness and its competitiveness, it is possible to sketch in broad outline some of the dynamics that have been unleashed.

The most striking change is in the level of uncertainty. The industrial licensing system meant that new competition emerged rarely and gave advance notice as licence applications slowly made their way through the government machinery and information about them leaked out. Similarly, advance notice of new imports was given when import licences were granted. Hence there was considerable time to react to competition either in economic ways or politically by seeking to block the granting of industrial or import licences to competitors. These political instruments of competition have vanished, and so have the devices of delay. The result is a considerable increase in the level of uncertainty. The pace has thus quickened and the objectives have been simplified to growth and profits.

Technology has traditionally played a crucial role in competition in this industry; but the content of technology is changing. Earlier, large firms filled slots: they identified the requirements of their buyers and found foreign models that would fit these needs. Often the clients themselves suggested the models which machine tool makers should license or copy. The search for technology abroad, however, takes time and involves uncertainty. Foreign companies are also bureaucratic organisations and take decisions slowly. Now that they are free to export to India, moreover, they are less inclined to license their technology. In the meanwhile, competition does not wait. So there is more making do, improvising, putting together of new models in–house — more innovative behaviour in other words. This was very evident in the 1995 Machine Tool Exhibition; there were many new machine tools, especially NC tools, which were produced without foreign collaboration. This does not mean that more R&D is being done; innovation includes the many technological improvements which do not require R&D. For instance, many small changes are done on the shop floor; often a firm takes up a design made outside; if the demand is brisk, a machine design is put together and improvements are made in it over time as buyers' reactions come in. Restructuring of production, changes in factory layout, redeployment of workers are done without any formal R&D. There are technological flows between supplier and buyer firms. Thus competition increases the output of technology, only a small part of which is met through R&D; an even smaller part is met by technology imports. In this way, as technological change has quickened, its sources have also changed.

Finally, the level of ambition has changed. The international competitive disadvantage of the Indian industry has declined and many in the industry even see chances of profitable production for export. Imports have increased and there are no limits on who can import. The implicit threat thus has been magnified. Hence the industry is reorienting itself outwards; and once it does so, its opportunity set will be greatly broadened. This does not mean that it will quickly become a significant exporter since it is still handicapped by import duties that are high, and higher on its inputs than on its output. For the moment, the industry is also experiencing full order books and is turning away orders. Hence a rapid shift to exports is not in the offing. But the world outside is no longer being ignored; nor is it being regarded as a pure threat. Industrial organisations by instinct tend to work against competition, both from imports and within the country. This tendency has quite disappeared for now, for the sudden outbreak of competition has opened up new opportunities for large firms. Nor is IMTMA any longer a monolithic body dominated by big firms. HMT is in deep trouble as its traditional import substitutes have been undermined; the new technocratic firms are rapidly expanding and increasing their weight in IMTMA. They are in favour of greater openness and freedom and less inclined to seek help from the government. This change in attitudes may well be the most important change brought about by the new policies.

If this is the impact on large firms, what is the prospect for small firms? For over four decades they thrived on low wages and on encroachment into the large firms' market. Now that new dynamism has been injected into large firms, can the small firms continue to feed on them? Is there not the opposite possibility that the large firms may, with rising efficiency and falling costs, begin to encroach on the small firms' markets?

It is no doubt true that the success of small firms was based on the built–in constraints and consequent inefficiency of large firms. But this differential advantage began to erode in the 1980s. First, broadbanding in 1984 made competition possible amongst large firms. Then came the terrorist campaign in Punjab in the late 1980s; it largely closed down Batala and brought considerable hardship to the machine tool makers of Ludhiana. As a result of their difficulties, small manufacturers in the centres further south — Rajkot, Surat, Madras, Coimbatore etc. — expanded. These manufacturers are much closer to the large firms of Bombay, Poona and Bangalore. They are also closer to the industrial culture of the peninsula — to higher engineering capabilities, better organised credit and capital markets, and international influences. In the ensuing shakeout, many small firms in Batala and Ludhiana have closed down; those that are left are the larger ones with wider contacts. In this way, small firms throughout the country have raised their technological and marketing capabilities. This is evidenced by the entry of an increasing number of small firms into IMTMA, and their participation in the biannual machine tool fairs. The products they exhibit show the same openness to outside influences. Hence it would be wrong to assume that small firms will react passively to competition from large firms or from imports and succumb like sitting ducks: they have already been reacting by enhancing their own capabilities.

Thus what matters is not that small firms are different from large firms in their motivation or behaviour; what matters are the factors that kept them small and perpetuated the duality in the industrial structure. This duality was created by the privileges of small firms — access to cheap bank credit, exemption from excise taxation, and reservation of some 800 products for small industry. The value of these privileges has declined with reform. Forty per cent of bank credit continues to be reserved for agriculture, small industry and other politically favoured borrowers, but the interest subsidy has declined with the removal of interest rate controls[11]. A small manufacturer still does not have to pay excise duty on its output as long as it is below certain limits. But duties on capital goods have now been made reimbursable to the buyer against excise duty payable on his own production, so if a machine tool manufacturer does not pay excise, it is no advantage to a customer who is not himself exempt from excise duty. And there is no machine tool amongst the products reserved for small industry. In this way, small industry concessions have lost their value for machine tool manufacturers and increasingly, small machine tool manufacturers will have to rely on their inherent advantages of flexibility and low labour costs. The erosion of their special privileges has gone far, as has the process of adjustment. Yet small firms have survived, and what seems clear is that they will no longer be boxed into a special corner; they are large firms in the making. Nor will their relations with large firms be necessarily competitive and complementary; other more supportive types of relationship are already emerging, and will likely be reinforced.

The emergence of an innovative and internationally competitive machine tool industry in Chinese Taipei was due less to domestic competition than to the stimulus provided by interaction with overseas clients. Once habits and practices of innovation had been developed, these firms were able to keep up with the changing requirements of their clients through in–house innovation and linkages to local R&D institutions. In India, regulatory policies that limited market entry created a disincentive for both large and small firms to innovate and discouraged small firms from competing in the product markets monopolised by large firms. As a result, the large domestic market did not provide the stimulus to innovation and competitiveness which it might otherwise have done. Deregulation was critical in breaking these traditional habits and practices and in stimulating firms to innovate. Although the Indian machine tool industry is still far behind the industries of Chinese Taipei, Korea and China, it is changing fast. Whether it goes on to become internationally competitive, however, will depend on whether tariffs are further reduced and rationalised, for tariffs are even now too high, and the tariffs on machine tools are lower than on metals. The future is uncertain; but the energy injected into the industry by the recent policy changes will keep it advancing for a few years at least.

Notes

1. Licensing is more common in oligopolistic structures, such as those which were created at the outset in the Korean and Brazilian telecommunications and petrochemical industries. See Chapters 4 and 5 in this volume.

2. It is invariably lower than the unweighted average since low–rated items have a larger share in imports; even in India whose tariffs are amongst the highest in the world, the collection rate was 30 per cent in 1993–94 (Ministry of Finance, New Delhi, 1995: 30).

3. Taiwan had been a Japanese colony until 1946 and there have always been many Taipei Chinese who could speak Japanese and had connections in Japan.

4. One manufacturer who gave out a proprietary component for outside manufacture, got a 20 per cent discount by allowing the supplier to sell the component to others (Lautier, 1994: 51–2).

5. The same cannot be said for the Chinese Taipei pharmaceutical industry as we shall see in the next chapter.

6. Premier Auto was a car manufacturer which started production in the 1950s with a licence from Fiat.

7. They were presumably concentrated at one time in a town called Ramgarh.

8. The machine tool industry in Gujarat is taking a particularly interesting turn. Gujarat has had a long tradition of goldwork and jewellery. The craftsmen turned to gem cutting in the 1970s, which today is India's second largest export after textiles. The gem cutters are now going into gem cutting machinery and thence into precision machinery; a number of them exhibited their machines in the 1995 Indian Machine Tool Exhibition.

9. See, for instance, the list of technology importers for machining centres in Jacobsson and Alam (1994: 138–39).

10. The greater role of Chinese Taipei R&D services to industry, when compared with India, is also evident in the biotechnology industry (see Chapter 3 in this volume) but the consequences for the level of R&D in the industry are quite different thus pointing to the importance not only of the policies themselves but of the dynamics they generate in different contexts and with respect to different actors.

11. Small loans up to Rs 200 000 ($6 000) still pay lower interest, but they are quite modest in relation to the business of even a small machine tool manufacturer, and the bother of getting them would incline most manufacturers to prefer straight bank credit.

Bibliography

AMSDEN, A. (1985), "The Division of Labour Is Limited by the Rate of Growth of the Market: The Taiwan Machine–Tool Industry in the 1970's", *Cambridge Journal of Economics*, 9.

AMSDEN, A. (1977), "The Division of Labour Is Limited by the Type of the Market: The Case of the Taiwanese Machine Tool Industry", *World Development* 5(3)217–33.

BELLO, W. AND S. ROSENFELD (1990), *Dragons in Distress: Asia's Miracle Economies in Crisis*, Institute for Food and Development Policy, San Francisco.

BUREAU OF INDUSTRIAL COSTS AND PRICES (1988), *Studies on the Structure of the Indian Economy: Strategies for Cost Reduction*, New Delhi.

CENTRAL MACHINE TOOL INSTITUTE (1989), *Machine Tool Census 1986*, Bangalore.

COUNCIL FOR ECONOMIC PLANNING AND DEVELOPMENT (1994), *Taiwan Statistical Data Book 1994*, Taipei.

FLAMM, K. (1990), *La Coopération et la concurrence dans l'industrie mondiale des ordinateurs*, rapport pour le Comité de l'industrie de l'OCDE, Paris.

FRANSMAN, M. (1986), "International Competitiveness, Technical Change and The State: The Machine Tool Industry in Taiwan and Japan", *World Development* 14(12) 1375–96.

GALENSON, W. (1992), *Labor and Economic Growth in Five Asian Countries*, Praeger, New York.

GOLD, T.B. (1986), *State and Society in the Taiwan Miracle*, M.E. Sharpe, Armonk, New York.

HSIANG, M.–H. (1971), *Taiwan: Industrialization and Trade Policies*, Oxford University Press, London.

INDIAN MACHINE TOOL MANUFACTURERS' ASSOCIATION (1994), *Machine Tools Industry in India*, Delhi.

INDUSTRIAL CREDIT AND INVESTMENT CORPORATION OF INDIA (1985), *Export Performance of ICICI–Financed Companies 1978–79 to 1980–81*, Bombay.

JACOBSSON, S. (1991), "Government Policy and Performance of the Indian Engineering Industry", *Research Policy* 20.

JACOBSSON, S. (1986), *Electronics and Industrial Policy, the Case of Computer Controlled Lathes*, Allen and Unwin, London.

JACOBSSON, S. AND G.A. ALAM (1992), *Liberalisation and Industrial Development in the Third World: A Comparison of the Indian and South Korean Engineering Industries*, Sage, New Delhi.

JETHANANDANI, K. (1985), "Historical Evolution of Machine Tools Industry in India", Discussion Paper No. 21, Indian Council for International Economic Research, New Delhi.

LAUTIER, M. (1994), "Competition, Innovation and Competitiveness in Taiwan's Machine Tool Industry", Paper presented at the Working Group Meeting on Competition, Innovation and Competitiveness, OECD Development Centre, Paris, 20 December 1994.

LEE, T.H. AND K.–S. LIANG (1982), "Taiwan", in BALASSA, B. (ed.), *Development Strategies in Semi–Industrial Economies*, Johns Hopkins University Press, Baltimore, 310–55.

LIN, C.–Y. (1973), *Industrialization in Taiwan, 1946–72: Trade and Import–Substitution Policies for Developing Countries*, Praeger, New York.

LITTLE, I.M.D. (1979), "An Economic Renaissance", in Galenson, W. (ed.), *Economic Growth and Structural Change in Taiwan: The Postwar Experience of the Republic of China*, Cornell University Press, Ithaca, 475.

MINISTRY OF FINANCE (1995), *Economic Survey 1994–95*, Delhi.

OECD (1982), "The Review of Available Case Study Material and Proposals for Additional Work on Technology and Competitiveness: The Machine–Tool Industry", mimeo, Paris.

SCIBERRAS, E. AND B. PAYNE (1985), *Technology and International Competitiveness: The Machine Tool Industry*, Longmans, London.

SCOTT, M. (1979), "Foreign Trade", in W. GALENSON, ed., *Economic Growth and Structural Change in Taiwan: The Postwar Experience of the Republic of China*, Cornell University Press, Ithaca, 308–83.

TSAI, S.D.H. (1992), "The Development of Taiwan's Machine Tool Industry", in WANG, N.T. ed., *Taiwan Enterprise in Global Perspective*, M.E. SHARPE, New York, 151–70.

UNIDO (1991), "The World Machine–Tool Industry", background paper, Vienna.

UNIDO (1989), *Industry and Development: Global Report*, Vienna.

WADE, R. (1990), *Governing the Market: Economic Theory and the Role of Government in East Asian Industrialization*, Princeton University Press, Princeton.

WOGART, J.P., A. KAPOOR AND A. MEHTA (1993), *Technology and Competitiveness: The Case of Brazilian and Indian Machine Tools*, Sage Publications, New Delhi.

III

Bio–Pharmaceuticals in Chinese Taipei and India

Rohini Acharya[1]

Introduction

Modern biotechnology is defined as "the industrial use of recombinant DNA, cell fusion and novel bioprocessing techniques" (US OTA, 1991). A broader definition which is used predominantly by developing countries describes biotechnology as "the application of scientific and engineering principles to the processing of materials by biological agents to provide goods and services" (OECD, 1982) and as "any technique that uses living organisms (or parts of organisms) to make or modify products, to improve plants or animals, or to develop micro–organisms for specific uses" (US OTA, 1991).

The growth of modern biotechnology in the industrialised countries has been most rapid in the pharmaceutical and agricultural sectors. Developing countries, recognising the speed with which the introduction of biotechnology is changing these two sectors, have begun to initiate programmes to develop and diffuse biotechnologies. Those with well developed technological capabilities in basic and applied research, such as India and Chinese Taipei, have been able to implement their programmes faster than others.

This chapter deals exclusively with the development of technological capabilities in the pharmaceutical sector[2]. Within therapeutic categories, pharmaceuticals is a classic oligopolistic industry. Globally this is supported by national patent systems and by considerable effort to enforce intellectual property rights through GATT and more recently the new World Trade Organisation.

Despite these barriers to entry, the pharmaceutical industry is important to countries like India and Chinese Taipei from both a welfare and a development perspective. A majority of India's population, the second largest in the world, does not have adequate access to health care and the need to ensure access to health care at affordable prices is high on the list of government priorities. Indian governments have thus brought pressure to bear on manufacturers to keep prices down. When, as a result of this and other policy constraints a number of multinational enterprises left India in the 1970s and 1980s, Indian producers stepped into the breach and developed substitutes which are cheaper and appear to be competitive internationally, judging from India's export surplus. In Chinese Taipei, although no direct attempts were made by the government to control pharmaceutical prices, the government has intervened in recent years either to orient R&D and product development or to provide financial and other support mechanisms for local industry.

Affordable medical care is not the only issue. Much of the R&D undertaken by pharmaceutical and bio–pharmaceutical firms in industrialised countries is targeted at their own health care needs and priorities such as cardio–vascular diseases. Developing country priorities, on the other hand, relate more to diseases which are predominant regionally, such as hepatitis B and C in Chinese Taipei or malaria in India. Although there are a few new products emerging internationally for hepatitis B, there is very little research on other diseases which are important for developing countries. Both Chinese Taipei and India have thus targeted the development of diagnostic tools and vaccines which concentrate on locally important diseases in order better to address the health care needs of their populations.

The choice of Chinese Taipei and India as case studies of the development of bio–pharmaceuticals in Third World countries is based on a number of commonalities and differences. Government in both countries, for example, remains a major factor behind biotechnology R&D today. But some evidence has emerged that inter–firm competition in India and Chinese Taipei has led to investment in new biotechnologies, either through licensing or expenditures on R&D. The nature of that competition, however, differs significantly across the two countries as a result of differences in the structure of the pharmaceutical industry and in the degree of exposure to changing international environments. The Chinese Taipei industry for example is composed mainly of small companies, whereas in India, the structure is mixed, with large indigenous companies controlling about 25 per cent of the national market. In Chinese Taipei, the top ten companies, including multinationals, control less than 18 per cent of the national market[3].

The pattern of development in the Chinese–Taipei bio–pharmaceutical industry resembles that in the United States during the early 1980s, although on a smaller scale; the industry has been led by small, dedicated biotechnology firms while the larger pharmaceutical companies have been reluctant to venture into the new technology. In India, the pattern was at first quite similar, but now large Indian pharmaceutical firms are investing heavily in biotechnology.

This chapter addresses three issues with regard to the relationship between competition, innovation and competitiveness: first, the nature of competition in the pharmaceutical sector in both countries and the incentive or disincentive system that shaped it; second, the degree to which technological capability had been built up by these companies and the extent to which it has led to innovation; and lastly, whether firms in India and Chinese Taipei can make the transition from pharmaceutical production to bio–pharmaceutical based R&D.

The nature of the technology itself is discussed first, especially the pace of its development, the international environment in which it is developing and the manner in which this may affect innovation in these countries. This is followed by a more detailed examination of the structure of the global pharmaceutical industry, the incentive system that has shaped it and its innovative capacity. The next section looks first at the structure of the pharmaceutical industry, globally and in each of the two countries, before moving on to a closer examination of biotechnology policies and industrial development in both countries. The rationale here is to see whether companies have been able to accumulate sufficient technological acumen to switch over from chemical–based processes to bio–pharmaceuticals. This leads into the final section which discusses the differences between the two countries in terms of the three basic questions posed above on competition and innovation and develops some conclusions on the role of government policies in these two case studies.

Global Patterns of Technological Change

The Technologies

Although biotechnology has been used by society for centuries, *modern* biotechnology is based on recombinant DNA, or as it is more commonly known, genetic engineering. The double–helix structure of DNA was first discovered by Francis Crick and James Watson of Cambridge University in England, in 1963, and was followed by a number of innovations which are generally classified as playing an important role in the development of modern biotechnology, namely monoclonal antibodies (MABs) and the splicing of a gene between two strands of DNA, to produce recombinant DNA (rDNA). The former, invented in 1975, were never patented because of the short–sightedness of the British establishment[4], while the latter was demonstrated in 1973 and after a long debate on the ethics of patenting, was finally granted a process patent in 1980 and a product patent in 1984. Both are currently held by Stanford University in the United States. These were the two technological ruptures of greatest relevance to most modern biotechnology techniques and especially to the pharmaceutical sector.

These two breakthroughs have also provided a window of opportunity for bio–pharmaceuticals in developing and industrialising countries such as India and Chinese Taipei. Monoclonal antibody–based diagnostic kits for example are becoming more widely available in both countries and companies are now slowly beginning to do their own research based on MABs. Work on recombinant DNA techniques is also being encouraged especially by the government, which sees a potential for this R&D in vaccine development. These techniques are however more sophisticated and costly than the MABs–based work and companies in Chinese Taipei and India are finding it more difficult to invest in genetic engineering. This is discussed further below when innovation patterns in pharmaceuticals and bio–pharmaceuticals are described in the two countries.

The initial breakthroughs in science in industrialised countries have led to three new generations of products based on rDNA research (Richards, 1992). The first generation was based on rDNA versions of natural products such as human insulin and interferon. It was soon discovered, however, that the safety and efficacy of natural products is based upon their administration in natural doses. Higher than natural doses soon led to side–effects, which were first associated with products such as interferon. The second generation resulted in products which used protein engineering to produce slight variations on the natural rDNA based products of the first generation. Protein engineering basically involves the identification of different functions performed by the different parts of a natural molecule, followed by a modification of specific parts of the molecule to improve its performance. Tissue plasminogen activator (tPA) used for cardiac arrest patients is an example of a first generation biotechnology product for which second generation variations are currently in use. Improvements on these products are continuously being made.

The third generation of rDNA–based products makes use of chemistry to build upon the understanding created by the development of first and second generation products. The objective is to produce chemical mimics of second generation products. Other new techniques include antisense technology which can be used to retard the production of disease–carrying cells (antisense is used for example in Calgene's Flavr Savr tomato to retard the ripening process in the fruit) and also gene therapy based on the pioneering work done a few years ago at the NIS in the United States to genetically correct cells which were then replaced in the body to strengthen the immune system (Coghlan, 1993). The NIS has also been at the forefront of research to map the human genome, a multilateral, multi–institutional effort which is also making extensive use of bioinformatics to ease sequencing procedures. Developing countries, especially those that have the scientific capability to use these techniques, have also joined international networks on basic research, although applied research of this nature is still some years away from their grasp.

As a result of these new techniques, companies such as Genentech, one of the more successful biotechnology firms, are moving out of the second generation of protein–based technologies, to concentrate on the "small molecule" which is considered to be more versatile especially in pinpointing problem cells and aids in understanding the disease mechanism, much more so than proteins which tend to have a number of disadvantages such as size and their inability to transfer across cell membranes. Thus, rather than using rDNA to produce natural products as in the first generation, or using rDNA to produce proteins as in the second generation, the third generation and beyond appear to be concentrating on the functioning of the body and the disease itself. The aim is to develop techniques which can interfere with problem cells and genes, to help the body to correct its own malfunctions.

The development of rDNA therefore has enabled industry to go from strength to strength and commercial applications are now becoming more readily available as new drugs pass their various stages of approval and clinical trials to enter the market. The biotechnology industry itself is moving into a consolidation phase as the results of initial investment in research become more widely available. The evolution of the global biotechnology industry, especially the phenomenon of the small firm which has dominated and greatly facilitated this revolution, is examined in more detail below.

From Invention to Commercialisation: Global Patterns of Development

The earliest efforts to commercialise the new discoveries were made in the United States market. Although pharmaceutical companies have had a long history of contracting research out to universities and research institutions[5], they were slow to commercialise the results of these R&D collaborations. Instead, university professors and researchers often found themselves on advisory boards of companies. The real push to commercialise modern biotechnology appears to have come in the early 1980s, when small firms specialised in biotechnology research or what became known as the new biotechnology firms (NBTFs) emerged.

These firms were often founded by members of the scientific community who recognised the commercial potential of their own research. One of the discoverers of the gene splicing technique, Herbert Boyer, for example, joined hands with venture capitalist Robert Swanson to form the first ever dedicated biotechnology company in 1980, devoted entirely to the use of genetic engineering to develop new products for the market. The company, Genentech, is now one of the more successful biotechnology companies. A number of other entrepreneurs followed and the 1980s were characterised by the formation of small companies using venture capital funds and then later going public to raise seed money to finance additional R&D. From 1980 to 1993, the number of NBTFs rose from 330 to 1 300 in the United States (Ernst and Young, 1993).

As Table 3.1 shows, most of the early innovators of products making significant revenues world–wide today in this industry were small companies that specialised in biotechnology R&D and relied on their research rather than marketing skills. This weakness in marketing and the manner by which the dedicated biotechnology companies have tried to overcome it has played an important part in the evolution of the industry and is discussed further below.

In comparison with the United States biotechnology industry, preliminary analysis (see Ernst and Young, 1994) has identified around 485 biotechnology companies in Europe. As with the United States, the majority tend to concentrate on the health sector, with 20 per cent in therapeutics and 22 per cent in other health care sectors. In Europe, where firms are strong in agriculture, however, 16 per cent of biotechnology activities are in ag–bio.

Table 3.1 **Top Ten Therapeutics Based on Biotech in the United States and Worldwide**
(1990, $ million)

Product	Inventor	Sales US	Sales Worldwide
Erythropoietin	Amgen, Genetics Institute	600	1 125
Hepatitis B vaccine	Biogen	260	724
Human Insulin	Genentech	245	625
Human Growth Hormone	Genentech, Biotechnology General	270	575
Alpha–Interferon	Genentech, Biogen, Wellcome	135	565
G–CSF	Amgen	295	544
t–PA	Genentech	180	230
GM–CSF	Immunex, Genetics Institute	50	70
Gamma Interferon	Genentech, Biogen	15	25
Interleukin–2	Immunex, Chiron	5	20

Source: Ernst and Young (1993).

Apart from the United States, the lack of a highly developed financial market was a barrier to significant investment in biotechnology and the early years were characterised by innovators in Europe and Japan trying to catch up with the United States especially in product development. In recent years, investment by large companies has increased significantly and European biotechnology is expanding rapidly (Ernst and Young, 1994). The different conditions of European biotechnology and its particular strengths especially in agriculture, however, may call for a different structure from that which developed in the United States and it is far from clear that the small biotechnology company is as crucial as it has been in the United States[6]. Despite the smaller size of the specialised biotechnology sector in Europe, for example, invention in terms of patents registered continued to increase[7].

In 1980, the United States was the first country to grant a patent to a living micro–organism: the famous Diamond vs. Chakrabarty case, in which a patent was granted to a non–genetically engineered "oil–eating" bacteria. The precedent set by this ruling in the United States Supreme Court allowed the United States Patent Office to begin examining its backlog of applications which related to organisms. A number of patents for new biotechnology innovations, including the Cohen–Boyer technique, were thus granted in the early 1980s. Although caution must be taken in interpreting data from the European patent office[8], Tables 3.2 and 3.3 show that the United States dominates patenting activity both in the European and the United States Patent Office statistics. Because of a preference for patenting in the United States, the gap in the

Table 3.2. **Pharmaceutical and Medical Biotechnologies Patents Granted by the EPO**

(Granted 1980–93)

Year	1980	1981	1982	1983	1984	1985	1986	1987	1988	1989	1990	1991	1992	1993
United States	2	103	198	378	437	448	534	464	458	576	674	756	1 037	1 148
United Kingdom	0	49	99	158	143	164	165	123	132	134	170	216	262	256
Germany	124	417	458	570	556	519	517	423	455	486	555	579	691	794
France	21	66	83	118	165	184	168	156	145	168	206	198	320	357
Japan	2	28	91	173	272	292	347	293	300	383	479	632	754	878
Total	158	812	1 199	1 649	1 875	1 978	2 059	1 752	1 802	2 179	2 512	2 927	3 714	4 132

Source: Acharya (1995).

Table 3.3. **United States Patents Granted for Biotechnology**

(Categories 435 and 424 for selected countries)[a]

Year	1965	1970	1975	1980	1982	1983	1984	1985	1986	1987	1988	1989	1990	1991
United States	177	217	412	430	514	413	537	528	598	830	856	1 222	1 167	1 298
United Kingdom	7	7	39	49	50	41	52	46	37	51	68	93	79	95
Germany	21	15	49	64	63	53	63	60	63	82	89	135	120	108
France	7	20	45	64	44	40	31	33	32	48	61	83	76	81
Japan	19	35	144	118	143	128	133	152	159	179	183	237	276	287

a. Categories 435 and 424 are broad cluster classifications which include a wide range of secondary biotechnologies as well as genetic engineering.

Source: Acharya (1995).

number of patents between United States and other firms is even wider in the United States patent office data. Germany, however, has had consistently high levels of patenting, perhaps demonstrating the traditional strength of its large multinationals in industrial biotechnologies, while Japan has been the most successful in catching up with European countries and now exceeds patenting levels registered by Germany. The United Kingdom and France have shown slow but steady growth rates in biotechnology patents, perhaps an indication of other weaknesses within their respective economies, especially in terms of spillover effects which tend to influence the next generation of inventions. The growing biotechnology industries in Europe, however, may reverse this trend in the future.

During the 1980s, the rise of the NBTFs filled a void in the effort to commercialise biotechnology. The NBTFs were specialised in research and brought in expertise, mostly from universities and other research institutions. As the data in Table 3.4 on the market value of several of these companies and the limited number of patented products which had reached the market by 1992 illustrate, the NBTFs were willing to undertake high risk investments where multinationals were still wary. The structure of the biotechnology industry especially in the United States was thus characterised by a growing number of companies and increasing competition during this period.

Table 3.4. **Market Value ($ mill.) and Product Estimates of Selected United States Biotechnology Companies (1992)**

Biotechnology Companies	Product Sales	Clinical Trials	Awaiting Approval	Patented Products on Market
Genentech	3 833	8	0	3
Amgen	645	6	1	2
Genzyme	81	6	0	1
Biogen	56	3	0	0
Chiron	28	11	1	2
Gensia	3	1	0	0

Source: Ernst and Young (1992), p. 22.

The stock market crash of 1987 marked a turning point in the structure of biotechnology R&D and since pharmaceuticals is the leading sector world–wide, these changes have been magnified here. The most significant difference between the periods before and after 1987 is in the number of mergers and strategic alliances that were signed by companies, both large and small. The first major change came in the late 1980s, when there was a sudden increase in the number of mergers and take–overs, the latter especially of smaller companies by MNCs. The take–over by Hoffman LaRoche of Genentech in 1990 was the most publicised of these cases. In 1991, the United States Congressional Office of Technology Assessment had predicted that the initial successes of companies such as Genentech, Amgen and a number of other successful NBTFs would prompt multinational corporations to take them over and benefit from their R&D skills (US OTA, 1991). While this has happened to a certain degree, it is being accompanied by an increasing number of alliances between small biotechnology firms and large established companies and multinationals. By the 1990s, Eli Lilly, for example, had ongoing alliances with over 11 biotechnology firms[9].

Both the larger pharmaceutical firms and perhaps more surprisingly the smaller NBTFs have initiated strategic alliances. The former were initially motivated by the need to gain access to the basic research capabilities, notably in the biological sciences, of the NBTFs. The latter were increasingly constrained by a lack of financing, especially for product approval and later stages of clinical trials which are especially lengthy in the health care field, and by their lack of vertical integration. With the notable exception of Amgen, one of the largest biotechnology companies in the United States, none of the most successful biotechnology firms has managed to achieve the degree of vertical integration required both to develop and to market biotechnology products. By the early 1990s, these roles had become blurred, especially as the number of mergers that took place between multinationals and biotechnology companies increased in this period, strengthening the in–house research capacity of the larger chemical–based pharmaceutical firms through acquisition of the small firm's expertise in the biological sciences. In addition these firms have increased their investment in biotechnology research. Three of the largest multinationals in pharmaceuticals, Glaxo, which acquired Wellcome recently, SmithKline Beecham, which is acquiring biotechnology companies in the area of cardio–vascular research, and Sandoz, have expanded their in–house R&D facilities while increasing their take–overs of smaller biotechnology companies.

The growth of mergers and acquisitions seems to support the general view of the pharmaceutical industry as an industry of extreme concentration, dominated by a few large companies which benefit from scale economies. Indeed as Table 3.5 shows, the annual sales of the small biotechnology companies are minuscule when compared to those of the largest pharmaceutical and chemical companies. Their initial success in spite of their relative "smallness" is even more surprising given the general view of concentration in the pharmaceutical industry and suggests that size may not be a critical factor in biotechnology development. The section which follows discusses briefly this perception of concentration in the pharmaceutical industry and the degree to which small scale biotechnology companies have been successful in overcoming some of the disadvantages of size associated with pharmaceutical R&D.

The Basis of Competitiveness in the Global Pharmaceutical Sector

In a seminal contribution, Lall (1974 and UNCTAD, 1975) discusses the sources of concentration in the pharmaceutical industry. In general, production technologies in pharmaceuticals, he argues, do not have to be large scale, since production volumes tend to be small. This is even more common in bio–pharmaceuticals where small scale production has been relatively successful. Thus economies of scale in production did not confer a decisive advantage on firms, and this is increasingly the case. R&D costs, however, have always been high in this knowledge–intensive industry and they have become higher in modern biological research. When we look at their annual investment in R&D, even the small biotechnology companies, however, are not that small. Pharmaceutical companies invest an estimated 15 to 20 per cent of annual sales in R&D. In biotechnology, the figure for 1993 ranges from 15 per cent to over 80 per cent (Ernst and Young, 1993)[10]. Size is thus becoming important in terms of the amount spent on R&D relative to the size of the firm, although to some extent this hurdle has been overcome by small companies in the United States through their access to venture capital markets. Size is also an important factor at the later stages of product development, in undertaking clinical trials and in marketing. Phase III clinical trials, where the subjects tested are human, are especially expensive and time consuming and small firms simply cannot raise the funding through venture capital. A similar constraint exists with respect to marketing and promotion which often involve providing free samples and service to hospitals and clinics. Here small firms are increasingly at a disadvantage as vertical and horizontal integration within companies seems to make for greater efficiencies in performing these functions.

Table 3.5. **Annual Sales of Companies**
(1993 figures for pharmaceutical firms and NBTFs)

Pharmaceutical Company	$ million	New Biotech Firm	$ million
Bristol Myers	11 413.000	Amgen	1 373.842
Merck	10 498.200	Genentech	608.189
Smithkline Beecham	9 246.000	Genzyme	270.371
Abbott Labs	8 407.843	Chiron	239.796
American Home Products	8 304.851	Alza	219.831
Glaxo Holdings	7 987.000	Biogen	136.418
Pfizer	7 477.700	Immunex	122.866
Warner Lambert	5 793.700	Genetics Institute	102.041
Lilly	4 452.400	Centocor	70.930

Source: *Bio/Technology*, 1994, various issues.

Pressure to increase investment in R&D is also coming from the growing involvement of large pharmaceutical companies in the emerging biotechnology industry. This reflects both their belated recognition of the importance of biotechnology and their continued pursuit of innovation–based competition as product life–cycles shorten and product patents expire. Glaxo's purchase of Wellcome, for example, was partly in response to the imminent expiration of its patent on Zantec, the world's most widely selling drug (*Bio/Technology*, 1995). Despite these pressures and the increasing number of mergers and alliances to which they are giving rise, however, small firms are apparently still valued for their ability to excel in high–quality R&D. Thus, the number of births and deaths of biotechnology companies has remained fairly constant over the years in the United States (Sharp, 1995), implying that while the small firm is increasingly threatened as it moves towards commercialisation of its product, there remain opportunities that it is effectively exploiting in order to survive.

For developing countries the problem of size in downstream operations is compounded by financial markets that are less efficient and innovative than those in the industrialised countries, particularly the United States. The long time lag before a product reaches the market and the company becomes profitable, moreover, is a factor pushing the small firm in industrialising countries to invest in diagnostics which require no clinical trials and are cheaper to research and bring to market, as opposed to products such as vaccines which involve higher costs for research and clinical trials.

Though the volume of production remains small, as Lall and others have argued, the novelty of the products being developed today has made the approval, trial and marketing process more complex and costly. The next section examines how industrialising countries such as Chinese Taipei and India are responding to these changes. In an attempt to understand the nature of innovation in the industry, we first examine the structure of the pharmaceutical sector in both these countries before moving on to an analysis of biotechnology applications to pharmaceuticals.

Technology Capability Development in India and Chinese Taipei

The Structure of the Pharmaceutical Sector in India and Chinese Taipei

While Chinese Taipei has found distinction as one of the "four tigers" whose pace of economic and technological development has astounded the world, India has often been portrayed as the giant in south Asia whose emphasis on self–sufficiency and import substitution has come at the expense of economic progress. Although a number of studies (Desai, 1988 and Lall, 1989, for example) have demonstrated the considerable technological capabilities that have been built up by Indian companies, India's economic growth rates have been much lower than those of the export–oriented economies, notably Chinese Taipei, in south–east Asia.

The pharmaceutical sector in India, similarly, has developed behind a wall of protection and internal restrictions[11]. Some of these policies, price controls on essential drugs for example, were a deliberate attempt to ensure affordable health care to the population. Others were developed to stimulate R&D and innovation in the pharmaceutical industry. In large part these measures were needed in order to open space for the emergence of domestic producers in an industry in which patent legislation that covered both processes and products was used by large oligopolistic firms to keep prices high and secure foreign markets for their products through import monopolies. To encourage local companies to develop their own technological capabilities largely through imitation, the Indian patent law, adopted in 1970, was thus kept deliberately weak, disallowing product patents, and permitting only seven years of process patent protection from the date of filing or five years from the date of sealing, whichever was shorter (compared to 16–20 years from date of filing in Europe and 17 years from the date of granting in the United States)[12]. This effectively meant little or no patent protection for the inventor since the process of granting the patent itself could take up to 6 years. In addition, royalties were restricted to a maximum of 4 per cent of the bulk selling price of the drug, compared to the traditional 30–45 per cent in European countries at the time[13].

By the 1990s, the Indian pharmaceutical sector was composed of about 250 large companies and some 15 000 smaller units (*Scrip Magazine*, 1994). Of these, the small units are exempt from price controls and licensing contracts. Over 100 bulk drugs are price–controlled and account for almost 50 per cent of all marketed drugs in terms of sales (*Scrip Magazine*, 1994), although this policy of price and licensing control is being gradually relaxed. The drug policy reforms of 1994 have pledged to bring down the number of price controlled drugs to 72. The new policy, however, penalises firms that unnecessarily raise prices by imposing an upper ceiling of Rs 4 crores on their turnover. While this policy protects consumers from sudden price rises, some analysts argue that it does not adequately compensate manufacturers for cost increases[14]. It has also been argued that one of the reasons for the low level of R&D investment by Indian companies, approximately 1.5 per cent of annual sales, compared to an average of 15.8 per cent invested by multinationals globally, is a lack of profit resulting from price controls (Redwood, 1994). But compared to R&D investments by firms from other developing countries, the Indian average of 1.5 per cent is well above the norm.

Since the early 1970s, India's pharmaceutical industry has thus grown up behind doors which were essentially closed. Being at a stage of technological development where innovation through imitation rather than innovation at the frontier was the major form of drug production, Indian firms benefited from the combination of weak patent protection and price controls to build technological and production capabilities in the pharmaceutical industry. Building upon their strengths at home, these firms gradually became competitive in export markets as labour costs remained low, quality improved and innovation made possible the introduction of new products and processes. In contrast, a large number of foreign companies, faced with these restrictions on prices, patents and investment and unable to compete with cheaper imitations which were being increasingly produced by their Indian competitors[15], pulled out of the Indian market in the 1970s and 1980s (Table 3.6) and the share of multinational ownership in the Indian pharmaceutical sector fell from over 80 per cent in 1970 to 50 per cent in 1982 and to a low of 39 per cent in 1993.

In direct contrast to the situation in other developing countries, by 1993 Indian companies controlled three–fifths of the Indian market[16]. A comparison of Tables 3.7 and 3.8 shows that amongst the largest firms, Indian companies tend to dominate the Indian market with only Glaxo having a larger market share than the largest Indian firm, Ranbaxy. Moreover, the Indian government estimates that in the mid–1980s, some 30 per cent of the bulk drug market was controlled by SMEs (Government of India, 1986).

Table 3.6. **Indian Pharmaceutical Sector (1970–93)**
(% share by corporate ownership)

Company	1970	1982	1993
Indian	10–20	50	61
Multinational	80–90	50	39

Source: Redwood (1994), p. 25.

Table 3.7. **Sales by Indian Companies in the Indian Market (1992)**

Company	Sales in Rs mil. ($ mill.)	Share (%)
Ranbaxy	1 689 (64.96)	4.4
Cadila	1 467 (56.42)	3.8
Cipla	1 175 (45.20)	3.0
Lupin	1 031 (39.65)	2.7
Alembic	1 008 (38.77)	2.6
Sarabhai	891 (34.27)	2.3
Torrent	818 (31.46)	2.0
Wockhardt	528 (20.31)	1.4
Aristo	527 (20.03)	1.4
Himalaya Drug	482 (18.54)	1.3
Total	9 616 (369.85)	24.9

Source: *Scrip Magazine* (1994).

The Indian government was able to achieve its objective of keeping prices relatively low by facilitating imitative innovation and stimulating firms to compete on the basis of price. In the process, Indian pharmaceutical companies were able to develop technological capabilities in chemical and pharmaceutical techniques. As the data in Tables 3.7 and 3.8 show, however, the large pharmaceutical companies have remained dominant. The top 20 firms thus account for 47.9 per cent of total sales but output in the industry has increased from Rs 10 crores (approximately $384.6 million) in 1947 to more than Rs 7 000 crores (about $2 692 million) in 1993 (*Business India*, 1994, 54). Exports of bulk drugs and active ingredients, however, have largely been led by small companies which are not subject to price controls and import licensing constraints and yet have been able to export at competitive prices.

During the 1970s and 1980s large pharmaceutical firms rose dramatically in importance and in 1993 accounted for 28.5 per cent of total output in the sector[17]. Since the early 1980s, moreover, the Indian pharmaceutical industry has been a net exporter, although this has to be qualified by the degree to which licensing contributed to the decline in imports during this period. Table 3.9 shows the substantial increase in the positive trade balance in pharmaceutical products that took place in 1989–90 and has been sustained into the 1990s, albeit with considerable fluctuations. These were most likely due to two main factors: the liberalisation policy which the government initiated during this period and which probably accounts for the increase in imports in 1990–91, and exchange rate fluctuations as the Indian rupee was devalued. Nevertheless, since the early 1970s, the Indian pharmaceutical industry, it can be argued, has become competitive on the international market.

Table 3.8. **Sales by Foreign Companies in the Indian Market (1992)**

Company	Sales in Rs mil. ($ mill.)	Share (%)
Glaxo	2 137 (82.19)	5.6
Pfizer	963 (37.04)	2.5
Hoechst	951 (36.58)	2.5
Boots	930 (35.77)	2.4
Burroughs Wellcome	826 (31.77)	2.0
Parke Davis	690 (26.54)	1.8
John Wyeth	624 (24.00)	1.6
Hindustan Ciba–Geigy	608 (23.38)	1.6
Eskayef	579 (22.27)	1.5
German Remedies	578 (22.23)	1.5
Total	6 886 (264.85)	23.0

Source: *Scrip Magazine* (1994).

Table 3.9. **India's Balance of Trade in Pharmaceuticals**
($ thousand)

Year	1969–70	1974–75	1979–80	1984–85	1989–90	1990–91	1991–92	1992–93
Exps	8 004	27 858	109 419	196 76	392 594	381 45	453 82	354 30
Imps	24 404	41 523	92 519	115 60	86 355	140 04	112 75	82 054
Blnc	–16 400	–13 680	16 900	81 160	306 259	241 41	341 07	272 25

Source: Monthly Statistics of the Foreign Trade of India.

In sum the growth of the Indian pharmaceutical industry was marked by the development of indigenous technological capabilities behind a barrier of weak patent protection which was meant to induce Indian companies to develop indigenous technologies, and strict price controls and licensing restrictions which were designed to ensure that products would become as widely and as cheaply available as possible. The large pharmaceutical companies, which to some extent have filled the void in the domestic market left by the multinational companies whose presence has become less influential since the 1970s, have been quite successful in imitating products and processes patented. In the process they have achieved a high level of technological capability in pharmaceuticals. Smaller firms, which are not subject to pricing and licensing controls have also been successful in harnessing this technological capability by building up a strong export base, although the products produced by these small companies tend to be based more on traditional competitive advantage from low cost labour and indigenously developed technologies. Nonetheless they have successfully transformed India from a net importer to a net exporter of pharmaceutical products.

The problem facing Indian companies today is how to move beyond imitation and incremental innovation, to the development of new products. As the vice–president of the Southern Petrochemical Industries Corporation's (SPIC) Pharmaceuticals division noted, the combination of price controls and weak patent protection contributed to the development of an indigenous industry which is internationally competitive in bulk drugs and formulations, but the industry has reached a point where it needs to progress beyond this in order to remain competitive internationally[18].

The new liberalisation programme moreover is opening up the Indian market to those very same multinationals which earlier had chosen to leave because of government policy. There is thus a danger that unless indigenous companies learn to invest in R&D as opposed to focusing on imitation based on reverse engineering and process innovations, they will lose their competitive edge as the market opens up. A number of industrialists also argue that while the lack of patent protection was beneficial to Indian companies during the 1970s and 1980s, especially by providing infant industry protection, what the Indian pharmaceutical sector needs now is better patent protection and fewer price controls. This, it is argued, will push Indian companies to break with old habits and practices which had proved successful in the past and to begin thinking in terms of investment in R&D to develop new products[19], a strategic approach needed for the future. Indeed, a speech by the Drugs Controller of India in 1994 emphasised this point and urged the Indian pharmaceutical sector to prepare itself for increased competition especially as India strengthens intellectual property rights (IPRs), eases import restrictions for a number of essential inputs and opens its market to foreign firms[20].

In contrast to the Indian case, the Chinese–Taipei pharmaceutical industry is much smaller and is dominated by small scale companies. According to surveys carried out by ITRI[21], there were about 406 registered manufacturers of western medicine along with 261 traditional Chinese medicine producers in June 1989. Table 3.10 shows that the majority of the Chinese–Taipei pharmaceutical companies are small, falling in the NT$30 to 50 million (about $1.25 million to $2.1 million) and below category.

Table 3.10. **Chinese Taipei's Pharmaceutical Industry (including MNCs)**
(Annual revenues, NT$ million)

Total Revenue	Number of Companies		
	1988	1989	1990
10	69	61	57
10 – 30	62	66	68
30 – 50	34	40	41
50 – 100	36	35	34
100 – 200	18	22	27
200 – 300	8	7	15
> 300	21	23	23
Sample size	248	254	265

Source: ITRI (1991).

Table 3.11. **Exports and Imports of Pharmaceuticals in Chinese Taipei**
($ thousand)

	1986	1988	1989	1990	1991	1992	1994
Imports	126 650	165 313	166 677	187 685	225 710	297 609	331 956
Exports	35 235	47 818	41 427	36 719	41 482	47 995	40 512
Net Balance (–)	91 415	117 495	125 250	150 966	184 228	249 604	291 444

Source: Monthly Statistics of Exports and Imports, Chinese Taipei Area, the Republic of China (Department of Statistics, Ministry of Finance, 20 April 1994).

The introduction of Good Manufacturing Practice standards is reducing the size of the industry further as companies which are unable to maintain quality standards, usually the smallest, are forced out. In a survey of 240 firms, ITRI found that only 22 had 100 or more employees[22]. There are also about 30 foreign firms active in the Chinese–Taipei pharmaceutical market.

Of the Chinese–Taipei–owned firms, the majority are generic drug producers and importers. Unlike India, where domestic pharmaceutical companies supply an estimated 70 per cent of the Indian market in finished formulations and 85 per cent in bulk drugs (*Scrip Magazine*, 1994), most bulk pharmaceuticals are simply imported and repackaged in Chinese Taipei. Chinese Taipei tends to import around five times as much as it exports[23] (Table 3.11). In fact, the gap between Chinese Taipei's exports and imports of pharmaceuticals has consistently widened in the 1980s and 1990s. Thus, in contrast to the large surplus Chinese Taipei has with other countries in other sectors, its trade balance in pharmaceuticals has been negative for a number of years, and

Table 3.12. **Registered Capital and Market Share of Pharmaceutical Companies in Chinese Taipei**
NT$ million 1988 ($ million)

Registered Capital	Number of Companies	Sales Revenue	Market Share (%)
> 100	19	7 500 (312.5)	40.7
50 – 100	21	3 300 (137.5)	18.0
10 – 49	100	7 000 (291.7)	38.0
< 10	35	600 (25)	3.3
Total	175	18 400 (766.7)	100.0

Source: *Taiwan Economic Research Monthly*, December 1988.

growing. If global competitiveness is measured in terms of trade surpluses, Chinese Taipei's pharmaceutical sector fares quite badly. Maintaining an open market has in fact been insufficient incentive for Chinese Taipei's pharmaceutical companies to compete globally.

Foreign trade is not the only area where this is reflected. In terms of R&D expenditures, it is estimated that only about 0.5 per cent of annual production revenues of this sector are invested in R&D, in contrast to the Indian average of 1.5 per cent, and the government has been trying to encourage companies to increase their spending on R&D. The level of investment in R&D compared to investment by the Indian private sector contrasts sharply with general public sector investment in R&D, where Chinese Taipei's investment is much higher (see Table 3.13 below). Part of the problem appears to be size: the emphasis on small scale in Chinese Taipei (it is estimated that there are more than 80 000 companies in the country), has resulted in only around 1 per cent of turnover being invested on R&D. In high–technology areas such as electronics, where Chinese Taipei has built up considerable capability, this is higher, at an estimated 4 per cent of turnover (Cross, 1989). The government, through the National Science Council, spends around 1 per cent of GNP on civilian R&D and is hoping that by encouraging increases in the industrial contribution, this figure will have doubled in the near future. This is also the emphasis of the programme to encourage biotechnology R&D in the country[24].

Thus, there are a number of similarities between the two countries' pharmaceutical sectors, especially in the presence of a large small–scale sector, more so in Chinese Taipei than in India, and also in the small percentage of sales which is devoted to R&D[25]. Unlike India however, Chinese Taipei has no direct regulations on drug pricing except for drugs reimbursed under a number of insurance programmes[26], although this may be changing as Chinese Taipei achieves its goal of creating a European–style national health system where the budgetary constraints of the national health body will make a certain degree of price control inevitable[27]. Despite the relative freedom in the market, the Chinese–Taipei industry has not built up a tradition of innovation, but has instead confined itself largely to imitating products based on chemical technologies. A lack of enforcement of intellectual property rights has also enabled small Chinese–Taipei companies to produce substitutes for patented products, thereby competing directly with foreign multinationals in the Chinese–Taipei market. R&D investment, however, especially in technologies at the higher end of the scale, remains low in the large Chinese–Taipei pharmaceutical companies.

A survey done by ITRI in 1988 on the market share of pharmaceutical companies in Chinese Taipei, shows that the largest companies control 40 per cent of the market. Small scale companies are not far behind, with 38 per cent of the market (see Table 3.12) although they are more numerous, 100 in 1988, compared to only 19 large companies in 1988. Nevertheless, in terms of market share, the degree of concentration found in Chinese Taipei does not appear to be as high as in India where the 20 largest companies (indigenous and foreign) alone control almost 50 per cent of the market (Tables 3.6 and 3.7 above). Below we examine the implications of size for this sector in both these countries.

The pharmaceutical sectors in Chinese Taipei and India have a number of similarities and dissimilarities. The similarities are:

— Low levels of R&D investment, although the Indian average is higher (1.5 per cent of annual sales in India and 0.5 per cent in Chinese Taipei compared to the global industry average of 15 per cent).

— A major role played by small companies, especially in Chinese Taipei but also in India where the small scale sector has become internationally competitive, exporting mainly bulk drugs and active ingredients.

— Weak patent protection in both countries, although this appears to have been a more deliberate policy choice in India than in Chinese Taipei.

— Incremental innovation especially in quality control in both countries.

In spite of these similarities however, there seems to be more of a tendency among Indian firms, especially the large companies, to imitate new technologies more effectively, i.e. to translate accumulated technological capabilities into new products. The Indian company Cipla, for example, was able to produce AZT by developing a different process from that used by the international patent holder and is currently exporting AZT to other developing countries. This innovative capability largely developed as a result of three Indian government policies, import substitution, restrictions on foreign ownership and weak patent legislation, which combined to stimulate Indian companies to imitate and reverse engineer foreign technologies at the same time as they created space for the emergence of such innovative firms by inducing foreign multinational companies to leave. Within the Indian pharmaceutical industry, large firms are investing in advanced R&D, while small companies invest in less ambitious R&D projects, concentrating instead on producing and exporting products at the lower end of the technology scale in India.

In contrast, while the basic research capability exists, research with the aim of developing new products remains relatively weak in Chinese Taipei (see also Yuan, 1990). Some incremental innovation does take place especially in quality control, but it appears to be largely restricted to this. Similar patterns of imitative activity can be seen in Chinese Taipei, but the size factor appears to be more important in determining the magnitude of investment in R&D. This is equally true of the large firms in Chinese Taipei which remain small by international standards in this sector.

Thus, while it can be argued that pharmaceutical companies in India will probably make the transition from chemical–based technologies to bio–pharmaceuticals because of their innovative ability, in Chinese Taipei it is not clear that the trend to adopt new biotechnologies will be led by the pharmaceutical companies. The next two sections examine this question in more detail.

The Development of Biotechnology Policies

Although R&D funding in developing countries is considerably lower than it is in industrialised countries, it is rising steadily. Because of its interdisciplinary nature it is often difficult to determine both the amount of funding provided for biotechnology and also the number of scientists working in this field. Private sector funding is also difficult to estimate because of the overlapping nature of R&D in companies which are moving from a different field into biological technologies. Even public sector funding is often difficult to determine, especially in developing countries, because of this interdisciplinary nature of the technology. Table 3.13 shows estimates of R&D funding for selected industrialising and industrialised countries along with estimated numbers of scientists in these countries.

Table 3.13. **A Comparison of R&D Expenditures Across Selected Countries**
($ million)

Country	Year	Total R&D expenditure	% of GNP	Researchers per 10 000 population	R&D per researcher ($ 1 000)
Japan	1991	101 557	2.77	41	186
Korea	1990	4 481	1.91	16	64
Chinese Taipei	1991	3 175	1.70	23	69
China	1988	3 873	1.01	4	9
India	1988	2 494	0.7	3.12	20.79

Sources: National Science Council, Chinese Taipei (1993); Report on the Survey of R&D in Science and Technology, Korea (1993); Dr Tae Ik Mheen, Director Genetic Engineering Research Institute (Personal Communication).

Both with respect to R&D funding and scientific personnel Chinese Taipei fares much better than India or China in the region and about the same as Korea. In addition, Chinese Taipei's recent emphasis on biotechnology is attracting Chinese–Taipei researchers back from abroad, especially the United States. Biotechnology policies were institutionalised in both countries relatively early for developing countries in 1982 in the case of Chinese Taipei which declared biotechnology to be one of eight key technologies, and 1986 in India, which established the Department of Biotechnology within the Ministry of Science and Technology. The Department of Biotechnology's main tasks are[28]:

i) to identify specific research and development programmes and biotechnology related manufacturing;

ii to identify and establish infrastructural support at the national level;

iii) to import new, recombinant DNA based biotechnological processes, products and technology;

iv) to evolve biosafety guidelines for laboratory research and production applications;

v) to initiate scientific and technical research priorities;

vi) to initiate programmes of manpower development in biotechnology; and

vii) to establish the International Centre for Genetic Engineering and Biotechnology.

In Chinese Taipei, the main science and technology policy–making and implementing body is the National Science Council (NSC). The NSC emphasises six key areas in biotechnology[29]:

i) using genetic engineering as a tool to develop a vaccine for hepatitis B and diagnostic agents;

ii) hybridoma;

iii) tissue culture;

iv) enzyme technology;

v) biochemical engineering;

vi) blood technology (Chinese HLA typing etc.).

In the pharmaceutical industry the technologies being encouraged by the NSC include:

i) biopharmaceuticals;

ii) physiological active compounds;

iii) diagnostic reagents and techniques;

iv) biomedical materials;

v) drug targeting and release.

In addition and in keeping with previous policy initiatives, the government in Chinese Taipei helped to set up the Development Centre for Biotechnology (DCB), a research institution established in 1984 to support commercial biotechnology R&D. For some time, the Chinese–Taipei government has provided assistance to new sectors in the belief that the size of Chinese–Taipei firms dissuades them from exporting or engaging in R&D investment. With regard to the former, Wade (1990) for example, has noted that in sectors as wide ranging as textiles, plastics and electronics a period of government intervention in the form of import substitution was needed before the industry was able to export competitively. With regard to the latter, fear that among the new high–technology firms small size would be a particular disadvantage has led to the establishment of a number of supporting public sector agencies to carry out R&D for the industry as a whole. The Industrial Technology Research Institute (ITRI), established in 1973, for example, does supportive research for a number of sectors.

The DCB had as its special mission to bridge the gap between academia and industry especially through technology transfer and R&D co–operation. It has three major programme streams[30]:

— biotechnology promotion and development projects which have a duration of approximately four years each;

— environmental biotechnologies which use the DCB's microbiology division and include projects primarily in waste treatment; and finally,

— pharmaceutical biotechnology which includes: *i)* elite compound screening from natural products and chemical synthesis; *ii)* pharmaceutical delivery systems and *iii)* pharmaceutical development.

The Chinese–Taipei pharmaceutical industry, it is estimated, consists of about 250 companies and not more than 20 of those are doing biotechnology R&D including vaccines, and plant and animal biotechnologies (Huang, 1992). At least two of the new biotechnology companies have been formed as a result of direct technology transfer from the DCB. In order to help small companies to invest in biotechnology and to overcome their problems of a lack of economies of scale, the DCB also provides troubleshooting services.

Other government initiatives designed to support high–tech industries include the creation of the Science Based Industrial Park (SBIP) at Hsinchu, south of Taipei and with efficient links to Chiang Kai Shek airport[31]. The SBIP which was originally established to support the electronics industry has recently pledged to set aside an area of 50 acres for biotechnology companies. It provides modern facilities, quick regulatory and customs clearance and a more generally efficient working environment than Taipei. An added attraction is that because of its status as an export zone, companies which locate there are exonerated from the payment of import taxes on inputs used to produce export goods. Venture capital funds have also been created and some firms have made use of this facility, although it is not clear if these funds will be sufficient to enable firms to grow over the longer term. One of the requirements for gaining access to the Science Park is that the company be R&D based. By 1994, 13 agricultural and pharmaceutical biotechnology companies had located in the SBIP.

The Department of Biotechnology in India is the biotechnology equivalent of the NSC in Chinese Taipei, in that it supports basic research activities and encourages collaboration between universities across the country. As with Chinese Taipei however, it was realised that supporting basic research would not be sufficient and in 1991 the Biotechnology Consortium India Limited (BCIL) was established to try to increase collaboration between academic research and commercial application, and also to provide technical and market related information for local entrepreneurs. However, unlike its counterpart the DCB in Chinese Taipei, the BCIL does not provide research facilities and cannot finance research projects. Instead, information dissemination appears to have been the main function of the BCIL until now, although this role is still being defined.

Thus both countries continue to support their academic research actively and have attempted to develop institutions specifically devoted to helping the private sector to commercialise the results of basic research. Below we examine how the private and public sectors are reacting to these supportive measures.

The Nature of Competition and Innovation in Biotechnology

Among the new biotechnologies, the techniques which have been most easily accessible to developing countries for reasons of financial cost and in terms of distance from the technological frontier, are diagnostic kits based on MABs. For these reasons, they are the technologies most developing — or more correctly, industrialising — countries, have utilised and are commercialising. Diagnostic kits are becoming more widely available, ranging from the simpler tests such as pregnancy detection kits to the quick diagnosis of diseases such as hepatitis B and C, particularly widespread in Chinese Taipei, and malaria which is prevalent in India. Moreover, imitation of these products through reverse engineering and indigenous technology development is also most widespread in diagnostic kits. While it is estimated that products such as vaccines and new drugs take between 2–3 years before they complete the required clinical trials and are approved for sale on the market, this is not the case with diagnostic kits for which clinical trials are not important. An average of only two months is required to bring a diagnostic kit from the laboratory to scale–up and commercial production. Thus, most small companies and indeed even the larger companies venturing into biotechnology have opted to use these products as a stepping stone to more sophisticated techniques which require larger investment and also involve more time before they can be commercialised.

In many developing countries diseases prominent in the region merit particular attention from a prevention perspective but the required research is rarely a priority in industrialised countries which do not face the same health problems, and when it is, the cost of treatment using imported drugs and vaccines is too high. Small private firms in industrialising countries, moreover, show less interest in this field because of the substantial initial investment, longer time lag before the product can be marketed and the requirement of clinical trials which is costly and time consuming. In addition, vaccines, unlike diagnostic kits, often form an integral part of government immunisation programmes and are therefore subject to strict price controls which reduce profit margins. This has been a particular disincentive for private firms in India to develop vaccines. Vaccines are thus one area in which developing countries have had to build up their technological capability by setting up either public sector research and development projects or publicly funded companies[32]. Lifeguard (Chinese Taipei) and the Indian Pharmaceutical Corp. are cases in point.

As in other targeted sectors, the Chinese–Taipei government has attempted to give the biotechnology industry a boost by helping to establish a large dedicated biotechnology company (DBC). Lifeguard, Chinese Taipei's largest such company, was established in 1984 and has a modern factory in the Science Park at Hsinchu. Its major product and the reason why the government and the Development Centre for Biotechnology were instrumental in helping to form it, was the manufacture of the hepatitis B vaccine. This was the beginning of a government programme to eradicate or greatly reduce the incidence of hepatitis B on the island by immunising newborn babies free of charge.

Lifeguard began by licensing the technology to produce hepatitis B vaccine from Pasteur Merieux which, since 1981, has licensed the technology to over 40 countries. The technology, based on blood plasma antigen, was imported and then produced in Chinese Taipei. The initial investment was about NT$240 million ($10 million approximately), over half of which came from the government (51 per cent). This initial capital has since tripled. Most of Lifeguard's output is used in the government's immunisation programme and purchased by the government at a price of $6 per dose. This contrasts with the $15 per dose at which hepatitis B vaccine is sold commercially.

Since the early 1990s, Lifeguard has run into financial difficulties. A number of factors have contributed to their current problems. The government's immunisation programme for newborns has been highly successful. Along with the availability of vaccines on the local market for children and adults, this has resulted in a sharp fall in the incidence of hepatitis B from approximately 30 per cent, when Lifeguard first began manufacturing the vaccine to 1.5 per cent or about the average in many European countries. Just as its domestic market was shrinking (Interview: Sr. Manager, Lifeguard, August 1994), fear of contamination by the AIDS virus forced the company to abandon the Merieux technology which was based on antigen obtained from carriers of hepatitis B, in favour of rDNA–based technology licensed from Merck[33]. The licence with Merck however carries with it the clause that Lifeguard is not to compete with Merck on the international market and hence once the Chinese–Taipei market was saturated, Lifeguard was unable to export. To make matters worse, during its first four years, the responsibility for new product development was assigned to the Development Centre for Biotechnology and not until 1988 was R&D capability localised on–site. Perhaps rather belatedly, the R&D Department was expanded into a Product Development

Table 3.14. **Estimated Assets of New Biotechnology Companies in Chinese Taipei**

Company	Year Founded	Assets 1989 ($ million)
Tai–Fu Pharmaceutical Corp.	1982	6.0
Tai–Da Pharmaceutical Co. Ltd	1982	1.5
General Biologicals Corp.	1984	12.0
BGH Biochemical Co. Ltd	1984	0.5
Lifeguard Pharmaceutical Inc.	1984	28.0
Ever New Biotechnology Co. Ltd	1984	8.0
Search Biological Technology Corp.	1987	1.5
King Car Biotechnology Co.	1988	1.5
Ming–Shing Pharmaceutical Technology Corp.	1988	1.5
Chinese Taipei Biotech Inc.	1989	3.0
Hwa–Yang Pharm Technology Inc.	1989	1.5
Grand Biotech Corp.	1989	5.0
TOTAL		70.0

Source: Soong (1991), p. 17.

Department in 1992 and Lifeguard began to invest in the development of alternative products, including diagnostic kits which it will be able to sell on the domestic market[34] or abroad. Lifeguard's experience points to the dangers for small companies of becoming over–dependent on one particular product and of not possessing sufficient financial resources and R&D capability to diversify its product range.

The Indian government's encouragement of public sector ventures in vaccine production has run into similar problems. A much publicised joint venture between the Department of Biotechnology, Pasteur Merieux and a public sector company, the Indian Pharmaceutical Corp. Ltd, to produce injectable polio vaccine for the national vaccine programme ran into trouble largely because the Department of Health under advice from the WHO (which believes that the oral polio vaccine is more appropriate for developing countries such as India) decided against buying the injectable vaccine from the company, thereby bringing the project to a halt after a three year investment and an estimated expense of Rs 120 crores ($50 million). The company is at present considering its options as its major foreign investor Pasteur is withdrawing from the project and another investor is being sought[35].

Both vaccines and diagnostics are based on technologies available to industrialising countries like India and Chinese Taipei. The question is, however, whether they can be commercialised effectively by private firms, or will face problems similar to those faced by companies in industrialised countries with respect to scale, especially in later stages of commercialisation.

Bio–pharmaceutical companies in Chinese Taipei are mainly small and they invest little in R&D (Table 3.14). Most dedicated biotechnology firms in Chinese Taipei, moreover, have either been set up with government support or formed as joint ventures with foreign multinationals especially those based in the United States. The availability of kits from their partners and the short term benefits derivable from the sale of diagnostic kits have thus led a number of small Chinese–Taipei companies to import and resell diagnostic kits.

Despite the government's concern with the small scale of firms in Chinese Taipei, size alone is not the most important problem facing Chinese–Taipei companies today. While the majority of small firms selling diagnostic kits are importing and reselling these products, there are a small number of R&D–based firms which have begun to use indigenous technological capabilities to innovate in biotechnology. General Biologicals, for example, is one of the small biotechnology firms established with the help of a foreign multinational corporation, Abbot, the inventor of the hepatitis B diagnostic kit. Like Lifeguard, General Biologicals is based in the Hsinchu Science Park and benefits from the efficiencies of services such as customs clearance and good infrastructure. But ten years after its creation, General Biologicals has expanded to over 70 employees, 80 per cent of whom are scientific staff, and only 20 per cent of its technology is licensed from abroad. The rest is based on in–house R&D, some of which is undertaken in collaboration with the Development Centre for Biotechnology (Interview: Sr. Management, General Biologicals, August 1994).

Facilities such as the Science Park mentioned above are certainly a factor in easing the initial difficulties of these companies, although access to investment capital (it can be a number of years before the company becomes profitable[36]) still appears to be a major bottleneck for many of them. But the problem mainly appears to arise after the research is over, i.e. when product development and clinical trials commence. Most of the firms that have built laboratories in the Science Park are, for this reason, either subsidiaries of multinationals or biotechnology companies in industrialised countries, or have collaboration agreements with them. This demonstrates that small scale need not necessarily be a disadvantage if there are funds from government or elsewhere available.

For those that have decided to remain independent and continue investing in R&D, the cost is undoubtedly high. Ever New Biotechnology[37], which concentrates on diagnostics and is now venturing into vaccines, has just patented a vaccine for hepatitis C in Chinese Taipei and also applied for a patent in the United States, Europe and Japan around mid–1994[38]. The cost of this success has however been high and today Ever New invests about 50 per cent of its annual sales of about $5 million in R&D. However, the Director argues that future success will largely be determined through continued investment in R&D and in maintaining diversity in research. Moreover, he also acknowledges the additional costs of marketing and other services which accompany the sale of a product. For this reason the company has decided to cut down on its manufacturing capacity and is offering R&D services for other companies to maintain its investment in further research.

The established companies, even the largest ones in the Chinese–Taipei pharmaceutical sector which have fewer difficulties in obtaining funding for R&D, have in contrast not shown any particular interest even in the relatively profitable field of diagnostics[39]. Most of the large companies in Chinese Taipei still produce bulk drugs and formulations which are either sold in Chinese Taipei or exported. Thus while the scientific and technological capability exists, and funding for basic research is actively provided by the National Science Council, there appears to be very little incentive for private pharmaceutical companies to invest in biotechnology R&D. A few of the largest companies are currently commissioning research or collaborating with universities and other public sector research institutions such as the DCB, although this seems to be in its early stages. Among foreign multinationals, Chinese Taipei seems to be attracting investment for manufacturing and assembling, with some R&D facilities for quality control research related to older technologies, but not for biotechnology R&D. United States–based biotechnology firms have however shown an interest in Chinese Taipei and of the 13 companies based in the Science Park, at least two are wholly owned subsidiaries of biotechnology companies in the United States. Genelabs, a research institute of Genelabs, California, was established in 1993, and more recently, Cephagen, which is a subsidiary of Biopure, a Boston–based biotechnology company, has decided to set up laboratories in the Science Park in Hsinchu (Interview, August 1994). Both are very recent investments and it is difficult to judge their success as yet, although Cephagen has already reached the production stage and is marketing 7 ACA, using a technique for which it holds a United States patent (Interview, August 1994)[40].

As in Chinese Taipei, small companies in India have tended to import and resell diagnostic products in the local market. Even large companies like Ranbaxy initially marketed imported products rather than do their own research, until recently. Currently, however, Ranbaxy is developing its own diagnostic kits and has invested heavily in a modern research laboratory which will facilitate more advanced biotechnology R&D. Ranbaxy, which employed some 269 people in R&D and spent 5 per cent of its sales in 1993–94 on R&D, expects its R&D spending to rise to 8 per cent by the year 2000 as it expands investment in biotechnology R&D (Interview: Sr. Manager, Ranbaxy, Sept. 1994).

The potential of biotechnology has moreover been recognised by a number of other large companies, including a number from outside the pharmaceutical sector. For example, the Vittal Mallya Scientific Research Foundation, which was established in 1987 by the large United Breweries Group, has successfully cloned insulin in genetically engineered yeast. The foundation has however run into problems in recent years, especially with funding for the commercialisation of some of its products. The UB Group, while happy to provide funding for basic research, appears to be unwilling to invest the large sums needed for upscaling and commercial production. For example, an initial investment of Rs 2 crores ($0.76 million approximately) is needed for the insulin project which includes pilot plant studies and clinical trials on animals and humans. Part of the problem is the length of time needed before production can actually commence and returns on investment can be made (Interview: Sr. Management of Vittal Mallya, Bangalore, Sept. 1994).

In response to this increasing demand for funding as companies become interested in biotechnology research, a number of venture capital funds have been set up although they have also been wary of financing high–risk biotechnology ventures, especially in pharmaceuticals[41]. The existence of the BCIL has also enabled an exchange of technology between companies and universities, although the BCIL appears to be concentrating on simple technologies, largely in the domain of agriculture. Biotechnology in pharmaceuticals has come to be regarded as more advanced, with a longer time span between initial R&D investment and returns to the investment, and therefore risky. Investment funds for these projects are therefore not as easily available as they are for example for agricultural technologies such as tissue culture and floriculture.

In addition, as in Chinese Taipei, many small and large biotechnology companies in India thus tend to take the short–term option of importing final products such as diagnostic kits for a number of diseases and distributing them in the country. This short–term policy would be ideal if there were longer–term plans to perform indigenous R&D. Among the hundreds of suppliers however, there are very few firms which are doing or even planning to do their own R&D. Public ventures which specifically fit into the national health policy and most of the large Indian pharmaceutical companies (see Table 3.7), however, are notable exceptions. Ranbaxy, Wockhardt and Cipla, for example, are building extensive research facilities in anticipation of a growing market for biotechnology products. Ranbaxy, in an attempt to compete with international firms, has ventured into Stem cell based research[42] which is presently being done by leading international biotechnology firms such as Amgen and Immunex (*Bio/ Technology*, October 1994). Wockhardt, on the other hand, has started an ambitious project to try to develop a new process to produce erithropoeitin, whose current patent holder is Genentech (see Table 3.1 above) and which is the largest selling biotechnology product in the world today. Similarly, Cipla built its reputation by producing two major drugs patented in the west: vincristine, an anti–cancer drug whose original patentholder, Eli Lilly, marketed the drug in India for about $3, in contrast to Cipla's price of $1, and AZT which was synthesised by scientists at the Indian Institute of Chemical Technology and transferred to Cipla.

Another new feature of the Indian biotechnology industry is the increasing foreign presence. One of the reasons for this is the recent liberalisation in India resulting in a number of alliances and joint ventures, the joint venture between Max India and Gist Brocades of the Netherlands and the link– up between Ranbaxy and Ciba Geigy being important examples. A number of small biotechnology companies have also emerged as a result of joint ventures between indigenous and foreign companies. In addition, the presence of a pool of indigenous skills and technological capabilities has attracted foreign multinationals, such as AB Astra of Sweden, to invest heavily in research.

The Astra Research Centre was established in the late 1980s. Because it was a wholly owned subsidiary of the Swedish company, the initial licence to invest was only granted on condition that the Centre be established as a non–profit society. The Astra Research Centre (ARC) is therefore restricted to research and cannot commercialise its own products. Its ultimate goal is new drug discovery. Commercialisation of these drugs by the parent company would, of course, be possible, but the products and processes developed at ARC thus far have been transferred to local companies (Interview: Sr. Management, Astra Research Centre, Sept. 1994). One such local company is Bangalore Genei[43].

Bangalore Genei exhibits some of the characteristics of university–industry collaboration common to the emergence of the small, dedicated biotechnology company in the United States. It was formed in 1989 by scientists, Dr P. Babu, a former Professor of Genetics at the Tata Institute for Fundamental Research, and Dr K. Prasad, a scientist in the United States, with the express purpose of commercialising technology developed by the Astra Research Centre. Its initial investment funding came from the venture capital fund of the Technology Development and Information Company of India (TDICI), which suggests that local venture capital firms may have more confidence in a company with close links to a foreign multinational that has a proven technology than in a local start–up whose research results and commercial potential are less certain. When Astra first began doing research in India, a number of basic enzymes needed for genetic engineering R&D were not available in the country and had to be imported. For climatic reasons, this was considered unfeasible. Astra therefore devoted itself initially to the production of these enzymes and other reagents. Bangalore Genei has now taken over this process and currently produces a wide range of restriction enzymes and speciality chemicals for rDNA research, thus providing an important input for Indian biotechnology (Interview: Sr. Management, Bangalore Genei, Sept. 1994).

Under the new rules agreed to in the Uruguay Round of trade negotiations, developing countries will be obliged to grant patent protection to products as well as processes within four years from 1 January 1995. While the impact of the new rules on the R&D strategies of firms like Wockhardt and Cipla, which have developed new processes for major drugs patented elsewhere, is not yet clear, it comes at a time when the progressive liberalisation of the Indian pharmaceutical market is creating new opportunities and constraints for Indian firms.

Under the liberalisation programme, diagnostic kits, for example, became easier and cheaper to import and an increasing number of small and also some large companies started to import these kits. Further liberalisation in foreign investment, however, has had the reverse effect of creating pressure on firms, especially those with large market shares in the Indian economy, to increase their R&D investment especially in the development of diagnostic kits in response to the pull of market demand. The high profitability of these kits in a market which includes not only government hospitals but private clinics and chemists' shops, their relatively low technological requirements and short cycle from R&D to production and commercialisation, have made them a very attractive product for new biotechnology firms. Moving beyond diagnostic kits to drugs and vaccines, however, involves costly R&D and long periods of clinical trials and in India, government assistance for companies has come relatively later than in Chinese Taipei. Indeed, until the formation of the BCIL in 1991, the Indian Department of Biotechnology largely concentrated on basic research and on expanding these facilities to increase biotechnology R&D[44]. Even today, the BCIL is unable to play as active a role in the commercial sector as the DCB in Chinese Taipei, which has created at least two companies since its formation. While large Indian firms are thus increasing their investment in R&D, like their smaller Chinese–Taipei counterparts, they are under increased pressure to enter into joint ventures or alliances with foreign companies. In this, they are increasingly successful as the availability of cheap, skilled labour in both India and Chinese Taipei and the presence of local firms with credible R&D bases are serving to attract foreign companies to both countries.

Innovation and Competitiveness in India and Chinese Taipei: Some Conclusions

The pharmaceutical sector has developed in different ways in Chinese Taipei and in India. In India, as a result of government policies and strict import and price controls, the pharmaceutical companies have developed significant technological capabilities. In Chinese Taipei however, this sector appears to have been dominated by foreign multinationals and local companies seem to have satisfied themselves with niche markets based on generic drugs. Very little investment is undertaken by pharmaceutical companies and there seems to be equally little incentive on the part of pharmaceutical companies to invest in the new biotechnology. This appears to be partly at least a response to strong competition from foreign multinationals which were allowed to invest quite freely in Chinese Taipei's open economy, restricting local pharmaceutical manufacturers to niche markets, or simpler activities such as importing and repackaging bulk drugs and formulations.

The relationship between competition and innovation in these two cases was thus far from straightforward. In Chinese Taipei, maintaining an open market proved to be an insufficient stimulus to innovation at the firm level, despite the fact that scientific capability as measured by skill levels and research facilities was built up within the economy. Most firms either licensed their technology from parent companies or imported, repackaged and distributed drugs. As a result, the gap between exports and imports of pharmaceutical products steadily widened over the 1980s and 1990s. In contrast, through a combination of protection and regulation, the Indian government was able to achieve its objective of keeping prices relatively low by facilitating imitative innovation and stimulating firms to compete on the basis of price. Competition thus developed within the protected domestic market. In the process, large Indian pharmaceutical companies strengthened their technological capabilities in chemical and pharmaceutical techniques, became competitive in some export markets and moved more quickly towards industry–financed bio–pharmaceutical R&D than did their Chinese–Taipei counterparts.

Despite this weakness in the Chinese–Taipei pharmaceutical industry, a biotechnology sector, led by small indigenous companies investing in biotechnology R&D is emerging. As in India, weak patent protection enabled these small companies to build their technological capabilities by imitating products patented in the industrialised countries. The number of these bio–pharmaceutical firms, however, remains small and given the lack of domestic investors among the larger pharmaceutical firms, many of these small companies face problems concerning funding, the result of which is collaborative projects with foreign multinationals and biotechnology companies to raise investment capital.

In India, the biotechnology sector exhibits a greater mixture of small and large firms, with small companies dominating biotechnology research until recently, when large indigenous companies stepped in to establish their own R&D centres and form collaborative arrangements with foreign multinationals. Foreign multinationals in turn are increasingly interested in the Indian market because of its size and the considerable pool of skilled labour present in the economy. The recent liberalisation has encouraged foreign companies to seek access to this market and has also made Indian companies more sensitive to competitive pressures from outside.

To date, Chinese–Taipei and Indian bio–pharmaceutical companies focus mainly on the development of diagnostic kits, which as we argued, require far less investment in clinical testing. In both countries, the government has had to support firms financially to encourage them to do R&D in vaccines and poor planning has sometimes produced disappointing results for the growth prospects of these companies, although the vaccine projects themselves such as the hepatitis B project in Chinese Taipei have been successful. Thus financing remains a constraint on the ability of companies in both countries to do their own R&D, but the uncertainties involved in doing R&D on new drugs, as opposed to reverse engineering established drugs, are clearly another.

The transition from the research stage to the development stage is also problematic. Clinical trials and marketing have become increasingly more difficult and costly for small biotechnology companies in all countries and significant financial assistance has had to be solicited from foreign multinationals and national governments everywhere. To some extent, the role that larger pharmaceutical firms are playing in funding R&D in India might be an advantage for the development of a bio–pharmaceutical industry in that country. Paradoxically, although small, flexible companies have been Chinese Taipei's strong point, increased consolidation of the indigenous industry may be required to give local firms the push they need to begin investing in R&D and become innovative there. Even then, although there are significant windows of opportunity in the early stages of biotechnology R&D for firms from industrialising countries like Chinese Taipei and India and increased innovativeness will certainly give these firms a greater chance to compete in this new technology, the nature of competition in bio–pharmaceuticals makes it far from clear that such companies will be able to survive the ordeals of product approval and clinical trials in the longer run.

Notes

1. This research was largely carried out while I was at the Maastricht Economic Research Institute for Innovation and Technology (MERIT) in the Netherlands and I would like to acknowledge the support of the institute during the course of the research and writing up of this paper. I am also grateful to Sandy Thomas of SPRU and participants of a workshop held at the OECD Development Centre in December 1994 for their comments. Any errors are however my own responsibility.

2. Biotechnology in agriculture is the subject of current research by a number of authors focusing on developing countries. A critique of older technologies such as the green revolution technologies is provided in Shiva (1989) while Hobbelink (1987) and Juma (1989*b*) provide analyses of the impact of biotechnology on developing country agriculture and the relationship between R&D in the industrialised countries and agricultural development in developing countries. At the OECD Development Centre the impact of biotechnology on cash and subsistence crops in developing countries has been examined by Brenner (1992).

3. In India, the top ten Indian and foreign companies in contrast would have a total market share of approximately 32 per cent. Thus, although a rough measure, the size of market share of the large companies in India and Chinese Taipei appears to show a greater degree of concentration in the former.

4. Monoclonal antibodies were never patented because of the failure of the British National Research and Development Corporation to recognise the potential of this technique and to file on behalf of the inventors. Subsequently, a number of key innovations following from the initial technique were patented by researchers in the United States (Fransman, 1991, p. 16).

5. Kenney (1986) describes the history of this relationship and the way in which it evolved over the years, leading finally to the formation of new biotechnology firms beginning with Genentech, and followed by a number of other successful companies such as Amgen, Transgene, Celltech and Biogen.

6. This is suggested by research on the evolving structure of biotechnology in three European countries being carried out by the author and several collaborators. The results of this analysis will be published in 1996.

7. Although European countries such as the UK, France and Germany have a strong tradition in basic research, the ability to translate this research into production appears to have been slower than in the United States. A number of reasons are given for this, including the "culture" in the United States, where the divisions between academia and industry are fewer and less rigid, and also the availability of short term venture capital funding to start new companies. While links between industry and academia in Europe go as far as contract research, there is less evidence than in the United States, of academics extending their contract research activities into commercial and applied R&D. In the United States,

the ability of academics to join hands with venture capitalists to form the small biotechnology company was instrumental in establishing modern biotechnology industries (Sharp, 1985; Kenney, 1986).

8. A word of caution must be added when examining patent data in this technology. There are a number of problems with the dataset provided by the EPO partly because of the newness of the EPO itself which makes data for the early 1980s relatively unreliable; the establishment of the EPO in Munich moreover may lend some bias to early data in favour of Germany when other countries in Europe still may have had a tendency to patent at home rather than at the EPO; similarly the United States data may show a bias in favour of the United States and Japan for the same reason, although this is less likely, since the United States has always been an important market for European countries as well. The data on patents are therefore used in conjunction with other measures and observations in order to provide support for the arguments in the paper. For a further discussion of the problems of using patent data see Chapter 3 in Acharya (1995).

9. *Bio/ Technology* (1994), vol. 12, July, pp. 652–653. See also Delapierre and Mytelka (1995) on strategic alliances in biotechnology.

10. Sales of dedicated biotechnology firms were estimated at $5 700 million in 1993 (Ernst and Young, 1993).

11. Some argue that it remains the most highly protected industry in India, whereas most other industries were significantly liberalised in the 1990s.

12. Like India, during the 1970s, Argentina's high court, at the request of the local pharmaceutical industry, eliminated product patents on the grounds that they constituted the basis for restrictive business practices (Chudnovsky, 1983). In Canada, to encourage competition in the domestic market the life of patent protection was shortened, thus stimulating the development of a generic pharmaceutical products industry in that country (Waring, 1987). Pressure from multinational pharmaceutical firms acting through national pharmaceutical industry associations and internationally through organizations such as GATT and the WTO have, however, reversed most of these policies since then.

13. Redwood (1994), pp. 15–21.

14. One method suggested to do this, would be to index prices of drugs to the wholesale price index which would ensure that consumer prices could rise when manufacturing costs rise (*Economic Times*, 25 August 1994, New Delhi).

15. Redwood (1994), p. 22.

16. *Ibid.,* p. 22.

17. *Business India* (1994), p. 54.

18. Interview with Dr M.D. Nair, August 1994.

19. A number of the companies interviewed in August 1994 in fact are going ahead with investment in anticipation of increased competition from abroad, as patent protection becomes stronger and a number of government controls, including on foreign equity ownership, are reduced. The 1986 drug policy for example allows foreign ownership up to 51 per cent and even above in some cases (Government of India, 1986).

20. Speech made by the Drugs Controller of India at a meeting of the Pharmaceutical Association in Bangalore, August 1994.

21. Huang (1992), p. 545.

22. I am grateful to ITRI for providing me with this information.

23. Interview with Dr Huang, August 1994.

24. Huang (1992), p. 546.

25. In India, it is likely that the small scale sector has a lesser tendency to invest in R&D than the industry average of 1.5 per cent of annual sales mentioned above.

26. *Ibid.,* p. 547.

27. Interview with Dr Huang, August 1994.

28. Based on Department of Biotechnology's Annual Reports from 1989–94.

29. Interview at the National Science Council in Taipei, August 1994.

30. Annual Reports from DCB (1991–94). I am also grateful to Dr Leah Lo and Dr Soong of the DCB for providing additional information on biotechnology companies in Chinese Taipei.

31. Based on interview at SBIP in August 1994.

32. This is changing somewhat as the case of Evernew Biotechnology discussed below illustrates.

33. Others (Yuan and Hsu, 1990) argue that this change in policy was actually the result of Lifeguard being sued by environmental groups in Chinese Taipei.

34. Because the company is based at Hsinchu, it would have to pay a sales tax of 5 per cent in order to sell on the local market and so it will probably try to export.

35. Based on an interview with senior managers in August 1994.

36. General Biologicals for example only began making a profit after its products were on the market for three years.

37. Interviewed in August 1994.

38. It is estimated that the time between application and decision as to whether the patent will be granted or not, is approximately 22 months for biotechnology.

39. The two large pharmaceutical companies interviewed for example, while acknowledging their interest in biotechnology R&D, had still not reached the stage where they were willing to invest in their own in–house R&D facilities and staff. At present the extent of their R&D extends to quality control facilities. This observation was supported by other institutions supporting national biotechnology R&D in Chinese Taipei.

40. Although it has only recently begun marketing its product, estimated sales in the 1993–94 period were $0.5 million.

41. Interview with senior managers at Canbank Venture Capital Fund, Bangalore and the Technology Development and Information Corporation of India (TDICI) in August 1994. The latter is an older venture capital institution and has made some investments in biotechnology, but mostly in agriculture as this is in general, less risky than in pharmaceutical and drug related biotechnology. Of the new biotechnology companies interviewed for example, only one had received venture capital funding.

42. Based on interview with senior managers at Ranbaxy, according to whom, it was the pioneering work of research at Ranbaxy on Stem cells which prompted the company to increase investment in biotechnology R&D. Diagnostic kits are therefore a short term source of profits while the long term goals are more ambitious.

43. Karnataka Antibiotics has licensed a DNA probe for detecting malaria from ARC.

44. The Indian government was instrumental in attracting the highly prestigious UN funded International Centre for Genetic Engineering and Biotechnology, which is the only developing country counterpart to the Centre in Trieste, Italy.

Bibliography

ACHARYA, R. (1995), *The Impact of New Technologies on Economic Growth and Trade: A Case Study of Biotechnology*, Universitaire Pers, Maastricht.

BRENNER, C. (1992), *Biotechnology and the Changing Public/Private Sector Balance: Developments in Rice and Cocoa*, OECD Development Centre Technical Papers No. 72, Paris.

CHANDRASEKHAR (1993), "Role of Biotech Consortium India Ltd. in the Commercialisation of Biotechnology Products/Processes — Status Paper", Paper presented at the Workshop on the Commercialisation of Biotechnologies in Agriculture and Aquaculture at IIM, Ahmedabad, 23–24 April.

CHUDNOVSKY, D. (1983), "Patents and Trademarks in Pharmaceuticals", *World Development*, 11 (3).

CHUDNOVSKY, D. (1979), "The Challenge by Domestic Enterprises to the Transnational Corporations' Domination: A Case Study of the Argentine Pharmaceutical Industry", *World Development*, Vol. 7.

COGHLAN, (1993), "Engineering the Therapies of Tomorrow", *New Scientist*, 24 April.

CROSS (1989), "Taiwan Tackles Its Past", *New Scientist*, 10 June.

DELAPIERRE, M. AND L. MYTELKA (1994), "Blurring Boundaries: New Inter–Firm Relationships and the Emergence of Networked, Knowledge Based Oligopolies", Paper presented at an EMOT workshop, Como, Italy, October.

DEPARTMENT OF STATISTICS, MINISTRY OF FINANCE, GOVERNMENT OF TAIWAN (1994), *Monthly Statistics of Exports and Imports, Taiwan Area, the Republic of China*, Taipei, April.

DESAI, A. (ed.) (1988), *Technology Absorption in Indian Industry*, Wiley Eastern Limited, New Delhi.

DEVELOPMENT CENTRE FOR BIOTECHNOLOGY (1994), *Biotechnology Information Service Report*, Development Centre for Biotechnology, Taipei.

ERNST AND YOUNG (1994), *European Biotech 95: Gathering Momentum*, Ernst and Young, San Francisco.

ERNST AND YOUNG (1993), *Biotech 94: Long–Term Value, Short–Term Hurdles*, Ernst and Young's Eighth Annual Report on the Biotech Industry, Ernst and Young, San Francisco.

ERNST AND YOUNG (1992), *Biotech 93: Accelerating Commercialisation*, Ernst and Young's Seventh Annual Report on the Biotech Industry, Ernst and Young, San Francisco.

FRANSMAN, M. (1991), "Biotechnology: Generation, Diffusion and Policy", United Nations University Institute of New Technologies (UNU/INTECH) Working Paper No. 1.

Gatoskar, S.S. (1983), "Drug Control: India", *World Development*, 11 (3).

GATT (1994), *Final Act of the Uruguay Round in Marrakesh on 15th April 1994*, Vidhi Publishing, New Delhi.

Government of India, Ministry of Chemicals and Fertilisers (1986), *Modifications in Drug Policy, 1986*, Government of India, New Delhi, September.

Griliches, Z. (ed.) (1984), *R&D Patents and Productivity,* University of Chicago Press, Chicago.

Hobbelink, H. (1987), "New Hope or False Promise? Biotechnology and Third World Agriculture", International Coalition for Development Action, Brussels.

Huang, W.F. (1992), "Taiwan Republic of China", in R.N. Spirey, A.I. Wertheimer, R.D. Rucker, (eds.), *International Pharmaceutical Services: The Drug Industry and Pharmacy Practice in 23 Major Countries of the World*, The Harworth Press Inc., New York, NY.

Juma, C. (1989*a*), *Biological Diversity and Innovation: Conserving and Utilizing Genetic Resources in Kenya*, ACTS Press, Nairobi.

Juma, C. (1989*b*), *The Gene Hunters: Biotechnology and the Scramble for Seeds*, Zed Books, London.

Kanavi, S. (1994), "Leaders in Technology", *Business India*, 4–17 July.

Kaplinsky, R. (1988), "Industrial and Intellectual Property Rights in the Uruguay Round and Beyond", Institute of Development Studies, University of Sussex, Brighton.

Kenney, M. (1986), *Biotechnology: The University–Industrial Complex*, Yale University Press, New Haven.

Lall, S. asst. by G. Wignaraja (1989), *National Capabilities to Master Technological Change: A First Look at Selected Developing Countries*, OECD Development Centre, Paris, June.

Lall, S. (1974), "The International Pharmaceutical Industry and Less–Developed Countries, with Special Reference to India", *Oxford Bulletin of Economics and Statistics*, August.

Marstrand, P. (1981), "Patterns of Change in Biotechnology", *Occasional Paper Series No. 15*, Science Policy Research Unit, University of Sussex, Brighton.

Nair, M.D. (1994), "It's Buying Power That Matters: Intellectual Property Rights and Drug Prices", *Business Line*, 21 May.

National Science Council (1993), *Indicators of Science and Technology: Republic of China*, National Science Council, Taipei.

O'Brien, P. (1974), "Developing Countries and the Patent System: An Economic Appraisal", *World Development*, Vol. 2, No. 9, September.

OECD (1989), *Biotechnology: Economic and Wider Impacts*, OECD, Paris.

OECD (1982), *Biotechnology: International Trends and Perspectives*, OECD, Paris.

Orsenigo, L. (1989), *The Emergence of Biotechnology: Institutions and Markets in Industrial Innovations*, Pinter Publishers, London.

Ranis, G. (ed.) (1992), *From Developing to Mature Economy*, Westview Press, Boulder, Co.

REDWOOD, H. (1994), *New Horizons in India: The Consequences of Pharmaceutical Patent Protection*, Oldwicks Press Ltd, Felixstowe, UK.

REPUBLIC OF CHINA (1993), *Indicators of Science and Technology: Republic of China*, Republic of China, Taipei.

RICHARDS, B. (1992), "New Ways from Biotechnology to Detect and Treat Old and New Diseases", *Biotechnology Education*, 3 (1).

SCRIP MAGAZINE (1994), "Unleashing the Indian Pharmaceutical Industry", March.

SEABROOKE, J. (1993), "The Reconquest of India", *Third World Resurgence*, No. 26.

SERCOVICH, F. (1991), "Industrial Biotechnology Policy: Guidelines for Semi–Industrial Countries", in *Issues in the Commercialisation of Biotechnology,* Proceedings of the Expert Group Meeting on the Commercialisation of Biotechnology, UNIDO, Vienna, 168–71.

SHARP, M. (1995), "The Science of Nations: European Multinationals and American Biotechnology", Paper submitted to the *International Journal of Technology Management (Biotechnology Review).*

SHARP, M. (1990), "Technological Trajectories and Corporate Strategies in the Diffusion of Biotechnology" in E. DEIACO, E. HÖRNELL AND G. VICKERY (eds.), *Technology and Investment: Critical Issues for the 1990s*, Pinter Publishers, London.

SHARP, M. (1985), *The New Biotechnology: European Governments in Search of a Strategy*, European Paper No. 15, SPRU, University of Sussex, Brighton.

SHIVA, V. (1989), *The Violence of the Green Revolution: Ecological Degradation and Political Conflict in Punjab*, Research Foundation for Science and Technology, Dehra Dun, India.

SIMON, D.F. (1992), "Taiwan's Strategy for Creating Competitive Advantage: The Role of the State in Managing Foreign Technology", in N.T. WANG (ed.), *Taiwan's Enterprises in Global Perspective*, M.E. Sharpe Inc., Armonk, NY.

SOONG, T.–S. (1991), "Current Industrial Biotechnology Development in Taiwan", *Agro Industry Hi–Tech: International Journal for Food Chemicals, Pharmaceuticals, Cosmetics as Linked to Agriculture through Advanced Technology*, 1991.

UNCTAD (1975), *Major Issues in Transfer of Technology to Developing Countries: A Case Study of the Pharmaceutical Industry*, United Nations, Geneva.

US CONGRESS OFFICE OF TECHNOLOGY ASSESSMENT (OTA) (1991), *Biotechnology in a Global Economy*, US Congress Office of Technology Assessment, US Government Printing Office, Washington, D.C.

US CONGRESS OFFICE OF TECHNOLOGY ASSESSMENT AND FORECASTING (OTAF) (1982), *Patent Profiles: Biotechnology, 1982 Update*, US Department of Commerce, US Government Printing Office, Washington, D.C.

VAITSOS, C. (1973), "Patents Revisited: Their Function in Developing Countries", in *Science, Technology and Development: The Political Economy of Technical Advance in Underdeveloped Countries*, Frank Cass, London.

WADE, R. (1990), *Governing the Market: Economic Theory and the Role of Government in East Asian Industrialization*, Princeton University Press, Princeton, NJ.

WARING, B. (1987), "The Canadian Experience with Compulsory Licensing of Pharmaceuticals: Its Relevance for LDCs", MA Thesis at Carlton University, Ottawa, Canada.

WORLD BANK (1993), *The East Asian Miracle: A World Bank Policy Report*, World Bank, Washington, D.C.

YUAN, R. (1986), "Biotechnology in Singapore, South Korea and Taiwan", Report prepared for the International Trade Administration, US Department of Commerce, Washington, D.C.

YUAN, R. AND M. HSU (1990), "Biostrategies in the Pacific Rim", *Genetic Engineering News*, November–December.

IV

The Telecommunications Equipment Industry in Brazil and Korea

*Lynn Krieger Mytelka**

Introduction

In the 1980s when Brazil and then Korea embarked upon major programmes to develop digital switching for the domestic public telecommunications network, the contribution of telecommunications to productivity and growth and its importance as a tool for meeting private and social needs were widely acknowledged[1]. As in France and Japan a decade earlier, the decision to press ahead with the development of this technology, the so–called "make or buy" decision, was taken by the state and given effect through the creation or strengthening of a public research laboratory[2] enjoined to collaborate with local firms. In all four countries specifications were set by the publicly owned telephone operating company[3] which acted as a monopsonist in domestic procurement.

As the case studies of Brazil and Korea presented here illustrate, inter–firm competition did not figure as a stimulus to innovation in the early catch–up phase. Despite this and in contrast to arguments advanced in the conventional literature[4], several of the resulting products were competitive in local and export markets. From there, however, the stories differ with regard to the pace of innovation, the relationship of competition to innovation and the resultant competitiveness of telecommunications products.

This chapter focuses on a number of factors that explain those differences. These include *i)* the opportunities and constraints posed by the pace and trajectory of technological change globally, *ii)* the changing pattern of international competition in this industry, *iii)* the structure of both the domestic telecommunications equipment supplier and the telecommunications operating company industries, *iv)* the historical practices of local firms with respect to competition and innovation, and *v)* the impact of government policies on firm behaviour and on the environment within which competition took place. The latter two factors are captured by the concept "policy dynamics" developed in Chapter 1.

Technological Change and the Pattern of International Competition

Until quite recently, telecommunications was considered to be a highly mature and thus very stable industry. Its principal activity was the transmission of voices in the form of electrical impulses over copper wire between terminals, mainly telephones. At its heart were two types of electromechanical switches, the rotary switch and the crossbar switch. Both were invented before World War I and the latter, in particular, remained in widespread use well into the 1980s[5].

The 1970s, however, witnessed a major rupture in telecommunications technology when fully digital switching and transmission technology became available. Though earlier attempts to introduce electronic exchanges had been under way since the late 1950s[6], the new time division switching techniques were the first to combine digital multiplexing with the use of "computers for both the control function and for translating the analogue signals via pulse code modulation into digital signals". This opened the way to a substantial increase in system capacity (Dang Nguyen, 1983). It also enhanced the system's functionality making possible the eventual development of an integrated services digital network (ISDN)[7].

Several firms pioneered this technology. In 1965 CNET, the public telecommunications laboratory of the French Direction Général des Télécommunications, working with a small company, SLE–CITEREL, a subsidiary of Ericsson and CGE (later CIT–Alcatel) developed the world's first fully digital switch, a small rural exchange known as the E–10 which was introduced into the French telecommunications network in 1972. Subsequent efforts to work collaboratively in the development of larger switches, however, proved problematic and by the late 1970s, CIT–Alcatel had fallen behind its competitors, AT&T (Western Electric) which had developed the 5–ESS, Ericsson, which had developed the AXE system at Ellemtel, its joint R&D centre with the Swedish PTT, and Northern Telecom which began to commercialise its DMS family of fully digital switches in 1977[8]. These firms, moreover, were shortly followed by others[9].

Within highly protected domestic markets, the new digital switching technology diffused quite rapidly. Both push and pull factors accounted for this. First, the very high R&D costs incurred in the development of the new technology[10] induced firms to amortise these costs as quickly as possible. Second, the clear technical superiority of these switches in terms of speed, maintenance and functionality led to an interest in their ready adoption.

By the early 1980s, however, the pace of technological change in the telecommunications industry had slowed down[11]. This lengthened the time horizon over which the costly R&D process could be amortised. An incremental and hence more predictable technological trajectory also seemed to be emerging. Space thus opened for newcomers to catch up in the low density digital switching area while front–runners forged ahead to develop larger central office switches.

Another factor encouraging the emergence of latecomers in the 1980s was the nature of the technology itself. Production of electromechanical switches had required the development of a large dedicated precision engineering capability and a high level of technical skills in manufacturing the multitude of specialised components that had to be interfaced mechanically and electrically (Hobday, 1990). This barrier to entry was considerably reduced by the introduction of microelectronics technology which has fewer moving parts, many more standardised components and is software–intensive. The latter significantly raised the social benefits to be derived from local development of digital exchanges since the opportunities for employment in Korea and Brazil had proved so low in the 1970s for electronics, software and systems engineers trained in the United States, that many had sought refuge at Bell Labs or in the research departments of major telecommunications multinationals abroad[12].

In addition "[p]roduction of microelectronics equipment is characterised by modularity of design and divisibility in manufacture... [and e]ngineering effort is concentrated mainly in the research, design and development stages of manufacture" (Hobday, 1990). The new technology thus contributed to changes in production which further reduced entry barriers making the moment appear ever more propitious for new comers from the developing world.

Competitive conditions reinforced this view. Domestic telephone operating company monopolies were still major barriers to entry by non–resident companies in the main industrialised country markets. Cross–market penetration through exports was thus difficult and exports[13] in this period accounted for only 10 per cent of world production (Dang Nguyen, 1983).

The need to ensure compatibility and system maintenance, however, favoured existing companies over new entrants. Nowhere was this more evident than in those developing country markets where electromechanical switches had already been installed and production facilities for their manufacture had been set up. Under pressure to expand sales, major telecommunications equipment suppliers were eager to maintain their footholds in these markets. As a result, it now became possible for developing countries to obtain better terms in licensing agreements to manufacture the new switches locally and consciously to set out to master the new technology[14].

As local technological capabilities began to emerge, the many opportunities offered by this new conjuncture encouraged governments in several developing countries to consider "making" rather than "buying" telecommunications technology. Brazil, Korea and India all took the plunge in this period. As latecomers, firms in these countries, however, would not only have to pool resources in order rapidly to achieve economies of scale and scope in R&D, production and marketing comparable to those of their competitors, but as Alfred Chandler pointed out, to maintain enough capacity utilisation to assure competitive unit costs, they would also have to take customers away from the first movers who dominated their domestic markets (Chandler, 1990). Investments in telecommunications infrastructure, market reservation provisions, tendering procedures and a host of tariff and non–tariff barriers were put in place to ensure that domestic procurement provided just such a stimulus to local R&D efforts. As in France, Japan and Sweden, public research laboratories were set up to develop the new technology and transfer it to industry.

In slightly more than a decade after beginning the catch–up phase, Brazil and Korea had moved from low to high density digital switches using indigenously developed technology. Korea had even begun to export its smaller switches to Asian and Eastern European markets. They thus appeared to have caught up. But could they keep up? Changes in the intensity and nature of competition and in the speed and direction of technological change suggest that this would become increasingly difficult.

In the mid–1980s, for example, competition began to intensify as the market for digital switching in the industrialised countries showed signs of becoming saturated. In the wake of the court–ordered dismemberment of AT&T in 1982, firms from Europe and Canada set their sights on the United States market while AT&T[15] itself sought new opportunities for expansion in Europe. The market crash for semiconductors which took place in 1985–86 intensified international competition in the telecommunications industry still further, since many telecommunications companies, particularly in Japan, were also semiconductor and computer manufacturers[16].

With the globalization of competition, pressure mounted everywhere for the liberalisation of markets[17]. Latecomers with large, protected markets were especially attractive targets as we shall see below. The newer cellular and satellite technologies became initial points of entry, but procurement practices for central office switches were not spared.

The nature of competition in the industry also began to change as the earlier emphasis on higher density switching gave way to a focus on innovations that increased the flexibility of digital switches to provide enhanced services[18]. This change in focus created new opportunities for collaboration among service companies, operating companies and equipment suppliers at the same time as it intensified the potential for competition among them. In 1993, for example, telephone operating companies (Telcos) were actively seeking to merge with cable television (CATV) firms. The two most prominent cases were the aborted merger of Bell Atlantic Corporation, the Philadelphia–based RBOC, and Tele–Communications, and the failed effort by South western Bell Corporation to form a joint venture with Cox Cable Communications, Inc. In 1994 the Telcos and the CATV companies became rivals when several of the "baby Bells" formed an alliance with Walt Disney Company to develop their own cable programmes, while four of the largest cable companies in the United States announced plans to invest massively in upgrading their networks so they could offer high–definition television, wireless telephone, video on demand as well as basic telephone and computer on–line services[19]. Cross–national alliances involving telecommunications operating companies are also on the rise[20].

Growing competition between telephone operating companies and providers of data and video services, where switching speeds and the volume of throughput are important, gave a boost to the development of asynchronous transfer mode (ATM) switching. Invented simultaneously by CNET and AT&T in the mid–1980s, ATM, by the early 1990s, had emerged as a potent competitor to the more traditional form of ISDN. The latter, which involved heavier capital investment, secured the dominant role of national telecommunication operating company monopolies, notably in Europe[21]. The former now became an element in competition within the more competitive US and Canadian markets where ATM switching developed and diffused more rapidly. As early as April 1993, Newbridge ATM switches were installed by BC Tel, the telephone operating company in Canada's most western province (Williams, King and Gerrad, 1994). Six months later, Time Warner, the second largest cable television operator in the United States began to introduce AT&T's ATM switches into its network.

During the 1990s the pace of technological change picked up and competition among telecom equipment suppliers to be "first in the market" with an advanced product or service intensified. ATM switching is being rapidly adapted to existing systems and to multiple uses from PABXs to central office switches. Major strides are also being made in transmission with cross–connects ensuring compatibility between the new synchronous digital hierarchy (SDH) techniques and the older synchronous transport module (STM), while the growing demand for cellular (mobile) telephony has generated a need to bring together radio signalling technologies with more conventional switching techniques. Costs per line are also falling, adding an element of price competition that plays havoc with R&D budgets and reinforces the need for collaboration in R&D[22].

As this brief discussion illustrates, competitive conditions in the 1990s bear little resemblance to those of the early 1980s when Brazil and Korea launched their telecommunications programmes. Below we look at some of the weaknesses in the catch–up strategies pursued by these two countries, and more importantly, analyse the extent to which the new competition has been a stimulus to the kind of innovation that would enable these firms to keep up as conditions changed.

Brazilian Telecommunications

By 1964, the year in which the military came to power in Brazil, state–owned enterprises (SOEs) were well established in sectors where private capital had been reluctant to invest, notably in the heavy and chemical industries. The SOEs, moreover, were quite successful. Petrobras, the Brazilian petrochemical holding company, figured on the *Fortune* list of the world's largest corporations, Companhia Siderúrgica Nacional (CSN) had an impressive record of profitability and the state–owned electric companies had overcome Brazil's hydroelectric power constraints.

Despite the positive record of state–owned enterprises General Humberto Castello Branco, the first post–1964 military President, sought to reverse earlier nationalistic policies and "base Brazil's economic development on internationalism and economic liberalism". In this he was supported by his principal economic advisor, Roberto Campos, "a devout economic liberal who believed that a return to competition was the only way out of Brazil's stagnation" (Evans, 1979). "The disastrous performance of the Brazilian economy from 1964 to 1967 discredited economic liberalism", however, and "instead of diminishing under the military, the number of state enterprises increased more rapidly than in any previous era" (Evans, 1979). For some, therefore, the expansion of state enterprise during the Brazilian economic boom of the late 1960s and early 1970s did not result from an explicitly statist ideology, although it was systematically justified by market failure (Evans, 1979; Tigre, 1983). Others, however, maintain that the creation of Embraer to manufacture light aircraft, Digibras and Cobre to strengthen Brazilian informatics capability, Telebras and its research institute CPqD to develop and diffuse digital switching and transmission technology, and Nuclebras to promote nuclear power generation were indeed expressions of a nationalist striving for scientific and technological autonomy (Adler, 1987; Baptista and Cassiolato, 1994), and all agree that the military's concern for national security[23] was a decisive factor.

In the case of telecommunications, both the market failure and the technological autonomy arguments are quite credible. But government policies and the practices of Brazilian–based firms, foreign and local, would differ from that in other sectors. In large part these differences grew out of the initial structure of this industry in the 1960s and the *policy dynamics* which developed over the next two decades.

Prior to the creation of Telebras in 1972 no overall authority was responsible for telecommunications services in Brazil, although elsewhere, the provision of telecommunications service was regarded as a natural monopoly and, with rare exceptions, was the purview of a single national supplier[24]. International telephone service was provided by four concessionaires, two of which were foreign. In the domestic market, the Companhia Telephonia Brasileira (CTB), a wholly owned subsidiary of the Canadian Traction Light and Power Company,

> operated approximately 68 per cent of installed telephones, and no less than 800 small private firms were responsible for the balance... The disorganised state of the telecoms service companies was reflected in the inefficiency and inadequacy of the network coverage. For example, in 1962 there were less than 1.3 million telephones servicing a total population of 74 million — i.e. less than two telephones per 100 population. Also there were less than 1000 telex terminals...[and this] was compounded by an inadequate local transmission network which only efficiently connected up four of the major cities (Hobday, 1990).

In addition, the small scale of operations and the unrealistic tariffs charged by these companies contributed to both the low levels of investment in the industry and to the slow growth in telecommunications traffic. Over the next three decades, successive Brazilian governments attempted to deal with this situation through a combination of protection, procurement, the promotion of domestic production and R&D, and the diffusion of telecommunications services.

The Demand Side

To rationalise and extend service and to bring tariffs down, the Brazilian government, beginning in 1962, acquired most of the private firms operating in the domestic market and in 1972 consolidated them under the newly established Telebras, a state–owned holding company[25]. Today, the Telebras system (STB) is composed of 28 local telecommunications operating companies, EMBRATEL which handles overseas operations and a research institute, the Centro de Pesquisa et Desenvolviment (CPqD). A constitutional amendment would be required to privatise the Telebras system.

Once consolidated and despite a major balance of payments crisis following the oil price hike of 1973, investment in telecommunications infrastructure doubled during Telebras' first five years. Although public investment fell in 1980 after the second oil crisis, it rose again in a sustained fashion from 1986 through 1992 (Table 4.1).

The diffusion of telephone services was also impressive. The number of main lines doubled between 1973 (1.6 million) and 1977 (3.6 million) and again by 1983 (6.2 million). From a business planning perspective, however, it is the number of lines installed per year that is important and as the data in Table 4.1 show, this varied considerably — averaging 374 000 per year in 1973–77, 542 000 over the period 1977–80, falling back to 395 000 lines per year in 1981–84 and 390 250 in 1985–88 as the debt crisis worsened and funding expansion of the network became more difficult[26] (Table 4.1).

While the telephone penetration rate in Brazil is not high when compared with Korea or the OECD countries[27], it did rise from fewer than 2 telephones per 100 persons in 1970 to a high of 9.5 in 1987 before declining to between 6 and 7 as the economic crisis deepened towards the end of the 1980s. More importantly, the number of localities reached by telephone rose dramatically over these two decades, with particularly rapid growth in the period 1980 to 1984 and again from 1987 to 1990. This was largely linked to extensive use of public telephones, a factor of considerable importance in a vast country such as Brazil where a large percentage of the population both rural and urban cannot afford a telephone (Table 4.1)[28].

Table 4.1. **Changes in Telecommunications Investment and Access in Brazil, 1972–92**

	Investment $ million	Installed telephone lines '000	Localities reached	Public telephones '000	Inter-urban traffic (calls) millions
1972	-----	142.000*	----	10.28	124
1974	796	312	2 554	13.67	177
1976	1 648	708	2 917	23.98	285
1978	1 454	589	3 112	36.42	400
1980	932	405	3 773	49.80	630
1982	1 523	393	6 119	63.88	842
1983	947	422	7 061	71.22	937
1984	964	474	7 995	87.33	1 069
1985	918	294	8 508	98.52	1 299
1986	1 245	346	8 815	141.25	1 623
1987	1 448	407	10 246	172.25	1 901
1988	1 977	514	11 908	200.40	1 984
1989	2 586	611	12 781	220.70	2 374
1990	2 121	463	13 900	227.00	2 499
1991	2 300	474	14 500	236.40	2 949
1992	3 063	857	15 400	259.60	3 131

* Cumulative to 1972, thereafter annual increments.
Source: Telebras (1990) and (1993).

The Supply Side

During the 1960s the provision of telecommunications services was gradually reorganised and an expansion of the network and of access to it was begun. But it was not until 1974, that balance of payments problems resulting from the first oil shock motivated the new Geisel government to launch an ambitious programme of import substitution in this and other industries. The new policy was contained in the Second National Development Plan (II PND).

With regard to telecommunications, government policies were aimed first, at reducing telecommunications imports by stimulating domestic production and second, at building the capabilities needed to reduce "the dependence of the sector on foreign technology" (Graciosa et Machado 1989). The latter led initially to the funding of research activities in five Brazilian universities[29] and subsequently to the creation of the CPqD in 1976 and the launching of major research programmes on digital switching and transmission technology.

The former gave rise to a debate over the desirability of creating a state–owned manufacturing facility in the telecommunications equipment sector. In August 1975 Portaria 661 authorised the creation of a Brazilian–owned equipment manufacturer which would be assured of 40 per cent of the public sector market for space division digital switches. Initially it was expected that Telebras would be a major shareholder (da Costa, 1991), but it was unclear whether it would be the majority shareholder.

Faced with the overwhelming dominance of multinational corporations as both technology suppliers and equipment manufacturers in Brazil and the need to rely on these companies over the decade or more that would elapse before Brazilian telecommunications technology would be available, the government subsequently opted against the creation of a state–owned manufacturing enterprise in the telecommunications industry (Interview: General Alencastro[30], Nov. 1992). To ensure a more effective transfer of technology and an increase in the domestic content of local production, however, foreign–owned manufacturing firms now came under pressure to transform themselves into joint ventures (Adler, 1987; Botelho *et al.*, 1993).

These pressures were given credibility by the monopsonist procurement position of Telebras and the implicit threat of exclusion which this presupposed (Fritsch and Franco, 1991). But they were balanced by the inducement of negotiated prices, market reservation and product normalisation which created barriers to entry to potential competitors, reduced the risks to the private sector and guaranteed its profitability. Portario 622 of June 1978, for example, reserved 40 per cent of the domestic market in space division switching for domestically manufactured equipment and such equipment had to be certified by Telebras before it could be included as part of a tender bid. In 1976 Ericsson, NEC and SESA (ITT) were certified for the domestic manufacture of space division digital switches.

Between 1978 and 1981 Ericsson, NEC, Equitel (Siemens), ABC [formerly Telettra (Fiat) and Italtel] and Multitel (GTE) ceded 51 per cent of their shares to local interests though, for the most part, the former parent company continued to shape technology and investment decisions within the joint venture (Interviews: Alencastro, Nov. 1992; Equitel, Nov. 1992 & May 1994; Ericsson, Nov. 1992 & May 1994; NEC, May 1994). ITT, then in the process of rethinking its strategy, sold SESA to local interests. In addition, a number of small wholly owned Brazilian equipment manufacturers emerged during the 1970s and 1980s. In 1978, three of these, Elebra, Embracom, later PHT–Promon, and IGB Control later replaced by SID/STC Telecomunicacões were designated domestic suppliers of the future national technology[31].

In 1981 Minicom ended the purchase of space division digital switches and since no Brazilian time division digital switches were yet available, it certified three foreign switches for use in the Telebras network – NEAX–61 (NEC), EWS–D (Siemens–Equitel) and AXE (Ericsson). To encourage domestic production of these switches Portaria 215 of 1981 allocated the markets of Brazil's three major cities to these companies: São Paulo to Ericsson; Rio de Janeiro to NEC/SESA[32] and Curitiba to Equitel. Markets in the rest of the country were left open to competition with the proviso that 50 per cent of the market would eventually be reserved for Tropico switches once these became available. Embratel's needs were also met through open tenders.

One result of the market segmentation policy was to structure market share amongst the three main foreign producers. With the São Paulo market reserved for Ericsson switches, that company was able to develop the largest installed base and held a decided advantage in being able to grow by providing extensions (Interview: Ericsson, Nov. 1992 and Equitel, Nov. 1992 & May 1994). Compared to markets in Western Europe and North America where a single supplier accounted for upwards of 80 per cent of the market, however, the Brazilian market appeared highly contestable. Through competitive pricing, for example, NEC early on took the largest share of the market for international switches (Interview: Embratel, Nov. 1992) and as Belo Horizonte, Brasília and other cities developed, there was room for growth. But over the 1980s, the basis for competition was less price than technicity and product differentiation.

As these firms began to produce locally and meet domestic content requirements through purchases from Brazilian suppliers, the value of domestically produced telecommunications equipment rose from $620.8 million in 1980 to $1 202.6 million in 1987 (Table 4.2), growing at the high rate of over 9 per cent per year despite massive devaluations in 1982 and 1983. Over time, the composition of domestic output also changed as the relative importance of electromechanical switches declined from 795 400 terminals in 1977 to 470 099 in 1983 and 165 000 in 1991 and the production of digital switches and digital transmission (Multiplex PCM) rose — the former from 110 600 terminals in 1983 to an average of 710 438 per year in the period 1986–88 and the latter from 54 134 channels in 1983 to a high of 205 709 in 1989 (GEATIC).

Table 4.2. **Brazil: Annual Production of Telecommunications Equipment: 1980–93**
($ million)

	1980	1983	1984	1985	1986	1987
Value	620.8	663.4	595.5	765.7	938.2	1 202.6
% change			-10.2	28.6	22.5	28.2

	1988	1989	1990	1991	1992	1993
Value	1 418.9	1 515.2	1 314.0	1 369.0	1 280.0	1 150.0
% change	17.9	6.8	-13.3	4.2	-6.5	

Source: GEATIC.

During the early 1980s, the rise in domestic production was accompanied by a steep decline in imports and a small beginning in telecommunications exports (Figure 4.1). As a consequence, the deficit in the balance of trade in telecommunications products declined from $352 million in 1975 to $151 million in 1977 and $78 million a year later. It reached its lowest point of $51 million in 1983. By 1987, however, it had begun to climb, jumping from $83 million in that year to $158 million in 1988 then averaging $118 million over the three year period 1989–91 before rising dramatically to $213 million in 1992. Overall growth in the domestic production of telecommunications equipment also slowed down after 1987 (Table 4.2), particularly in the production of electronic exchanges, which declined to an average of 668 546 terminals per year in the period 1989–91, and multiplexers, which fell to an annual average of 177 029 channels over the same period.

Figure 4.1. **Brazilian Imports and Exports of Telecommunications Products: 1976-92**
($ million)

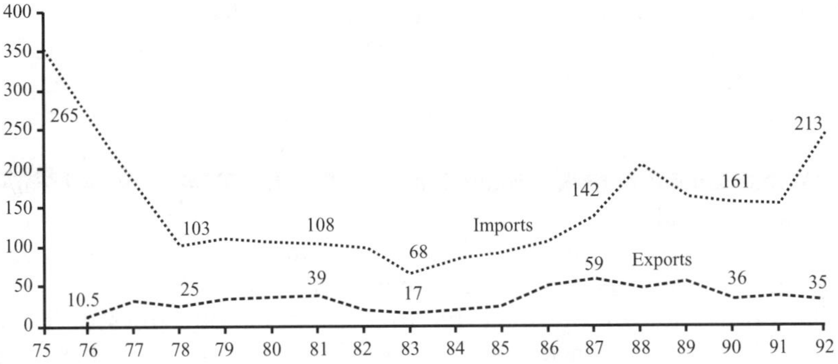

Source: GEATIC.

In a recent publication, Claudio Frischtak suggested that the sharp decline in domestic production towards the end of the 1980s can be explained by foreign exchange– induced shortages in imported inputs and a fall in public investment (Frischtak, 1990). As the data in Table 4.1 show, however, investment in the telecommunications network began to rise in 1986 and reached an average of $2 518 million per year in the period 1989–92. Imports also began to rise in the mid–1980s despite a foreign exchange shortage. In what follows, therefore, it will be argued that the decline in production and the rise in imports are both related to changes in telecommunications policies which made possible a substitution of imports for domestic production notably after 1988, when imported data and satellite communications equipment were introduced into the network, and in the early 1990s as the Collor deregulation and liberalisation policies took effect.

Two factors lay behind the change in telecommunications policy and hence in the trade–off between imports and domestic production. One was the slower than expected progress in developing Brazilian telecommunications technology. The second was the impact of the changing global competitive environment on the pricing, production and innovation strategies of large multinational firms operating in the Brazilian market.

The Slow Pace of Innovation in Digital Switching

The research programmes initiated under the new telecommunications policy were very successful in developing *low density* time–division electronic switches destined for rural areas or urban localities with low traffic. They were also successful in transferring this technology to industry. But they were not able to develop and commercialise high density digital switches during the brief period when a window of opportunity had opened for doing so.

Growing out of the work begun at the University of São Paulo under contract to Telebras, CPqD launched a programme of research on digital switching in 1977. Many of the researchers at USP who had produced a prototype of a small digital switch moved to CPqD to continue their research. By 1982 they had field tested the Tropico C, a small, 192 line, 30 channel stored programme control (SPC) time–division digital switch. A year later it entered production. In 1984, the Tropico R, a local/tandem switch with a total traffic capacity of 320 Erlangs and able to handle about 4 000 users was field tested. Three wholly Brazilian owned firms — Promon, Elebra and P&D Sistemas Electronicas — participated in its development (Hobday, 1990). The Tropico R entered production in 1986 and by 1988 over 380 000 lines of Tropico R, manufactured by wholly owned Brazilian firms, had been ordered by local telephone operating companies of the Telebras system.

Research on a 20 000 line Tropico switch, then called the Tropico L, was well under way in the mid–1980s when it became evident that such a switch would be too small to handle the anticipated increase in subscribers and traffic and the new features which were rapidly being introduced by foreign manufacturers. This did not present an insuperable problem for Tropico because it had been conceived as a modularised and decentralised system and could be extended more easily than the centralised AXE, NEAX and EWS–D systems, whose expansion was limited by the size of the central processor (Interview: Equitel, Nov.1992). The Tropico L and the Tropico RA programmes were thus combined and in 1987, CPqD completed "the hardware integration for the lst Prototype of the SPC–T (Tropico–RA) telephone exchange" (Telebras, 1987), a time division local/tandem switch with a total traffic capacity of 12 600 Erlangs (typically 80 000 to 100 000 subscribers).

Where the problem in a decentralised switching system lies, however, is in its very complex software. In the absence of a hierarchy, software problems rise exponentially with size. This significantly adds to the cost and lengthens the development time of such systems, as ITT discovered in developing its System 12 — a problem which Alcatel inherited when it acquired ITT's European subsidiaries. Thus, although the prototype of the Tropico RA was field–tested in 1989, it was far from ready to be introduced into the network. None of the 100 000 lines of Tropico RA sold by Alcatel in 1990 and 1991, for example, had been delivered in 1992 because 80 of its engineers were still working in Campinas with CPqD on software development (Interview: Alcatel, Nov. 1992). Between its inception and the development of a prototype, moreover, the number and kinds of features demanded by the Brazilian market for digital switches had considerably changed (Interview: CPqD, Nov.1992 and May 1994). The technological frontier was also advancing faster than anticipated[33]. Between 1987 and 1992 when the burden of further development fell most heavily on CPqD[34], its financial capabilities were being seriously undercut by political developments.

In 1984 the military stepped down and was replaced by a civilian government the following March. Already divided over the need for liberalisation, faced with a debt crisis and buffeted by pressures to open the domestic market in informatics products, the new government found it virtually impossible to develop a coherent industrial policy (Bastos, 1992; Erber, 1985; Ventura–Dias, 1989; Meyer–Stamer, 1992). Following several years of low public investment in the telecommunications system, however, the wait for a telephone line had grown to over two years[35]. Priority was thus given to new capital investment.

In 1987, CPqD's budget was "held down to 1.5 per cent of net exploration revenue and the Centre did not manage to meet the target of 2 per cent that had previously been established...[As a result,] the resources allocated to...CPqD were insufficient fully to meet its needs" (Telebras, 1987). By then, moreover, CPqD's research programme was spread too thin — some 44 projects grouped into 8 major research programmes: electronic switching, satellite communications, digital transmission, optical communications, components and materials, communications of data and texts, network development and studies, telephone technology. In the absence of a serious effort to narrow the scope of its activities[36], debt, inflation and economic crisis began to take its toll on CPqD's research programme. Between 1987 and 1992, just at the critical juncture in developing the Tropico RA switch, the number of professionals working at CPqD fell by 17 per cent (Table 4.3) and while Telebras waited for the Tropico RA, large segments of the public exchange network remained inefficient[37], fuelling the demand for liberalisation.

Table 4.3. **CPqD Budget and Professional Workforce: 1986–93**

	1986	1987	1988	1989	1990	1991	1992	1993
Employees	n.a.	1 364	1 421	1 340	1 357	1 282	1 134	1 298
Budget–$ million	32.6	36.0	67.1	70.6	72.6	46.2	65.4	113

Source: CPqD.

Competition and Competitiveness

Over the 1980s international competition heated up driving world prices down for digital switches and widening the gap between Brazilian and international prices for telecommunications equipment[38] (Table 4.4). Because local manufacturers were overwhelmingly foreign and there was considerable under–utilised capacity in the industry at this time, one might have expected these firms to respond to international competitive pressures by improving domestic productivity and exporting through their world–wide network. A few firms did export electromechanical and later digital switches to neighbouring Latin American countries. But as Figure 4.1 illustrated the rise in exports between 1983 and 1987 was not sustained and indeed there was little reason for these firms to reduce costs and export when higher profits could be made in the domestic market.

Table 4.4. **Brazilian Telecommunications Equipment Industry International Price Comparisons: 1983–86**
(dollars)

Equipment	Unit	Avg. unit price: 1983	Int'l unit price: 1983	Avg. unit price: 1986	Int'l unit price: 1986
Electromech. exchanges	Lines	360	330	286	....
Electronic exchanges	Lines	420	300	400-450	120-180
Multiplex PCM	Channel end	380	360	200	360
Microwave radio-analogue	Transceiver	40 000	22 000	40 000	22 000
Microwave radio-digital	Transceiver	60 000	22 000	60 000	22 000
Radio UHF	Transceiver	7 500	5 000	6 000	5 000
Radio VHF	Transceiver	1 800	1 200	900	1 200
Telephone handset	Instrument	30	50	32	30
Public telephone	Instrument	400	600	450	600

Source: 1983: Ministério da Ciencia e Technologia (1993), 50; 1986: Frischtak (1990), 44.

Prior to 1989 when the first Tropico RA switches were tested, no alternative to foreign technology in large scale digital switching and transmission technology or in the newer cellular technology was available. In 1985, the new civilian government thus issued policy directives which opened the domestic market for large public switches to locally based firms using foreign technology. Because of earlier import substitution and market segmentation policies, Ericsson, Equitel (Siemens) and NEC were well placed to benefit from this policy shift. All three companies, moreover, had developed substantial in–house engineering capability. This coupled with their long years of experience in adapting their technology to Brazilian specifications gave them a clear advantage over their global competitors — AT&T, Northern Telecom and Alcatel — who were not then established in the domestic market. The major consequence of this change in policy was to shift the balance of power in negotiating the purchasing price for large digital switches from the Brazilian government to the firms. Practising oligopolistic pricing policies within the context of a domestic market which remained highly protected, these firms successfully pushed up prices on locally manufactured equipment to new heights (Figure 4.2).

Figure 4.2. **Effect of Competition on the Price of Digital Switches in Brazil**

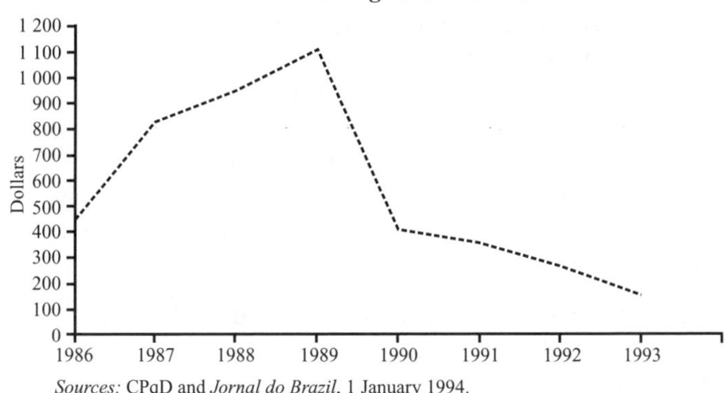

Sources: CPqD and *Jornal do Brazil*, 1 January 1994.

The dominance of Ericsson, NEC and Siemens, however, would be short–lived. The market crash for semiconductors in 1985–86 intensified global competition in the telecommunications industry, increasing R&D costs, accelerating the speed with which products were developed and moved to market, and leading firms to adopt product differentiation strategies (Ernst and O'Connor, 1992). In this new context, the potentially large and still protected Brazilian market for telecommunications products became highly attractive to foreign investors, thus adding to the pressure on Brazil's new civilian government to relax foreign investment restrictions. The surge of new entrants that followed significantly altered competitive practices in the domestic market.

Beginning in 1987 Alcatel acquired five wholly Brazilian–owned telecommunications equipment suppliers — Elebra, Multitel (ex–GTE), SESA and SESA Rio (ex–ITT) and ABC–Teleinformation (formerly Telettra and Italtel). Virtually overnight it became a domestic equipment supplier and a direct competitor to the foreign technologies of its global rivals — Ericsson, NEC and Siemens (Equitel). In addition, through its take–over of Elebra and SESA, Alcatel acquired two of the licences to manufacture the Tropico family of switches. These were worth 50 per cent of the market reserved for Tropico and put Alcatel in direct competition with Promon and SID/STC, the only remaining nationally–owned producers of the Tropico system. By 1990 large orders of Tropico R and RA and the new presence of Alcatel in the market led to a sharp drop in average prices per line for digital switches (Figure 4.2)[39]. The continued fall in international prices for digital switches enabled Telebras to negotiate lower prices for Tropico switches, pushing average prices below $500 in 1991 and below $300 by 1992, though the domestic market was still closed to imports from least cost suppliers such as AT&T and Northern Telecom.

In the short term, the fall in prices augured well for the competitiveness of the Tropico family of switches. In the longer term, however, the take–over of Elebra and SESA created a potential conflict of interests for Alcatel, since the large Brazilian market offered a unique opportunity to help amortise the high cost of developing its System 12[40]. The conflict of interest became a reality once changes in telecommunications policies eliminated the market reserve for Tropico switches, leaving Promon and SID/STC the sole companies with an interest in developing the Brazilian technology. Neither of these firms, however, had the financial resources to maintain and develop the Tropico system and how far either was prepared to invest in Tropico was uncertain, given the alliances they were then concluding with Northern Telecom and AT&T[41]. Though neither company had penetrated the domestic market for central office switches by 1992, both had become active in supplying equipment for the newer and fast growing cellular market[42].

After Alcatel's entry, though prices continued to decline and market shares changed, concentration in the telecommunications market actually worsened. In 1987, for example, Ericsson held 50 per cent of the market for digital switching but the three foreign firms collectively [Ericsson, NEC, Equitel (Siemens)] accounted for only 74 per cent of the digital switching market, while three domestic firms (Promon, Elebra and SID/STC) accounted for the remaining 26 per cent. In 1992 Ericsson's share of the switching market had fallen to 36 per cent, but the four foreign firms then in the market accounted for 90 per cent of the switching market and the share of the two remaining Brazilian–owned firms had fallen to roughly 10 per cent (Table 4.5).

Table 4.5. **Concentration in the Telecommunications Market: 1987 and 1992**
(percentages)

	1987 Electrom.switch	1987 Digital switch	1987 Multi– plexer PCM	1987 Multi– plexer FDM	1992 Switches	1992 Multi- plexers	1992 Satellite	1992 Cellular
Ericsson	46	50	--	--	36	7	<1	12
NEC	22	17	15	2	21	27	38	65
Equitel	14	7	--	34	16	11	16	<1 with Motorola
Elebra	11	63			Alcatel			
SESA	18				Alcatel			
ABC			12	28	Alcatel			
Alcatel					~17	~35	14	<1
Promon	--	12	--	--	~5	--	--	10 with Northern
SID /ST<C	--	~3	--	--	~5	--	--	13 with AT&T

Sources: 1987: GEATIC; 1992: NEC (1993).

Liberalisation, Deregulation and Innovation

It was in this changed international environment that the new Collor government began, in 1990, to develop its monetarist policies and its programme of deregulation and market liberalisation. The former, undertaken in the hope of reducing inflation, had the negative impact on small telecommunications firms of making credit scarce. The latter, aimed at increasing competitiveness (Ministério da Ciencia e Technologia, 1994), led to radical changes in the rules of competition as the regional market segmentation policy was ended[43], the level of domestic content in locally produced equipment was reduced, and the market was opened wide to imports (Lei 8248 of 1991).

Then in October 1992 the 50 per cent market reservation for Tropico technology was eliminated, altering the trade–off between domestic production of a locally developed switch (which Telebras estimated would still need 400 researchers and $20 million per year to maintain and develop, especially CCITT No. 7 channel signalling needed to support ISDN capability; Interview: Telebras, May 1994), and imports, sharply in favour of the latter. The result, as we have already seen (Table 4.2 and Figure 4.2), was a sharp increase in imports and a continued drop in domestic production of telecommunications equipment[44].

Deregulation and liberalisation also stimulated a shift in the mode of competition from competition based on technical proficiency, product differentiation[45] and an effort to search for exploitable domestic market niches to competition on the basis of being "first" into the market. Equitel, for example, had developed a micro–PABX for small businesses and in 1992 still envisaged the possibility of selling this product abroad through the Siemens sales network (Interview: Equitel, November 1992). By 1994, however, the emphasis was on the number of new products they had introduced — 42 per cent of their sales in 1993 consisted of products that were less than two years old and a further 33 per cent were products between two and five years old (Interview: Equitel, May 1994).

Since gearing up to manufacture new products locally would delay their introduction, the adoption of a "first in the market" strategy reinforced the tendency to import. Alcatel, whose component companies had a long series of locally developed products to their credit, for example, began replacing these with Alcatel products. In 1993, Alcatel introduced 14 new products, only three of which were locally developed. SDH transmission and telecom network management products were all imported and domestic production would, in future, be limited to low order PCM multiplexers and switches smaller than the Tropico R for use in villages and condominiums (Interview: Alcatel, May 1994). Similarly NEC, in preparation for the future installation of ATM switches, had begun to send Brazilian engineers to its ATM centre in the United States (Interview: NEC, May 1994).

Several consequences of the radical liberalisation of the domestic market and the changed nature of competition have a bearing on the ability of Brazilian firms to maintain the telecommunications R&D capacity that was created over the 1980s and sustain the future development of the Tropico family of switches. *First*, by emphasising imports, the "first into the market" strategy undercut the market for local component suppliers, most of which lacked the resources needed rapidly to development alternative markets (Pessini, 1993). According to GEATIC, nearly 80 per cent of the component manufacturers went bankrupt as imports began to rise in the mid–1980s (Interview: Wanjberg, May 1994). One indication of this is the sharp fall in the market share of domestically owned telecommunications firms between 1986 and 1992 (Table 4.6).

Table 4.6. **Telecommunications Equipment Suppliers: Evolution of Market Shares**
(percentages)

	1972	1986	1992
Indep. Brazilian firms	<5	~45	~30
MNCs installed before 1990	>95	~55	~50
MNCs installed in or after 1990	-	-	~20

Source: Telebras, CPqD cited in Graciosa & Gomes (1994).

Second, the speed with which new products were being introduced into the market and prices were falling made keeping up much more difficult for the smaller Brazilian companies than for their larger foreign competitors since they were unable to offset losses on switching with revenues from other stronger product lines. Without a "mother company" to supply technology, these smaller firms faced the double problem of needing financial resources to invest in production technology to match that of their global competitors[46] at the same time as they were now forced to accelerate the pace of new product development in order to compete domestically. The new mode of competition, therefore, reduced the incentive for local firms to innovate, pushing the few remaining Brazilian–owned companies into alliances and joint ventures with foreign partners. Promon's decision to license technology from Northern Telecom is a case in point[47].

An employee–owned company, Promon began life in the 1960s as an engineering firm. During the 1980s it moved into digital switching and worked with CPqD to develop the Tropico family of switches. To compete in the new cellular market, however, it sought out a foreign technology partner. While it is currently working to add a cellular capability to the Tropico R, it is unlikely that this will be extended to the RA. Indeed, Promon is now also licensed to make Northern Telecom's DMS switches and it acknowledges that its licences with Northern have become a mainstay of its telecommunications business[48]. Promon has thus become vulnerable to a Northern take–over (Interview: Promon, May 1994). Other small firms face a similar dilemma — develop indigenous technology that might be technically superior and price competitive but arrive on the market too late to take market share away from the front runners, or license technology from abroad. Monytel, for example, despite an excellent track record in developing and commercialising a number of telecommunications products such as PBXs and voice mail systems, has also recently concluded an agreement with a foreign technology supplier (Interview: Monytel, May 1994).

Third, being first in the market also meant being quickest in adapting imported switches to Brazilian specifications. Rather than waiting to adapt products that had been fully developed by the parent firm, Brazilian–based companies are now sending engineers to work in the parent company to adapt the new technology as it is being developed, thus, in effect, subsidising the development process in their parent firm. Thirty of Alcatel's 300 engineers previously dedicated to R&D in Brazil are now working in Alcatel companies in Europe to ensure that future Alcatel products include Brazilian specifications from the start (Interview: Alcatel, May 1994). Both Equitel and NEC are pursuing similar strategies (Interview: NEC, Equitel, May 1994), thus locking in their new product development to that of their parent firm and reducing the need to develop new products in Brazil. The new mode of competition has thus become a major barrier[49] to the future development of the Tropico system, not least because firms currently manufacturing Tropico switches are also manufacturing a competitor switch and with the exception of Promon, all are multinational subsidiaries that have little interest in subsidising CPqD's development costs when they are being asked to do the same with respect to their parent firms.

In 1993, Collor was forced to resign the Presidency to face corruption charges. Though concerned about the impact of Collor's reforms on the telecommunications industry, the government of Itamar Franco was initially disinclined to slow the process down. Then, in November of that year the government opened a tender for 720 000 telephone lines and the established players agreed to bid at between $220 and $230 per line which they described as the minimum price needed to keep their companies alive (Interview: Alcatel, NEC: May 1994). The tender called for all bidders to hold the Telebras technical quality certification (AQT) and there was a tacit assumption that this implied some degree of domestic content. A few days before the bids were due, AT&T received the AQT for imported 5 ESS switches and, to make matters worse, entered the bidding with a price $100 below that of its rivals, thus effectively disrupting the oligopolistic pricing practices which the "new" insiders had sought to re–establish as a barrier to the entry of still newer entrants[50]. Although a lawsuit initiated by NEC to block AT&T's bid was rejected by the courts, an appeal to the President resulted in the tender's cancellation pending an evaluation by Telebras. The incident was sufficiently shocking, however, that a task force was assigned to look into revisions to the tendering process that would both enhance its transparency and rekindle an interest in domestic manufacture and local innovation.

The result was Decreto 1070 of April 1994. The new policy takes the "buy American" act as its model, thereby side–stepping outcries of renewed protectionism. Rather than protect firms through high tariffs or prohibit them from importing, Decreto 1070 encourages firms to produce locally and engage in R&D through a set of incentives that can reduce the firm's tax burden by as much as 40 per cent and can lower the purchasing price to clients by exonerating them from a number of duties. In addition further tax reductions result if the firm invests 5 per cent of its turnover in R&D and training, of which 2 per cent can consist of work contracted out to universities and research institutions. The new policy also restructures the bidding process so as to introduce both technical and price grounds for selecting prospective suppliers. In a first cut, bids are regrouped into "similar" proposals and of this group, the difference between the highest and lowest price cannot exceed 12 per cent. Within the group, preference is then given to products developed in the country by a Brazilian–owned firm and following that by a foreign–owned firm. Foreign products produced locally come third and imported products fourth in the preference hierarchy.

While it is far too early to assess the significance of this new policy change, the data presented above suggest that Decreto 1070 may have come too late since many Brazilian–owned firms have already failed or have abandoned efforts to develop new products and processes in–house, preferring to license them from abroad. Others, however, have begun to reconfigure themselves as "systems integrators" taking advantage of the convergence between computers and telecommunications and between producers and users of telecom services to develop networking products for local firms in the retail, banking and manufacturing sectors where customisation and hence user–producer links are critical (Cassiolato *et al.*, 1995). To the extent that telecommunications software capabilities are fungible skills, their development over the past decade through CPqD programmes might now serve as the basis for rapidly developing systems integration activities.

Opportunities to maintain and further develop existing technological capability in telecommunications might also emerge if the large multinational firms choose to use Brazil as their manufacturing base for Latin America, thus re–creating a market for components. Recent exports by Alcatel and Ericsson suggest some movement in this direction. But there is also counter evidence, particularly in the case of Alcatel which is under pressure to increase capacity utilisation at its Spanish plants and has placed its Brazilian subsidiary under the general direction of Telfonica. Decreto 1070 might, nonetheless, have a positive impact on the persistence with which these firms seek to maintain existing R&D capacity by promoting their services within the corporate group. Equitel, Alcatel and Ericsson have all tried to move in this direction with Ericsson having made considerable headway in becoming a development service provider within the Ericsson group. Seventy–five per cent of their R&D effort is now undertaken for the group — some 70–80 000 man–hours in 1994 (Interview: Ericsson, May 1994). Since Alcatel has no central laboratory but conducts research in 20 centres around the world, there is some hope that a similar arrangement will emerge there. But this alone may not be sufficient to induce the local subsidiary to do more than adapt foreign products for the local market and use its adaptive capabilities to service the marketing needs of the parent firm around the globe. Local production would remain imitative, locking them into overseas component suppliers and limiting the possibility for positive spillovers in Brazil. Over time, in these and other companies, R&D staffs would be reduced as many engineers were shifted to marketing and maintenance activities.

Korean Telecommunications

As United States aid declined in the early 1960s, the new military government of Park Chung Hee chose to borrow rather than rely on direct foreign investment (DFI) for development funds. Like the Japanese before them, the Korean government initially barred direct foreign investment and after a brief period of liberalisation following recognition of Japan in the mid–1960s, exercised tight control over direct foreign investment and technology transfer well into the 1980s[51]. Unlike Brazil, direct foreign investment thus played a relatively small role in Korean development and its effect was limited to only a few sectors — chemicals and petrochemicals in the 1970s, electronics and transportation equipment in the 1980s (Mytelka and Ernst, 1998). Much of this investment, moreover, was in joint ventures and only 31.5 per cent of cumulative DFI in 1978 consisted of wholly foreign–owned companies (Westphal, Rhee and Pursell, 1979, 368). Not until the Foreign Capital Investment Act was revised in December 1984 did the investment process become more transparent. By that time, however, the large diversified firms known as chaebols had become powerful economic forces both at home and abroad[52] and in the joint ventures and licensing agreements they initiated with ITT, AT&T, Alcatel, Ericsson and Northern Telecom during the 1980s, they emerged as the dominant partners.

In large part the rise of the chaebols was stimulated by state policies, co–ordinated by the Economic Planning Board (EPB) attached to the Prime Minister's office, and their ability to bargain successfully with multinational firms owes much to the role of the state (Enos and Park, 1988). With its control over the domestic banking system, over the inflow of foreign capital, which accounted for a high percentage of the corporate borrowing in Korea, and over interest rates in the formal banking sector, the Korean government could exercise considerable influence over private firms by rationing longer–term domestic and foreign loans (Rhee, Ross–Larson and Pursell, 1984). Very high debt–equity ratios in these companies then meant that domestic firms were constrained to return to the banks for loans, thus giving the banks considerable leverage over them[53].

For nearly a quarter of a century, Park Chung Hee and his successors used these financial levers not to engage in the single minded pursuit of a neutral trade regime as some have argued[54], but to combine "vigorous export expansion in highly labour–intensive products, and selective import substitution in capital–intensive intermediate products and consumer durables" (Westphal, 1979)[55]. This was particularly important during the 1960s when, as several studies have shown, export production remained less profitable than production for the domestic market and many exporters would have been operating at a loss without government subsidies (Amsden, 1989, 1992; Hamilton, 1986; Kim Seung Hee, 1970; Lim Youngil, 1981)[56]. Government was thus obliged to exercise considerable coercive power over business in the form of tax penalties, loss of import licences and access to credit during the 1960s and 1970s in order to achieve its export targets. But in exchange it offered subsidies and tax concessions, erected barriers to imports thus protecting the domestic market and granted exclusive import rights to manufacturing firms[57]. Indeed, during the 1970s and 1980s, imports of textiles, automobiles, refrigerators, television sets, VCRs and other consumer durables were virtually prohibited until such time as they could be produced locally (Mytelka and Ernst, 1998).

With Korea's first and second economic development plans (1962–66 and 1967–71) both of which focused on building productive export capabilities in light, labour–intensive industries such as textiles, large companies became the preferred partners of the state. The first of many public research institutes, the Korea Institute for Science and Technology (KIST) was also set up in this period.

By 1973 the five largest chaebols contributed 8.8 per cent to gross domestic product (GDP) in the manufacturing sector and the top 10 contributed 13.9 per cent. As privileged partners of government, the emerging chaebols were thus able to take advantage of the shift towards heavy and chemical industries promoted under the Third Five Year Plan (1972–76). Legislation was adopted to attract Japanese chemical and petrochemical companies, then in the process of internationalising, and loans were granted to large Korean companies to encourage their entry into these new industrial activities as licensees and joint venture partners. Shipbuilding, steel and automobile production were also encouraged by sector–specific policies in this period. Thus began a pattern in which Korean firms grew through diversification rather than by deepening their technological capabilities in any one domain, and they grew rapidly. In 1978 the five largest chaebol contributed 18.4 per cent of manufacturing GDP, while the top 10 accounted for nearly one quarter. It is to the chaebols that the government would turn when looking for partners to develop the telecommunications industry under the Fourth Five Year Plan (1977–81).

The Demand Side

Building a telecommunications network requires huge investments over an extended period of time. But staying in for the long haul has been characteristic of all major state–initiated undertakings in Korea, and telecommunications was no exception as the figures for investment in Table 4.7 show. Thus, unlike the dramatic fluctuations in investment that took place in Brazil, "an average annual growth rate of 17.8 per cent in the number of main lines from 1966 to 1990 raised the number of main lines from a mere 300 000 to over 15 million in Korea" (Hansuk Kim, 1992) and increased the penetration rate to 20.5 lines per person by 1987 and 37.8 in 1993. By the late 1980s the backlog in meeting the demand for telephone service had been eradicated and the growth in the number of new lines being installed peaked. This affected both the nature of competition in the domestic market and the need to export.

Table 4.7. **Evolution of the Korean Telecommunications System**

	1982	1983	1984	1985	1986	1987
Telephone supply[a]	n.a	1.0	1.1	1.4	1.6	1.6
Investment[b]	n.a	1.2	1.2	1.4	1.4	1.5
Backlog	427	464	498	280	160	1.0
R&D/sales(%)[c]	1.7	1.9	2.4	3.0	3.0	3.3

	1988	1989	1990	1991	1992	1993
Telephone supply[a]	1.2	2.0	2.8	2.7	2.0	1.7
Investment [b]	1.3	1.8	2.0	n.a	n.a	n.a
Backlog	51	2.0	0.7	0.2	0	0
R&D/sales (%)[c]	3.1	3.3	3.5	3.5	4.1	n.a

a. Millions of lines.
b. $ billion.
c. For Korea Telecom only.
Sources: Hansuk Kim (1992), p.14 and KTRC.

The Supply Side[58]

The rapid expansion of telecommunications services which took place over the 1980s was largely based on the growth of domestic production of digital switching systems. Neither Oriental Precision Company (OPC) nor Goldstar, both of which were producing electromechanical switches, were able to make the transition to digital switching on their own. Neither, moreover, was inclined to do so and their position was shared by the Ministry of Communications (MOC). Yet, the costs of rapidly developing and modernising the telecommunications network would be prohibitive if all equipment were to be imported. Since the Korea Telecommunications Authority (KTA) was then a part of MOC and did not have its own budget, the Economic Planning Board and the Ministry of Trade and Industry (MTI) took the initiative in attempting to persuade Goldstar, Samsung and OPC to form a joint venture to produce digital exchanges. When this failed, the government of Park Chung Hee moved to its second option[59] and, in 1975, created a state–owned enterprise, the Korea Telecommunications Company (KTC), and following an international tender, licensed the M10CN, an analogue electronic switching system, from Bell Telephone, the Belgian subsidiary of ITT.

Licensing would be the primary vehicle for KTC and its successors to build technological capabilities in digital switching. But indigenising production was not far behind. To accelerate the process of domestic sourcing, on 10 January 1977, the Ministry of Trade and Industry announced a list of the components which were to be covered in a plan for the domestic production of electronic telephone exchanges.

The process of learning through licensing began in 1977 when KTC sent nearly 200 engineers, many from Seoul National University[60], to Belgium for training. Bell had been chosen over a lower cost bid from Fujitsu precisely because of its willingness to transfer more technology. But the costs of technology transfer accelerated when the new, and as yet untested, M10CN switch encountered software problems. Long delays were thus incurred as these problems were worked out, but with the result that learning was significantly increased, making possible subsequent changes by KTC engineers as the network evolved.

By 1979, when KTC's new factory in Kumi was operational, the huge cost overruns and the inefficiency of its management convinced the government to sell the company. As part of the imitative diversification strategy practised by Korea's chaebols, Samsung, which until then only produced a PBX, bought KTC and in 1983 went on to license the all digital S1240 switching system from ITT/BTM (later Alcatel). The basis for Samsung's later R&D strength in the telecommunications sector lay in the ITT/BTM–trained engineers it acquired when it took over KTC[61]. To balance this sale, Goldstar was allowed to form a joint venture, Goldstar Semiconductor (GSS) with AT&T (56 per cent Goldstar, 44 per cent AT&T) the following year, and to license AT&T's No. 1A ESS, a small, electronic switch. Daewoo Telecommunications, still prohibited from entering the digital central office switching market, was permitted to acquire Teihan Telecommunications, then producing an electromechanical PABX under licence from Fujitsu in 1981, and to license the SL–1 digital PABX from Northern Telecom, making it first in the market with a digital PABX. Using its relationship with Northern Telecom to build a research base in PABX technology, the 24 engineers trained at Northern in SL–1 technology became the nucleus of Daewoo's Research Centre. By 1989 the centre employed 700 persons in testing Northern products, localising high volume components like subscriber boards (PCBs), CPUs and memory chips and subsequently in innovating by increasing the number of subscriber lines per card in the SL–1 from 4 to 8 and then to 16[62]. Until 1984 Samsung and Goldstar were the only local suppliers of central office switches (Table 4.8).

The Samsung–Goldstar duopoly in central office switching began to break down in 1983 when the government allowed Oriental Precision Company to form a joint venture with Ericsson. Otelco (OPC, 51 per cent, Ericsson, 49 per cent) licensed the digital AXE–10 switch and began marketing it domestically in 1984 (Table 4.8)[63]. A few years later GSS licensed ATT's No. 5 ESS, completing the move to the licensing of all digital switching systems. By 1981, the year in which the Korean TDX programme was launched, all potential collaborating firms were thus producing switches, whether electromechanical or electronic, under licence from the world's major telecommunications equipment suppliers, and each had newer licences for more sophisticated digital switches in the pipeline.

Until 1989 switches based on foreign technology accounted for over 80 per cent of all switches purchased by Korea Telecom (Table 4.8) with the balance between older M10CN and No. 1A switches and newer AXE, 5 ESS and S1240 switches shifting from 2.5:1 in favour of the former in 1986 to 1.4:1 in favour of the latter in 1989. By the end of 1993, 58.9 per cent of all switches had been digitalised and of these, 35 per cent were TDX (MOC, 1994).

Table 4.8. **Value and Type of Switches Purchased by Korea Telecom: 1982–93**

(in million Korean won)

Type of Switch	1982	1983	1984	1985	1986	1987	1988	1989	1990	1991	1992	1993
M10CN	62 997	72 329	103 388	137 420	120 737	94 282	117 125	83 294	16 420	8 293	5 003	4 937
No.1A	26 412	44 592	90 428	106 740	103 854	74 705	94 779	55 273	15 431	7 131	4 392	2 768
AXE 10			3 776	32 297	91 697	60 014	64 743	34 434	17 214	14 478	25 013	9 954
TDX-1A[a]				6 740	26 824	77 660	68 752	18 551	8 970	3 019	5 716	2 421
TDX-1B[a]							7 083	200 414	187 382	114 004	100 478	46 398
5 ESS							31 060	95 822	116 493	63 801	45 412	32 224[b]
S1240							19 176	65 021	134 087	66 343	42 790	24 536
TDX-10[a]										90 277	189 527	202 836
Total	89 409	116 921	197 592	283 197	343 112	306 661	402 718	552 809	495 997	367 346	418 331	326 074

a. Samsung, Goldstar, Daewoo and Otelco in roughly equal proportions from 1988-92.

b. Includes 10 235 million won of direct sales by AT&T.

Sources: Korea Telecom, KTRC, MOC and company interviews.

The Development of Korean Switching Technology

Beginning in 1970 the Ministry of Trade and Industry announced a series of measures to promote domestic production of electrical and electronic equipment and develop scientific and technological capabilities in these sectors. The latter, for the most part, were located in the Korean Institute for Electronics Technology (KIET) created under MTI in 1976 and merged with the Korean Telecommunications Research Institute (KTRI) of the Ministry of Communications (MOC) in 1985 to become the Electronics Technology Research Institute (ETRI)[64]. As such, it played a major role in the development of digital switching in the telecommunications industry.

Finding partners, however, would not be easy since Samsung and Goldstar had invested heavily in foreign switching systems and believed they would face difficulties in recovering their investment if an indigenous digital switching system came on line too soon. From the government's perspective, however, since the terms of their licensing agreements required them to import proprietary integrated circuits from ITT and AT&T, there were limits to the technology they could master. Moreover, the price of foreign switches produced locally was higher than MOC expected local switching technology to be. With an eye to the way indigenous telecommunications technology had been developed in Japan, notably the relationship between NTT and its four–firm Den Den family of suppliers[65], and wielding its procurement lever[66] once again, the government thus pushed these two firms and subsequently OPC and Daewoo into collaborating with ETRI in the development of what became known as the TDX family of switches.

In 1981 a team was assembled at ETRI to develop the TDX 1, a switch with up to 10 000 subscriber lines. Within the first year, 50 people were recruited and both GSS and Samsung sent ten of their engineers to work at ETRI. Later, they would be joined by a similar contingent of engineers from OPC and Daewoo. The bulk of the development costs, however, were paid by KTA. Unlike the subsequent TDX1B and TDX 10 switches, the TDX 1 used exclusively off–the–shelf chips and owed a lot to the research undertaken at KIST during the 1970s on a digital PBX, funded by the US telecommunications firm GTE[67] and later transferred to Samsung (Interview: Kyong Sang–Hyon, May 1990), and to the know–how acquired through licensing and exchanges of personnel with Ericsson (Interview: Choi Byung–il, May 1990; Kim, Cae–One *et al.*, 1992). The TDX 1 was field tested and commercialised in 1985.

By 1986, 310 engineers were working on the TDX project and KTA had grown reluctant to authorise additional spending. Taking the lead, ETRI successfully lobbied for a change in its financing legislation. Henceforth KTA would be obliged to spend 2 per cent of its revenues on R&D. Over the next several years this was revised upwards and in 1996 was expected to reach 6 per cent. Unlike CPqD which at precisely the same juncture found its finances at the mercy of an economic crisis, ETRI was able to maintain and indeed to intensify the pace of development, expanding the TDX 1A, as it now came to be known, into the TDX 1B, a switch with up to 20 000 subscriber lines suitable for suburban areas and medium–sized cities, and launching a programme to develop the TDX 10, a large switch with over 100 000 subscriber lines and 60 000 trunk lines.

With TDX 1A in production and some experience in research and development under their belt, it became easier to convince the companies to collaborate with ETRI on an expansion, the TDX 1B. Most of this work was, in fact, done by the firms. During the late 1980s and early 1990s, some 200 ETRI engineers and 600 engineers from the four companies were involved in the TDX 1B and TDX 10 programmes. Despite the heavy involvement of these four firms in the development effort, no single firm was able fully to master the technology since each company's team engaged in a distinct development task and ETRI co–ordinated the process.

Although there was some expectation that a full transfer of the technology would take place, neither ETRI nor KTA had a real interest in doing so: the former because it would lose control over the development process and the latter because the costs of dealing with various versions of a TDX switch when there were already a large number of different switches installed in the network, appeared prohibitive[68]. As a result, the emergence of differentiated versions of the TDX 1A and 1B was delayed and competition between the companies in the domestic market remained limited.

This was reinforced by the pricing and market allocation practices of KTA. In principal, KTA allocated the market for TDX switches equally to each of the four producers, with penalties as a function of the number of faults the switch had in the field. Each year, moreover, KTA did a cost analysis and allowed a 10 per cent margin over the least cost supplier on the purchase of its switches. The system thus contained some incentives to reduce costs over time but not to innovate. This is reflected in the gradual and rather predictable loss of market share by Samsung and Goldstar to Otelco and Daewoo as the TDX switches were phased in (Table 4.9).

Table 4.9. **Korea: Market Shares in Central Office Switching: 1982–93**

(in percentages)

	1982	1983	1984	1985	1986	1987	1988	1989	1990	1991	1992	1993
Samsung	70	61.9	52.3	48.7	35.9	39.1	38.6	36.7	40.2	34.4	29.1	28.4
Goldstar	30	38.1	45.8	38.0	31.1	32.8	36	37.2	36.5	33.4	29.5	26.9
Otelco	-	-	1.9	13.3	33	28.1	20.7	16.2	13.4	18.1	23.7	22.3
Daewoo	-	-	-	-	-	-	4.7	9.9	9.9	14.1	17.7	19.3
AT&T	-	-	-	-	-	-	-	-	-	-	-	3.1

Note: TDX shares were divided for 1985 and 1886 in accordance with Goransson's estimates of 80 per cent to Otelco and 20 per cent divided among the remaining three. Thereafter, in line with interview estimates, shares were divided equally among the four companies.

Source: Based on the data in Table 4.8 and Goransson (1991), 108.

By the end of the 1980s, when the TDX 10 was under development, the companies had thus settled into a comfortable pattern. Telecommunications accounted for only a small share of the overall business of these chaebols — 5 per cent in the case of Samsung and Goldstar, 20 per cent in the case of Daewoo — but it had become a kind of cash cow, providing a stable market for which production could be planned ahead and for which a highly subsidised flow of technology could be expected from ETRI. ETRI encouraged the latter practice by doing many of the key development tasks in-house. The ISDN component for the TDX 10 switching system, including the network, terminal and transmission equipment components, for example, was done by ETRI in the early 1990s, and was transferred to industry in 1993. The commercialised version of the TDX 10 thus has circuit/packet and CCITT No.7 channel signalling capabilities, putting it on a par with its competitors and ahead of Tropico RA. In the mid–1990s, ETRI has focused many of its telecommunications activities around the design of application–specific integrated circuits (ASICs) for the prototype of its ATM switches and for the CDMA (code division multiple access) digital cellular system that it is developing (ETRI, 1994). Its ATM project was being run much as the earlier TDX collaborative ventures had been, in a hierarchical fashion, with ETRI allocating the work and setting the pace — a pace which some of the chaebols regard as too slow.

Competition and Competitiveness

Unlike Brazil, KTA did not wait until the indigenous TDX 10 technology was available but continued to purchase large quantities of switches based on AT&T, Ericsson and Alcatel technologies although some of these were noticeably more expensive. The growth of market share for AT&T's No. 1A switching system in 1984, for example, led to a steep increase in the average price of lines in that year, as did the introduction of the 5ESS in 1988. Competition in the form of Samsung's introduction of the S1240 and the impact of switches based on indigenous technology such as the TDX 1B, which became a credible competitor in 1989, and the TDX 10 in 1991, brought prices down considerably in the 1990s[69] (Figure 4.3). The latter parallels the Brazilian experience and suggests that simply having an alternative is a powerful bargaining tool for government in its negotiations with the firm while the threat of open competition from a comparable switch cannot be taken lightly. By putting firms on guard, it provides a stimulus to cost reductions that make competitive pricing possible if the threat becomes a reality.

In 1990 the number of new lines installed per year peaked at 2.8 million and by 1994 had fallen to a low of 800 000. For the firms, growth would have to come either from taking market share away from one of the other four firms manufacturing the TDX family of switches or through exports. The former, however, was discouraged by Korea Telecom which allocated roughly equal market shares to each of the four companies and used its purchasing power to push prices lower. ETRI, moreover, had embarked on a number of longer–term research projects in ATM and cellular (CDMA) switching, and needed to share costs with the firms. Collaborative work on a standard product, moreover, was favoured by Korea Telecom both to avoid the problems of having to deal with many different kinds of switches, as we saw above, but also because it did not want to be dependent on only one or two big chaebols for digital exchanges.

Figure 4.3. **Effect of Competition on the Average Price of Central Office Switches in Korea**
(in dollars)

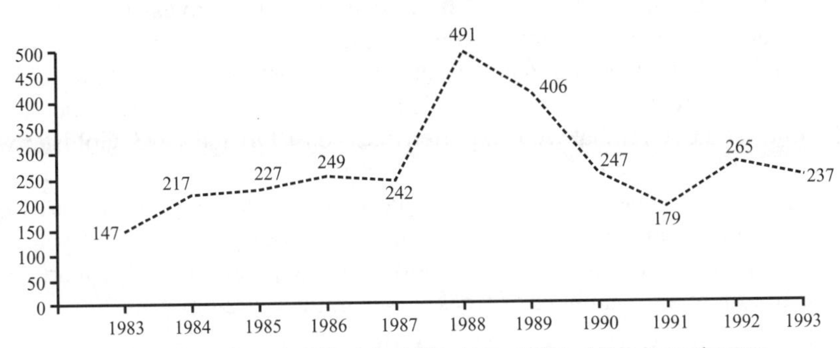

Source: Calculated from data in Tables 4.6 and 4.7 and converted into dollars at annual average won/dollar exchange rates.

Pressure to export also came from another source. During the latter half of the 1980s, Korea's export growth had given rise to demands, notably from the United States, that it open its domestic telecommunications market to imports Bark, 1991. Unlike the Brazilian case where a weak civilian government was attempting to deal with a major debt crisis and unsatisfied demand could add its voice to the chorus of those seeking liberalisation, the Korean government successfully resisted opening the domestic market to imports of central office switches until 1993. But the writing was on the wall.

With expansion through sales in the domestic market increasingly less likely, the chaebols were obliged to look for export markets. As in the past and in other sectors, the Korean government moved to help by setting up Korea Telecom International to prospect for markets, negotiate, and do the engineering needed to install Korean switching systems abroad. The Economic Development Co–operation Fund provided financing, particularly for sales to developing countries.

Despite this assistance, export growth has been relatively slow when compared to textiles and clothing in their heyday or more recently Dynamic Random Access Memory chips (Mytelka and Ernst, 1995). One of the key problems the chaebols faced in going abroad, was that Korea Telecom, like NTT in Japan, had set its specifications too high. Telecom switches were thus over–engineered making them too costly for export. The cost of producing switches to that standard was initially borne by the state which financed most of the research and provided a secure market for the output. But to be price competitive abroad Samsung and Goldstar had to cut their costs. One way to do this was to strip down the TDX and target poorer markets. But, as competition had intensified globally by this point, Korean firms had to compete in export markets not only by providing cheaper "solutions" but on the basis of new features. This required considerably higher expenditures on R&D both to reverse–engineer the TDX switches and to accelerate the introduction of new functions. It also required closer links between marketing and R&D than had been practised in these firms in the past.

By the early 1990s, this link had been forged and Korean firms began to develop their own versions of the TDX switching system and to invest more heavily in telecommunications R&D. In moving towards innovation in central office switching, Samsung and Goldstar were far ahead of Otelco and Daewoo, and the latter's share of Korean TDX exports reflects their lack of innovation–based competitiveness. Of the 315 250 lines of TDX 1B that were exported between 1990 and 1993, Goldstar was in the lead with 51.7 per cent, Samsung followed with 31.2 per cent, Daewoo lagged with 17.2 per cent and Otelco registered no exports at all (Interviews: KTI, June 1994)[70]. Samsung and Goldstar have also gone furthest in developing a market penetration strategy that includes investments in assembly plants in potentially large markets such as China. But there are a number of weaknesses in their strategy.

While manufacturing and testing have been the strong points of the Korean production system, R&D in core components has not. Until 1990, for example, most chip sets for the TDX system were imported. In 1994, Yang Seung Taik, President of ETRI (Interview: June 1994), estimated that 20–25 per cent of the microprocessors in the TDX 10 were imported, but the ASICs, which are critical in differentiating a product, were of ETRI design. This, however, merely points to the fact that the firms are still very dependent upon ETRI for their technology and in the newer products, such as ATM switching systems, they are convinced that the pace of development is too slow to meet the needs of global competition. To accelerate the development of products that their competitors can already offer, Samsung and Goldstar have thus begun to enter into strategic partnerships with a number of overseas firms, some of which may only be thinly disguised OEM arrangements. To the extent that they are, it is unlikely that even Korea, once having caught up, can successfully keep up in an industry whose technological frontier continues to advance with great rapidity. As the domestic market opens further, moreover, firms that have not made the transition from recipients of ETRI technology to innovators in their own right will find it increasingly difficult to remain in the market[71].

Conclusion

Over the past three decades, Korean policy–makers in collaboration with Korea's large conglomerates, the chaebols, invested in industries such as steel and semiconductors where the costs of entry were prohibitive and static considerations of allocative efficiency should have been a restraining factor. But Koreans have long preferred to base development choices on the dynamic growth prospects of an industry and the extensiveness of its linkages to the economy. From this perspective, the decision to develop a domestic telecommunications equipment industry in the 1980s followed established practice and did so despite the fact that, with its relatively small population and area and its buoyant exports, Korea could have expanded and digitalised its telecommunications network rapidly through imports.

Brazil, however, faced a very different set of choices. In the early 1980s the smallest exchanges then being built could accommodate from 4 000 to 10 000 lines. Installed in small towns and rural areas around the world, these switches were inevitably under–utilised. As Sam Pitroda commented with regard to India, "(t)his kind of waste may be tolerable in a country where the number of small exchanges is tiny. In India... waste on such a scale was unthinkable" (Pitroda, 1993, 5). The investment costs of building a telecommunications network in Brazil would also have been exorbitant, especially if we consider that Brazil in 1983 had only 8 telephone sets per 100 people as compared with 15 in Korea (Mody, 1990, 80) and only 30 per cent of its toll switches and 23 per cent of its local switches had over 3 000 lines connected to them[72]. Low density was also a disincentive to upgrading the network from mechanical to digital exchanges (Mody, 1990, 81). Given the debt crisis and the decline in import capacity that this engendered from the mid–1980s on, there was little likelihood that Brazil could have significantly increased the speed with which its network was expanded and digitalized in the absence of the TDX programme. Yet from a growth perspective, rapid expansion of the telecommunications network and the extension of digital switching capabilities became increasingly more important over the 1980s. Brazil's range of choices was thus narrower than that of Korea and the cost of failure was correspondingly greater.

Both Korea and Brazil moved rapidly through the first phase of their catch–up strategy in this industry. Although firms in neither country were innovative at the outset and all R&D fell to the public research institutions, ETRI and CPpD, small rural switches were quickly developed and work on larger digital switches immediately followed. From then on, however, the trajectories began to diverge.

One key difference lay in the clarity and consistency with which Korean and Brazilian policy–makers held to their development objectives and the policies that were derived from them. With regard to telecommunications this was translated into differences in the size and the sustainability of funding for their respective public R&D institutions, the extensiveness of preferences favouring goods produced in the domestic market with local technology, the speed with which they were reduced and the kinds of performance criteria imposed. A second lay in the traditional habits and practices of telecommunications firms in these two countries and the policy dynamics that were thus generated by these preferences and performance criteria.

In the case of Brazil, there is no doubt that an ability by CPqD to sustain the pace of development beyond the Tropico R and, in particular, to move the Tropico RA to market sooner would have made a major difference in its survivability. Over time, MNCs, joint ventures and local firms became somewhat more innovative in both countries, with smaller local firms in Brazil moving quite quickly to innovate new products on their own and to innovate and commercialise products developed at CPqD. Many of these firms, however, were relatively small component manufacturers and their livelihood was closely linked to the larger, multinational telecommunications equipment manufacturers. When radical trade liberalisation led the latter to reduce domestic production in favour of imports, the ripple effect was catastrophic. In Korea, sustained R&D funding, greater participation by local firms in the development of the TDX 10 system, and a more gradual process of market opening accompanied by considerable assistance in developing export markets are slowly being rewarded by growing Korean exports of telecommunications products. More importantly, the major leap forward towards building a culture of innovation within the firm taken by Samsung and the LG Group (Lucky Goldstar) by bringing marketing and R&D capabilities together to adapt and develop new products for the domestic and export markets, is critical for the sustainability of this export drive.

The price of telecommunications switching equipment in the domestic market was also differentially affected by the policy dynamics that resulted from the preferences and performance criteria in these two countries. As the case studies demonstrate, it is not the number of firms in a market that makes that market competitive but their behaviour. In both Korea and Brazil markets in the 1980s were highly protected and import substitution was encouraged by the state, with public research institutions underwriting the costs of developing indigenous technology. In each case, an effort was consciously made to develop a competitive market by supporting the emergence of four supplier firms. The Brazilian case, however, shows that a set of large multinational firms, operating in this environment and acting as an oligopoly, were able to drive prices up. As affiliates of large foreign firms, moreover, these companies were responsive to changes in international competitive practices. Over time they became transmission belts changing the mode of competition within the domestic market, a change which became increasingly more negative for innovation as the trade–off between imports and domestic production shifted sharply in favour of the former.

In Korea, large locally based chaebols were unable to affect prices in the same way. The role of the state was critical here in creating the pressures and inducements that led local firms, irrespective of size, to lower prices. But competition amongst these firms, as the case study argues, was minimal during this period. It was not inter–firm competition in the market itself which drove prices down but rather threats and promises and the presence of alternatives that made them credible. Although the highly integrated Korean chaebols remained protected longer than firms in Brazil, they had a tradition of exporting encouraged and sustained by government policy in other sectors and other products. Telecommunications firms were thus able to move more quickly towards exports, and it was the pressure to export that provided the principal stimulus to innovate. While their technological capabilities had developed over the previous decade thanks to their relationship to the public sector research institution, ETRI, there was little need to be innovative in the domestic market. Competing in export markets, however, clearly required attention to innovation in costs, quality, features and functions. As the window of opportunity for catching up in digital switching technology closes and the knowledge frontier moves forward, not only rapidly but discontinuously, shifting the sphere of competition to cellular, ATM, multimedia and services, confidence in the quality of products and in the capacity of firms to keep up has become critical for competitiveness in the telecommunications industry[73]. While Korea's dominant chaebols might be able to keep up under these conditions, it is doubtful that Brazilian firms can follow suit.

Notes

* The author wishes to thank José Cassiolato, Fabio Erber, Martin Fransman, Staffan Jacobsson and Han Suk Kim for their comments on an earlier draft of this paper.

1. For a summary of this literature see Saunders, Warford and Wellenius (1983); ITU/OECD (1983); Hoffman (1989) and from a broader perspective, Freeman and Perez (1988).

2. These were Nippon Telegraph and Telephone's (NTT) laboratory in Japan, the Centre National d'Etudes de Télécommunication (CNET) in France, the Centro de Pesquisa et Desenvolvimento (CPqD) in Brazil and the Electronics and Telecommunications Research Institute (ETRI) in Korea.

3. Respectively, NTT, the PTT (Poste, Téléphone et Télégraphe, now La Poste for postal and banking services and France Télécom for telecommunications services) Telebras and Korea Telecom Authority now Korea Telecom.

4. See Chapter 1 for a review of the literature on competition, innovation and competitiveness.

5. Rotary switches were the most commonly used exchange in the UK in the mid–1980s with new installations taking place as late as 1985 (Hobday, 1990, p. 59 fn. 4).

6. Earlier efforts included a prototype pre–transistor based computerised exchange installed by the British Post Office in 1961 and AT&T's space division switch, the 1–ESS tested in 1964 and installed in 1966. Unlike the former, the latter was based on solid state devices and stored programme control which replaced electromechanical controls, but it transmitted analogue signals.

7. This is a network that can switch data and video as well as voice.

8. Northern Telecom, for example, commercialised its first space division switch, the SP–1 in 1971, its 10 000 line DMS–10 switch in 1977 and a full range of high density DMS switches in 1979 (NT, 1991, 7–12).

9. Neither ITT which through STC, its British subsidiary, and Standard Electric Lorenz, its German subsidiary, began working on System 12 in 1975, nor Siemens, which abandoned efforts to develop a space division switch in 1979 and accelerated R&D on its fully digital EWS–D exchange, were ready to introduce a fully digital switch into their domestic networks until the early 1980s. GEC/Plessey also took an excessively long time to develop its System X. NEC which had collaborated with NTT and by the 1970s had developed a fully digital switch, the NEAX, actually lost international market share between 1973 and 1982 (Dang Nguyen, 1983, 83).

10. These ranged from a low of $500 million in the case of Ericsson and NEC to between $700 and $750 million for Siemens, Northern Telecom and AT&T to over $ 1 billion for ITT (Dang Nguyen, 1985, 108; Gorenson 1991, Tab. 5.8, p. 137).

11. Writing in 1983, Godefroy Dang Nguyen, for example, argued that "[s]witching equipment has lasted 20 to 30 years and transmission equipment 10 to 20 years. New equipment was therefore only gradually taken up to replace the old"(Dang Nguyen, 1983, 88).

12. By way of illustration, José Ripper who headed the government's first optical communications research programme at UNICAMP and later was in charge of Elebra Telecommunications, Kyong Sang Hyun, President of ETRI and Yang Seung Taek responsible for technology development at KTC when it was taken over by Samsung and later head of the first digital switching programme at ETRI were "graduates" of Bell Labs.

13. In an anti–trust suit during the 1920s, AT&T "was forced to sell off its overseas subsidiaries (most of which subsequently formed ITT...) and Western Electric was restricted to sales within the United States" (Dang Nguyen, 1983, 88). As a result, most exports in the early 1980s came from European firms.

14. The key point here is the consciousness with which local firms seek to master imported technology. Many companies simply use licences as a substitute for local innovation as an analysis of 90 Latin American companies in the chemical, petrochemical and metalworking industries revealed (Mytelka, 1978). Siemens' involvement in Chinese Taipei (Hoffman, 1989, fn. 39), the KTC (later Samsung) licence to manufacture ITT's M10CN switch and the ensuing relationship of KTC to ITT's Belgian subsidiary BTM (Interview with Dr Yang Seung Taek, President of KTAI, Seoul, May 1990) and Ericsson's relationship with Ericsson do Brazil (Interviews with Paulo Castelo Branco, Ericsson, São Paulo, Nov. 1992, May 1994) illustrate the process of technology mastery.

15. Western Electric now took on the AT&T name. AT&T thus remained both an equipment supplier and an operating company.

16. A decline in the rate of growth of computer sales in the US market and over–investment in semiconductors in Japan created the over–capacity that drove many companies into bankruptcy or take–over and pushed the US balance of trade in semiconductor products into deficit for the first time in the mid–1980s. Seeking to defend its home market, the United States signed an agreement with Japan setting a floor price for semiconductors in the US market. In a contradictory fashion, the Semiconductor Trade Agreement further strengthened low cost Japanese producers by assuring them of a windfall profit that made possible new investments in R&D and in plant and equipment. Competition thus intensified, R&D costs rose still higher and the speed with which new product generations reached the market accelerated. These changes augured poorly for latecomers pursuing a catch–up strategy both in the European telecommunications industry where semiconductors were a vital input (Mytelka, 1994) and in Korea where, as in Japan, the same firms were involved in both the semiconductor and telecommunications industries.

17. Pressures to liberalise domestic markets initially came through the lengthy GATT Uruguay Round negotiation process but more recently telecommunications operating companies are taking matters into their own hands. The European VPN Users' Association (EVUA) is a case in point. Thirty major multinational firms with operations in Europe, including both US–based Rank Xerox, Digital Equipment Corporation and European firms such as ICI, Philips and ABB formed the EVUA to negotiate more favourable terms for the

provision of international voice services. In 1994, EVUA signed agreements with UK operator BT and a partnership of AT&T and Unisource to provide Europe–wide private voice traffic thus undercutting monopolies in France and Germany.

18. In addition to services such as call forwarding and voice messaging, enhanced 800 and 900 service, virtual private networks and credit and calling card services are among the functions now at the cutting edge of international competition (Pedersen, 1994).

19. "Cable Companies Move In on Telecommunications", *Globe and Mail*, 10 August 1994.

20. In 1993 NTT and Nextel Communications Inc. a US mobile communications carrier, formed an alliance which will enable NTT to enter the US telecommunications market (*International Herald Tribune*, 3 July 1994), while KDD, Japan's international carrier has teamed up with US firms, MCI and ITT to provide an international frame relay service for data transmission between the United States, Japan and Singapore (*Telecommunications Magazine*, May 1994, p. 16).

21. Choices made in the European Union's RACE programme reinforced this.

22. *Telecommunications,* International edition (June 1994, p. 10) reported that the Japanese government and industry have become concerned that Japan is lagging behind the United States in building up an information super highway. "As a result, the government is to help establish a company to develop high–speed data transmission technology: Ultra High–Speed Network and Computer Technology Labs. This company will consist of NEC, Hitachi and Fujitsu, each of whom have provided 10 per cent of the 30 million Yen capital. The company is scheduled to begin increasing its capital to Yen 3.5 billion by the fiscal year 1998."

23. Adler and others, for example, argue that the origins of Brazil's informatics policy lie in the Navy's recognition that new ships required sophisticated electronics capabilities that only foreign firms could provide.

24. The Direction Général des Télécommunications (DGT), later France Télécom, the Bundespost, now Deutsche Telekom, and Nippon Telegraph and Telephone, were typical, and the United States, where a private sector firm, AT&T, was a regulated monopoly supplier, and Canada, where one large (Bell Canada) and several smaller private–sector firms provided telecommunications services across the country, were the exceptions. Deregulation, privatisation and the break–up of AT&T during the 1980s, however, have considerably altered this picture.

25. By law, all those who have telephones own non–voting shares in Telebras.

26. In part this was a result of Minicom's decision in the early 1970s to make up for Telebras' lack of investment capital by obliging subscribers to pay for the installation of a telephone line and thus contribute to the expansion of the system. By the late 1980s, the cost of such lines, however, had risen to $2 000 (Interview: Equitel, Nov. 1992). As a result, "lower–income users were denied access to the system because of their lack of capital...[and overtime inflation] limited the ability of the middle class to pay, reducing the rate of growth of subscribers" (Botelho *et al.*, 1993).

27. Comparable figures for 1987 were 0.45 in India, 20.5 in Korea and an average of 40.3 for the OECD countries as a whole (Göransson, 1991, 127). By 1993, Korea had 37.8 lines per person (MOC, 1994, 16).

28. In 1990, per capita GDP in Brazil was approximately $2 060 but income distribution was highly inegalitarian. Twenty–seven per cent of the population barely earned the minimum monthly wage, 8 per cent had no income and a further 21 per cent had between 1 and 2 times the minimum wage. By Brazilian calculations, therefore, in the absence of public telephones, more than 50 per cent of the population would have no access to a telephone at all and for a further 25 per cent who earn between 2 and 5 times the minimum wage, access to a telephone would be problematic (Telebras, Dec. 1991, 19–20). As a result, Telebras has designed and installed public telephones, developed cheap telephone calling cards (Interview: João Mello, Telebras, 11/1992) and is currently developing fixed satellite systems to service low density rural areas.

29. The research focused on antennas and microwave radio propagation at Rio de Janeiro Pontifical Catholic University's telecommunications studies centre, on semiconductor lasers, voice signal digital encoding and TDM at UNICAMP in Campinas, on digital switching at USP in São Paulo and on microwave radio propagation at the Institute for Electronic Engineering of the Brazilian Air Force (Graciosa et Machado, 1989, 34).

30. General Jose Antonio de Alencastro e Silva was president of Telebras in the late 1970s and early 1980s. He was heavily implicated in the development of telecommunications policy in this period.

31. Other Brazilian owned firms included, Autel, Microlab, Unitel, Daruma, Splice, Schause and Icatel (now I.C.A. Telecommunicacoes). Data provided by GEATIC in 1994.

32. The market was at first allocated to ITT (SESA) which was beginning to withdraw from the telecommunications industry. ITT, therefore, sold its rights to NEC and later sold SESA to Alcatel.

33. This was also the period when ATM switching was emerging as a challenger to ISDN.

34. Although Promon and Elebra had established research facilities in Campinas and had individually worked closely with CPqD on the Tropico R and RA switches (Interview: da Costa, Promon, May 1994 and J. Ripper, AsGa, Nov. 1992), the need for a consortium to implicate the companies more fully and, more importantly, financially in the process of development had become increasingly evident. By the early 1990s, however, the predominantly foreign–controlled switching manufacturers had become reluctant partners at best.

35. Although the cost of a line was excessively high relative to incomes in Brazil (see note 26), the monthly tariff was far too low, about $1.00 per month with 90 pulses free (Interview: Equitel, Nov. 1992) and during the 1980s and early 1990s as inflation rose, the rates fell in real terms by over 30 per cent (Interview: Minicom, Nov. 1992). This added to the problem of generating revenues for investment in network expansion.

36. Several years later CPqD would undertake an internal evaluation that led to a reconceptualisation of its role in the telecommunications sector. Whereas previously it has "acted more like a development lab transferring product technology to the industrial sector", it would henceforth generate technology for the Telebras system — studies on service and network evolution, joint development with the operating companies of software for operation support systems — and only secondarily would it undertake "selective action" to develop "strategic and competitive products" and provide "technical support to industry" (Graciosa and Gomes, 1994).

37. The Nomura Research Institute, for example, estimated that in 1991 only 13 per cent of the lines in Brazil were digital as compared with 31 per cent in Mexico, 64 per cent in Chile, 42 per cent in the United States and 40 per cent in Japan (Nomura, 1991, 8). The quality of telephone service was also in decline with the rate of completed calls falling from an average of 54 per cent in the period 1982–85 to 43 per cent in the period 1986–89 (Telebras, 1992, 76–78). The international average is 60 per cent.

38. In some products, UHF and VHF radio receivers, telephone handsets and public telephones, Brazilian products were price competitive.

39. Graciosa and Gomes (1994, 5) note that average prices of digital transmission equipment (2 MBIT/s PCM) fell 50 per cent after the introduction of CPqD products, packet switching systems developed by CPqD (Compac) were sold for 1/4 of the imported system price and the price of CPqD developed telex switching exchanges (CETEX) were half that of similar imported equipment.

40. Alcatel President Pierre Suard insisted that his company intended to maintain and develop both Alcatel's E10 and ITT's System 12 but planned only to market System 12 in Brazil (Siqueira, 1992, 46).

41. Northern Telecom had first entered the Brazilian market through a partnership with Elebra but when the latter was acquired by Alcatel, Northern licensed Promon to produce its switches. AT&T attempted to break the import barrier by entering into a joint venture with SID/STC through which both its 5 ESS and its cellular system would be sold.

42. The Brazilian Telecommunications Code of 1962 had decreed a state monopoly over basic telecommunications services thus giving rise to a debate over whether newer services such as mobile cellular, paging, cable TV and data were "basic" or could be opened to private national and foreign companies. It was expected that this market would grow even faster once private vendors could enter.

43. This opened the entire Brazilian market to competition and made it possible to envisage a strategy of enlarging the domestic base so as to sustain future growth in switching through expansions, a strategy of importance to the established companies (Interviews: Equitel, Nov. 1992 & May 1994; Ericsson: Nov. 1992 & May 1994; Alcatel: Nov. 1992 & May 1994; and NEC: May 1994).

44. Firms producing packet switching using CPqD technology substituted imported technology in this period (Interview: Telebras, Nov. 1992).

45. Even in the case of Tropico R, each of the suppliers has developed its own version but fewer Alcatel engineers were involved in developing the Tropico system in 1994 than in 1992 (Interview: Alcatel, Nov. 1992 and May 1994). In Promon, however, work was being done in 1994 to add cellular capability to the Tropico R but its extension to the RA was uncertain (Interview: da Costa, Promon May 1994).

46. Ericsson, for example, reduced the time from the moment an order reaches the factory to the moment of sale from 42 days in 1989 to 3.5 days in 1992 by outsourcing some components locally and speeding up the process of ordering and storing imported components close to their factory (Interview: Ericsson, May 1994).

47. This includes packet switching for data communications, cellular and some DMS central office switches.

48. Promon began as an engineering firm and this remains a major economic activity for the firm. However, by 1993, 60 per cent of Promon's $146 million income was related to Northern Telecom products and Northern Telecom researchers were already working in Promon's facilities to develop SDH transmission which Telebras decided to buy for the first time in 1994 (Interview: da Costa, Promon, May 1994).

49. As opposed, for example to price or technical qualities.

50. Goldstar's TDX system was given a positive evaluation by Telebras engineers in the early 1990s but no certification was forthcoming (Interview: Goldstar–GSIC, June 1994). AT&T's AQT, however, was received just days before a strategically important tender in November 1993.

51. The history of the petrochemical, synthetic fibre and steel industries in Korea, for example, is marked by a continuous pattern of government intervention to ensure that technology was transferred and that plants achieved high output and foreign exchange savings (Enos and Park, 1988).

52. In 1985, the top ten Korean chaebols ranked as follows among the *Fortune* 500: Samsung Group (23), Hyundai (25), Lucky Goldstar (43), Daewoo (49), Sunkyong (67), Ssangyong (137), Korea Explosives (180), Hyosung (204), Pohang Iron and Steel (206) and Doosan (412). *Fortune* (4 August, 1986).

53. In addition, the state could reward well managed companies with new licences to expand or to enter new sectors, could refuse to bail out poorly managed firms in healthy industries and allow better managed firms to take them over (Amsden, 1989).

54. See, for example, Rhee, Ross–Larson and Pursell (1984).

55. Similarly, Luedde–Neurath (1986) demonstrates that the liberalisation of the 1963–64 period to which many neo–classical economists had earlier attributed the Korean "miracle" concealed an intricate system of import controls that protected the domestic market.

56. Amsden, for example, argues that "As late industrialisation has unfolded, it has become clear...that low wages are no match for the higher productivity of more industrialised countries...governments have to intervene and deliberately distort prices to stimulate investment and trade. Otherwise industrialisation won't germinate" (1992, 53).

57. Thus brewers could import beer, and spinners but not weavers could import yarn.

58. The account of changes in Korean telecommunications policy and the development of the TDX switching system contained in this and the following section, unless otherwise indicated, is based on interviews with: Kyong Sang–Hyon, President, ETRI 5/90 and Vice–Minister, MOC 6/94; Yang Seung Taek, President, KTAI 5/90 and President, ETRI, 6/94; and Suh Jung Wook, President, KIST, 2/93; Lee Man Yong, former President GSIC, 2/93 Chung Jang Ho, President, GSIC, 6/94 Park Sung Kyu, President, Daewoo Telecom, 5/90 and Yong–Min Kim, General Manager, Samsung, 5/90; Ji Young Man, Manager, Samsung, 5/90 and Myung Yun Shin, Senior Manager, Samsung, 6/94; Sonu Suk–Ho, director, KIET, 5/90 and Choi Byung–il, KISDI, 5/90.

59. This model of entry had already been used in the steel industry with the creation of the Pohang Steel Company (POSCO), a minority state–owned enterprise.

60. Korea's elite university.

61. In 1982–83, for example, KTA asked Samsung to expand the M10CN from 20 000 to 30 000 subscriber lines. This required a bigger CPU, which meant altering the architecture of the ITT 1602 computer to integrate new memory chips. Once expanded, through software changes they were able to introduce new services such as traffic measurements and maintenance. This went beyond what BTM was offering and as a result they were able to export their improved M10CN to Norway in 1986. Because BTM was short of engineers, considerable technology was also transferred when they licensed System 1240.

62. By the terms of their licensing agreement with Northern Telecom, these innovations were shared with Northern.

63. In 1992 Ericsson sold its shares in Otelco to Korea Explosives.

64. ETRI was under the Ministry of Science and Technology from 1985 to 1992 and then became an affiliated research institute of the MOC.

65. NEC, Fujitsu, Hitachi and Oki (Fransman, 1990, 14).

66. This involved the promise of a guaranteed market but the threat that only firms collaborating in the TDX programme would be permitted to sell switches based on foreign technology in the domestic market.

67. GTE funded this research to the tune of $500 000 with a view to getting a foothold in the Korean market.

68. One continues to hear this litany from KTA though some have argued that the problem in interconnecting electromechanical switches is nowhere near as serious in digital switches where signalling is subject to international standards and the process is entirely computerised.

69. Fluctuations in exchange rates over the years do not account for these dramatic upswings or downswings in prices.

70. Interviews at Samsung (6/94) and Goldstar (6/94) give considerably higher figures for exports and suggest that there is almost no difference between them in the number of lines exported.

71. This opens up a number of questions that go beyond this paper, such as *i)* whether the Korean government would be willing to bail out these firms as it has done in the past for shipbuilders, for example, or will it be willing to see them go out of business, or *ii)* will current practices be abandoned and Korea Explosives sell Otelco to Samsung, Goldstar, Daewoo or Hyundai which is now pushing to enter the market?

72. Comparable figures were 100 per cent and 60 per cent respectively in Korea (Mody, 1990, 80).

73. Rising costs have meant that NTT will reportedly spend $1.5 billion to develop its ATM switches in collaboration with Fujitsu, Hitachi, Oki and Northern Telecom (Martin Fransman: personal communication).

Bibliography

ADLER, E. (1987), *The Power of Ideology: The Quest for Technological Autonomy in Argentina and Brazil*, University of California Press, Berkeley.

AMSDEN, A.H. (1989). *Asia's Next Giant: South Korea and Late Industrialization*, Oxford University Press, New York.

AMSDEN, A.H. (1992), "A Theory of Government Intervention in Late Industrialization" in L. PUTTERMAN AND D. RUESCHEMEYER (eds.), *State and Market in Development: Synergy or Rivalry?,* Lynne Rienner Publishers, Boulder, Colorado.

BAPTISTA, M. AND J. CASSIOLATO (1994), "Liberalisation and the Recent Development of the Brazilian Information Industry", paper prepared for the Liberalization and Competitiveness Conference, Center for U.S./Mexican Studies, University of California, San Diego (5–7 May).

BARK, T. (1991), *Anti–Dumping Restrictions Against Korean Exports: Major Focus on Consumer Electronic Products*, Korea Institute for International Economic Policy, Seoul.

BASTOS, M.I. (1992), "State Policies and Private Interests: The Struggle over Information Technology Policy in Brazil", in H. SCHMITZ AND J. CASSIOLATO (eds.), *Hi Tech for Industrial Development*, Routledge, London.

BOTELHO, A. (1987), "Brazil's Independent Computer Strategy", *Technology Review* (May/June).

BOTELHO, A., J. FERRO, L. MCKNIGHTT AND A. OLIVEIRA (1993), "Telecommuications in Brazil", manuscript prepared for E. NOAM, (ed.), *Telecommunications in Latin America*, Oxford University Press, Oxford.

CASSIOLATO, J.E. *et al.* (1995), "Redes de Telecomunicações na Economia Brasileira" a report for the "Estudo das Relações de Networking entre Productores e Usuarios de Telecomunicaçois", IE/UNICAMP, Campinas.

DANG NGUYEN, G. (1983), "Telecommunications: A Challenge to the Old Order", in M. SHARP (ed.), *Europe and the New Technologies*, Frances Pinter, London.

ENOS, J. AND W.H. PARK (1988), *The Adoption and Diffusion of Imported Technology: The Case of Korea*, Croom Helm, London.

Erber, F. (1985), "The Development of the Electronics Complex and Government Policies in Brazil", *World Development,* No. 14.

Ernst, D. and D. O'Connor (1992), *Competing in the Electronics Industry*, OECD, Paris.

Ernst, D., T. Ganiatsos and L. Mytelka (1998), *Technological Capabilities and Export Success in Asia*, Routledge, London.

ETRI (1989), *Annual Report 1989.*

ETRI (1994), *Annual Report 1994.*

Evans, P. (1979), *Dependent Development: The Alliance of Multinational, State, and Local Capital in Brazil*, Princeton University Press, Princeton.

Evans, P. (1994), *Embedded Autonomy: States and Industrial Transformation*, Princeton University Press, Princeton, forthcoming. manuscript version.

Fransman, M. (1990), *The Market and Beyond: Cooperation and Competition in Information Technology in the Japanese System*, Cambridge University Press, Cambridge.

Freeman, C. and C. Perez (1988), "Structural Crises of Adjustment: Business Cycles and Investment Behaviour", G. Dosi, C. Freeman, R. Nelson, G. Silverberg and L. Soete (eds.), *Technical Change and Economic Theory,* Pinter Publishers, London.

Frischtak, C. (1990), "Specialization, Technical Change and Competitiveness in the Brazilian Electronics Industry", OECD Development Centre Technical Papers, No. 27, October, Paris.

Fritsch, W. and G. Franco (1991), *Foreign Direct Investment in Brazil: Its Impact on Industrial Restructuring*, OECD Development Centre, Paris.

Ghedini, F. (1992), "Um condominio para garantir o futuro do Trópico", *Jornal de Telecomunicações,* No. 49 (Julho).

Göransson, B. (1991), "Catching Up in Technology: A Comparative Case Study of the Telecommunications Equipment Industry in Brazil, India and the Republic of Korea", Ph.D. Thesis, Lund and Aalborg, December.

Göransson, B. (1987), *Telecommunications and Economic Development in Tanzania*, Research Policy Institute, University of Lund.

Graciosa, H. and M. Matchado (1989), "Telecommunications Research and Development in Brazil", *IEEE Communications Magazine*, Vol. 27, No. 9, September.

Graciosa, H.M.M. and L. Gomes (1994), "Telecommunication Technology in a Changing Economic Environment: Brazil's Case", presentation to Workshop #4 , Supercom, ICC '94.

Hamilton, C. (1986), *Capitalist Industrialization in Korea*, Westview Press, Boulder, Colorado.

Hobday, M. (1995), *Innovation in East Asia: The Challenge to Japan*, Edward Elgar, UK.

Hobday, M. (1990), *Telecommunications in Developing Countries: The Challenge from Brazil,* Routledge, London and N.Y.

HOFFMAN, K. (1989), *Technological Change in Telecommunications: Implications for Industrial Policy in Developing Countries*, UNIDO, Vienna, Technology Case Study No. 1, 4–7 April.

ITU/OECD (1983), *Telecommunications for Development*, International Telecommunications Union, Geneva.

KIM C.–O., Y.K. KIM AND C.–B. YOON (1992), "Korean Telecommunications Development: Achievements and Cautionary Lessons", *World Development*, Vol. 20, No. 12.

KIM C.–T. (1994), "Picking Teams", *Economic Report* (Korea), Vol. 9, No. 4, May.

KIM H. (1992), "Financial Aspects of Korean Telecommunications", *Telematics and Informatics*, Vol. 9, No. 1.

KIM L. AND C.J. DAHLMAN (1992), "Technology Policy for Industrialization: An Integrative Framework and Korea's Experience", *Research Policy*, No. 21.

KIM L., JANGWOO LEE AND JINJOO LEE (1987), "Korea's Entry into the Computer Industry and Its Acquisition of Technological Capability", *Technovation*, 6.

KIM, S.H. (1970), *Foreign Capital for Economic Developoment: A Korean Case Study*, Praeger, New York.

KOREA TELECOM INTERNATIONAL (1994), *KT International.*

LEVY, J. AND R. SAMUELS (1990), "Institutions and Innovation: Research Collaboration as Technology Strategy in Japan" in LYNN K. MYTELKA (ed.), *Strategic Partnerships and the World Economy*, Pinter Publishers, UK.

LIM, Y. (1981), *Government Policy and Private Enterprise: Korean Experience in Industrialization,* Institute of East Asian Studies, Korea Research Monograph No. 6, University of California, Berkeley.

LUEDDE–NEURATH, R. (1986), *Import Controls and Export–Oriented Development: A Reassessment of the South Korean Case*, Westview Press, Boulder, Colorado.

MEYER–STAMER, J. (1992), "The End of Brazil's Informatics Policy", *Science and Public Policy*, April.

MINISTÉRIO DA CIENCIA E TECHNOLOGIA E MINISTÉRIO DAS COMUNICAÇÕES (1994), *Decreto 1.070 Como o Governo compra bens e serviços de Informática e Telecomunicações*, Brasília 20.04.

MINISTÉRIO DA CIENCIA E TECHNOLOGIA, FINANCIADORA DE ESTUDO E PROJETOS–FINEP, PROGRAMA DE APOIO AO DESENVOLVIMENTO CIENTIFICO E TECHNOLÓGICO–PADCT (1993), *Estudo da Competitividade da Indústria Brasileira, Competitividade da Indústria de Equipamentos de Telecomunicaçoes*, IE/UNICAMP–IEI/UFRJ, Campinas.

MINISTRY OF COMMUNICATIONS (MOC) (1994), *Telecommunications in Korea.*

MODY, A. AND R. SHERMAN (1990), "Leapfrogging in Switching Systems", *Technological Forecasting and Social Change*, No. 37.

MOREIRA, M.M. (1989), *Progresso Técnico e Estructura de Mercade: o caso da indústria de telequipamentos,* BNDES, Rio de Janeiro.

MYTELKA, L. (1978), "Licensing and Technology Dependance in the Andean Group", *World Development*, Vol. 6.

MYTELKA, L. AND D. ERNST (1995), "Catching Up, Keeping Up and Getting Ahead: The Korean Model under Pressure" in D. ERNST, T. GANIATSOS AND L. MYTELKA, (eds.), *Technological Capabilities and Export Success: Cases from Asia,* UNCTAD, Geneva.

NEC DO BRASIL (1993), Offering Circular, NEC do Brasil S.A., 22 October.

NOMURA RESEARCH INSTITUTE (1991), "Telebras" Research Report, 27 November.

NORTHERN TELECOM (NT) (1991), "The BNR Story", *Telesis* (Northern Telecom Journal) Vol. 92, July.

PEDERSEN, K. (1994), "Intelligent Networks: The Competitive Edge", *Telecommunications,* International edition, June.

PESSINI, J.E. (1993), "Competitividade da indústria de telecomunicações – nota técnica setorial do complexo electrônico", a report for the "Estudo da Competitividade da Industria Brasileira", IE/UNICAMP, Campinas, and IEI/UFRJ, Rio de Janeiro.

PITRODA, S.G. (1993), "Development, Democracy, and the Village Telephone", *Harvard Business Review,* November–December.

RHEE, Y.W., B. ROSS–LARSON AND G. PURSELL (1984), *Korea's Competitive Edge Managing the Entry into World Markets*, published for the World Bank, Johns Hopkins University Press, Baltimore.

RIBEIRO DIAS, L. (1992), "A Telebrás Quer Contrato de Gestão", *Journal de Telecomunicações*, No. 49, Julho.

SAUNDERS, R.J., J.G. WARFORD AND B. WELLENIUS (1983), *Telecommunications and Economic Development*, World Bank and Johns Hopkins University Press, Baltimore.

SIQUEIRA, E. (1992), "Alcatel Chega ao Brasil", *Revista Naçional de Telecomunicações (RNT 154)*, June.

TELEBRAS (1990), "Avaliaçao do Desempenho do STB 1985–89", *Revista Telebras*, Março.

TELEBRAS (1991*a*), *Relatorio Annual 1991.*

TELEBRAS (1991*b*), "Telecommunications in Rural Areas: Support for Rural Development", *Telebras Review*, 15 (54), December.

TELEBRAS (1992), *Def–Tendencias Indice Apresentatção*, Banco de Dados, Ano XVI, No. 61, January/March.

TELEBRAS (1993), *Principais Dados 1972–92.*

TIGRE, P. (1983), *Technology and Competition in the Brazilian Computer Industry*, Pinter Publishers, London.

Ventura–Dias, V. (1989), "The Old Logics of the New International Economic Order", *CEPAL Review*, No. 37.

Westphal, L. (1979), "Manufacturing", in P. Hasan and D.C. Rao (eds.), *Korea: Policy Issues for Long–Term Development*, Johns Hopkins University Press for the World Bank, Baltimore.

Westphal, L., Y.W. Rhee and G. Pursell (1979), "Foreign Influences on Korean Industrial Development", *Oxford Bulletin of Economics and Statistics,* Vol. 42, No. 4, November.

Williams, A., D. King and S. Gerrad (1994), "ATM: Fact or Fiction?", *Telecommunications,* International Edition, April.

V

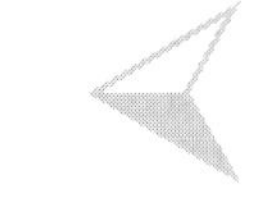

Petrochemicals in Korea and Brazil

François Chesnais and Hwan–Suk Kim

Introduction and Overview

The petrochemical industry permits a particularly close comparison between Korea and Brazil. The building of an indigenous capacity started in both countries in the mid–1960s. While Korea, for political reasons related to its strategic international position, seemed to have enjoyed more favourable relationships with foreign firms than Brazil, the move involved, at least in appearance, a fairly similar mix of reliance on foreign technology and know–how and on strong local government action. Neither country possessed important oil or gas resources[1]. In both countries the large investments required were undertaken for the purpose of import substitution in large–tonnage products, notably commodity thermoplastics, synthetic fibres and synthetic rubber. The initial decision to enter an industry characterised by important economies of scale and relatively accessible technology was based, here as elsewhere, on relatively straight- forward calculations concerning the size and rate of growth of domestic demand, the cost of imports and the cost of and estimated return on the projected investment. In both countries, at the beginning of the 1960s, such parameters appeared to justify the decision to finance the necessary investments, which were also expected to have additional technology pull effects on related equipment–supplier industries. In the case of Korea, the products derived from petrochemicals were viewed as the source of vital intermediary inputs to industries — first textiles, later automobiles and electronics — on which Korea's autonomous industrial growth and a large part of her exports were to depend. As a result the Korean government had less hesitation than the Brazilian authorities in deciding that the industry was strategic for overall industrial development, would be part of the public sector and would receive, unrestrictedly, all available forms of state support.

During a decade or so, the expansion of productive capacity as well as the process of technological learning took place at a fairly similar pace. Then divergence set in: first as a result of very different national macroeconomic environments (in the case of debt–burdened Brazil the 1980s were a "lost decade"); second as a consequence of significant differences in the pattern of corporate ownership and industrial organisation and so in the building up of an indigenous entrepreneurial capacity. In Korea, centralised management in the context of large hierarchies, the chaebols, allowed the industry to reap the full advantages of scale economies. In contrast, the Brazilian industry has suffered since the 1960s from divided and finance–dominated ownership, weak petrochemical entrepreneurial capacity and under–sized plants. These differences existed to some extent from the start; over the years they have tended however to increase rather than to lessen.

The expansion of productive capacity continued in Korea over the 1970s and 1980s, but stagnated in Brazil until the early 1990s. Within limits which will be explained below, technological catching up proceeded in Korea leading to the development of an endogenous capability increasingly based on R&D expenditures. In Brazil this process started to take place in the 1970s, but it came to a halt towards the mid–1980s, suffering a regression from which it has never been allowed to recover.

The privatisation of the industry and the liberalisation of trade in petrochemical products have also taken place in both countries. But they have occurred at very different points in the trajectories of each industry and been marked by even greater differences in the way the process was handled by governments. In the case of Korea, trade liberalisation took place progressively over a long period stretching from 1984 to 1993. This move was preceded by a number of carefully planned steps, dating back to the mid–1970s, aimed at preparing the private sector to meet this challenge. Over a number of years the role of the state was progressively reduced, the degree of internal competition increased and full responsibility progressively transferred to the chaebols. In Brazil on the contrary, trade liberalisation took place in 1988 after little prior preparation and was closely followed in the early 1990s by the enaction of a hastily prepared privatisation programme. This programme has had none of the characteristics of a planned transition; it has been more akin to a flight by the Collor Administration and its two successor governments out of an industry where the state had assumed strong responsibilities for nearly 30 years. Almost from one day to the next, the state took steps to shift total responsibility for the future of the industry onto the private sector, without considering whether it was in a position to support this responsibility. It has refused to contemplate the kind of measures, notably a forceful restructuring of the private sector, that other governments (including several in the OECD) have taken, in similar circumstances, to guarantee their domestic petrochemical industries' long–term viability in the new competitive environment of international oligopolistic rivalry that has resulted from the twin processes of liberalisation and globalisation[2].

In Korea, this viability is certainly assured for the next 15 years or longer. Even if output from the huge capacities built in Korea after 1988 may not always be able to find an outlet, implying that there are likely to be some serious corporate casualties along the way, Korea's role as a purveyor of petrochemical products, notably plastics, to nearby fast growing Asian markets is unchallengeable in the medium term. The relative weakness of the chaebol member firms operating in this industry lies elsewhere, namely in the low level of their technological investment and of their R&D outlays, not in petrochemicals *per se*, where the level attained is adequate, but in biotechnology and the fast growing, high value–added areas of fine chemicals towards which the large diversified chemical corporations of OECD countries have moved. However successful the chaebols have shown themselves to be in petrochemicals production *stricto sensu*, this fact differentiates them qualitatively (places them in a "different league") from their major OECD competitors. In point of fact, petrochemicals are no longer a high–technology industry, but one where technological change moves along known trajectories. Paradoxically, in petrochemicals one measure of success is the capacity to prepare exit strategies based on R&D investment in high value–added segments of the chemical industry and in biotechnology. Because the chaebols lack the capacity to do this, Korean firms do not, at least at present, possess in fine chemicals and pharmaceuticals the profile of potential entrants into the closed circle of the corporations forming the network of world oligopolistic relationships — a profile which they have acquired in semiconductors or even automobiles. In the case of Brazil this is an issue that cannot even be raised, since the medium–term viability of domestic chemical firms there is not certain even in petrochemicals.

Factors Influencing Competitiveness Internationally

Some essential facts regarding the nature of competition and sources of competitiveness in petrochemicals will be of help in assessing the comparative competitiveness and long–run viability of the Korean and Brazilian industries. An important distinction can be made between short–term profitability and competitiveness in basic petrochemicals; long–term sustainability within a broader range of products in the same industry; and long–term sustainability and competitiveness within the most advanced segments of the chemicals–related "complex of industries" viewed as a whole.

Competitiveness in Core Petrochemicals

In petrochemicals short–term competitiveness depends on costs. These do not depend just on the choice of technology, the price of inputs (oil and gas), the level of wages and the rate of interest. They are also strongly influenced by the way in which the opportunities and constraints stemming from the technical parameters related to economies of scale and the use or sale of co–products (briefly discussed below) are handled, and the extent to which vertical integration occurs within a single hierarchy.

The petrochemical industry produces synthetic organic chemicals using petroleum or gas fractions. The most widely taken route starts with the high temperature breakdown or "cracking" of hydrocarbons from naphtha, a derivative of oil (obtained through refining). Natural gas is a direct feedstock that does not need treatment before "cracking". While gas is less flexible and can be used to produce only a limited range of products, for these it leads to a qualitatively cheaper value chain than the one starting with naphtha, the price of which depends both on that of crude oil and on the cost of refining. A small number of countries and firms can build their competitiveness on the price of feedstocks. This is the case for the Persian Gulf countries where natural gas otherwise is simply burnt off in the desert. Their situation is, however, exceptional, while for others, the onus of competitiveness is shifted onto technology, economies of scale and corporate organisation[3].

The petrochemical industry is one in which large, lumpy investments with long gestation periods prevail, and where technical and economic parameters affecting performance and cost are stringent. Even though value added per unit of output rose again in the 1980s after a severe drop in the 1970s, it remains fairly low. In countries not endowed with the same resources as the Gulf states, the profitability of firms depends on their capacity to ensure, at each step of the processing chain, large downstream vertically integrated markets for outputs which retain throughout many phases the character of intermediate products. Petrochemical production includes more than a thousand products that form part of an original industrial chain, which combines segmentation and strong technical and economic interdependencies. Throughout the chain, processing leads to different categories of what are known as "co–products". Profitability requires that the maximum number of these products be either sold or used for further in–house elaboration. This is why upstream–downstream vertical integration is particularly developed in petrochemicals and operations concentrated on very large sites under a single hierarchy (see Figure 5.1 which reflects the way the United States group Du Pont approaches this issue).

The high degree of interdependency in the chain is attested by the fact that in the United States industry, for instance, 26.6 per cent of the industry's total output is consumed within the industry itself. Technical interdependency starts straight from the initial central "cracking" production phase. In the case of naphtha the typical pattern of "first generation" co–products includes: olefins such as ethylene, propylene and various butanes; aromatics such as benzene, xylene and esthyrene; and synthetic gases such as methane and hydrogen. In the second phase, the olefins, aromatics and synthetic gases are transformed into "second generation" products such as styrene, vinyl chloride, caprolactam and monomers, which are "intermediary inputs" to the chain. In the third phase, a large range of "final" products, which are this time true intermediate inputs to other industries, are obtained. These "third generation" petrochemical products are generally divided into five main sub–groups: thermoplastics such as polyethylene, PVC, polystyrene and polypropylene; synthetic rubbers; synthetic fibres, like nylon and polyester; fertilisers, like urea; and detergents.

Figure 5.1. **Simplified Representation of the Production Structure and Technological Relationships in the Chemical Industry**

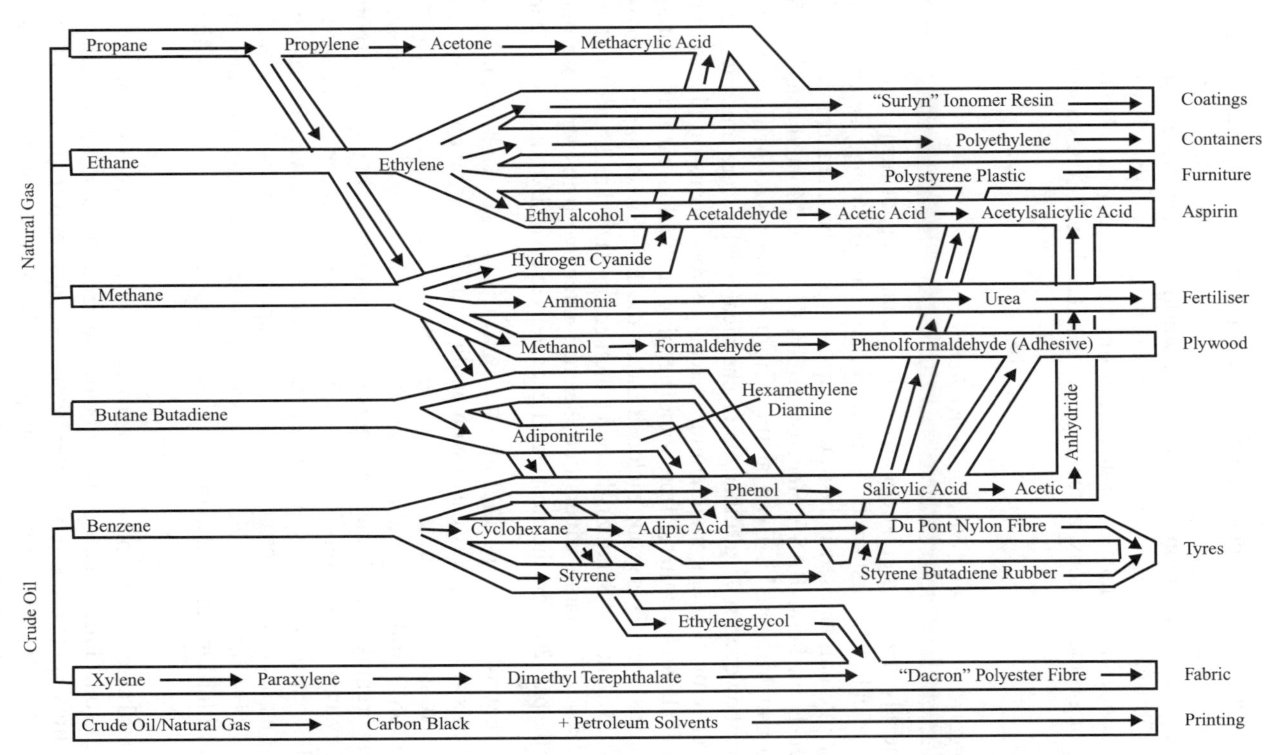

Source: From *Du Pont Context,* No. 2, 1974, E.I. du Pont de Nemours and Company, Wilmington, Delaware, as presented in Rudd, Dale F., "Modeling the Development of the Intermediate Chemicals Industry", in Richard H. Day and Theodore Groves (eds.), *Adaptive Economic Models,* Academic Press, Inc., New York, 1975, p. 417.

Investments are very large, while returns on capital outlays are slow and subject to fairly unstable market conditions. The industry is also characterised by strong endogenous cyclical movements as well as being highly sensitive to overall economic conditions. Each time a new world–scale naphtha "cracking" plant, e.g. a plant with 350 000 to 600 000 tonnes per annum (tpa) nameplate capacity, producing ethylene and the other main first generation co–products, comes on line, clearly observable disturbances occur in regional and often in world markets. Since the mid–1970s, moreover, the industry has been marked by latent excess capacity, which becomes overt in times of industrial recession. As a result the industry has also been the locus of quite strong trade tensions, especially between the United States and the European Union.

Categories of Firms Active in Petrochemicals

In the advanced capitalist countries, three categories of firms have been active in petrochemicals. The first are the very large, diversified, strongly science–intensive and highly internationalised industrial groups, notably the chemical–related MNEs, such as Du Pont, Dow, BASF, Hoechst, Union Carbide, Montedison, ICI, Solvay, Monsanto and Mitsubishi. Even at the height of the petrochemical paradigm's domination, however, several other major chemical MNEs were much less involved in the petrochemical chain, maintaining instead a strong focus on pharmaceuticals, agro–chemicals and synthetic fibres and keeping technological routes other than petrochemicals open. This group included Bayer, the three Swiss majors (Ciba–Geigy, Hoffman–La Roche and Sandoz), the two Dutch groups (DSM and Azko) and France's Rhône–Poulenc. The large, diversified, science–intensive firms are those that have made over the past 20 years the most significant steps to diversify out of petrochemicals.

The second category includes comparatively smaller firms active in petrochemicals alone, in many cases with public or mixed capital ownership. In some cases they were specialised firms that produced downstream high value–added products. During the 1980s, following radical restructuring, most of these firms disappeared as independent organisations through mergers with larger firms, notably oil corporations, of which they are now divisions. These firms (sometimes referred to as "independents"), though still large, usually operated within regional markets and were internationalised for only one main product, thermoplastics. At the time they included Huls, USI/National Distillers, CdF Chimie and Hercules (later Himont, following the merger of PP operations with Montedison and the subsequent sale of Hercules' assets to the Italian TNC).

The third category comprises the petrochemical divisions of the major oil MNEs: Shell, BP, Exxon, Gulf, Armco (Standard Oil) and Arco (Atlantic Richfield). By 1970, oil companies in the United States were already major producers of some petrochemicals. They used large windfall profits, in the wake of the oil shocks of the 1970s, and their privileged access to feedstocks to increase their share of the United States market and also to make important inroads into European petrochemicals markets. In France, during the restructuring of the chemical–related complex, petrochemicals were incorporated into the state–owned oil company, Elf Aquitaine. The petrochemical divisions of oil companies are particularly active both in the upstream stages (e.g. ethylene, propylene, benzene and styrene) and in several of the main commodity thermoplastics.

Technology Acquisition and Endogenous R&D–Based Competitiveness

In the core parts of the production process, petrochemicals technology reached maturity in the early 1960s. Most of the products/processes in the industry are well–known and standardised (in particular in the upstream segments of the technical production process). In thermoplastics for instance, the improvement in grades continues all the time, but new, radical product developments are rare, in contrast to special plastics and new materials where radical product development is vital for competitiveness. Most production technologies of the petrochemical industry are equipment–embodied. This has led to a supply structure marked by the presence of large engineering firms. These are either independent corporations or firms belonging to non–chemical conglomerates (e.g. Badger, Lummus, C.F. Braun, Stone and Webster). Others (for instance Uhde, a subsidiary of Hoechst, Snam Progetti, a subsidiary of ENI chemicals, Technimont of the Montedison group) are specialised engineering affiliates of some of the major chemical firms. Still others (like Technip, which was created by the French Petroleum Institute) are linked to OECD–based public–sector or public–enterprise R&D centres.

As a result of this supply structure, access to technology is rather open and highly reliable. The intense competition between suppliers and the need for the large engineering firms to defend their reputations act as strong deterrents to "opportunistic" behaviour in the provision and transfer of technology. Developing country firms can import embodied process technology from developed countries through turnkey contracts and/or licensing agreements[4]. They can of course subsequently learn and adapt the technologies through on–site operating experience or "learning–by–doing", which can later become the basis for incremental process innovations and productivity improvements. The danger however is that owners of recipient firms will regard easy access to technology as a factor dispensing them from funding any significant in–house technological effort, notably in the form of R&D. As we shall see below, this is indeed the case for many Brazilian firms. More generally it is in R&D that one finds the largest gap between the situation in the advanced countries and that in the newly industrialised ones, not only in R&D expenditure *per se*, but in the capacity to think ahead in technological terms.

R&D expenditures by the chemical–related MNEs are among the highest within the business enterprise sector. These outlays furthermore are backed by the work of some of the oldest science–related academic institutions as well as by that of large scale government laboratories[5]. Over several decades, petrochemicals attracted a large part of the expenditure on R&D and engineering. Since the start of the 1970s, independently of the impact of the "oil shocks", the history of the chemical–related complex has been marked by the emergence of rival, partly substituting technological paradigms in the form of new materials technology and the increasingly strong biotechnology. This redeployment has involved a significant increase in R&D expenditure. At the heart of MNE strategies aimed at long–term sustainability and competitiveness, therefore, lies not the pursuit of technological change in petrochemicals, but that of innovation within the broader chemicals–related "complex" of industries. United States chemical firms, for instance, almost doubled their R&D outlays in relation to turnover between 1979 and 1986 and have maintained this level since.

High Value–Added Plastics and User–Producer Relationships

The move downstream into specialities and fine chemicals in high growth and high value–added segments and into new products derived from scientific breakthroughs in new materials and biotechnology can be appropriately illustrated by the case of high value–added plastics, into which many MNEs previously active in large–tonnage thermoplastics have moved.

The better known engineering plastics such as ABS, PC, PBT or PPS have now been in use for over 20 years. However plastics have continued to evolve under the impact of the "new materials revolution", triggered by the irruption of information technology into the "design" process of industrial materials. This development has been marked by the advent of composites, e.g. fibre–reinforced plastics, and of new generations of polymers, engineering plastics and more recently special plastics. Composites are obtained by reinforcing a matrix (polymer, metal or ceramic) with fibres (carbon, glass, aramid, boron, ceramic and more recently polyacrylonitrile)[6]. These new materials have characteristics superior to those of the initial compounds and through computer–aided design and manufacture, can be tailored to meet user specifications. R&D has thus made it possible to produce stronger and especially lighter composites, totally "made–to–measure". Applications have progressively moved from space and aircraft to other industries requiring less sophisticated composites, but representing greater tonnage. Engineering polymers (polyacetal, polycarbonate, fluoropolymer, hybrid polyamide, etc.) can withstand extreme operating conditions and often have special properties such as transparency or autolubrification. They have many expanding markets, in packaging, transport, medical equipment, electronic consumer products[7].

Stimulus to technological progress in specialities has come from user industries. In particular in new materials technology involving plastics, user–producer relationships based on important co–operation agreements and partnerships between the chemical–related MNEs and very large firms in key user industries such as aerospace or motor vehicles, have been central to the ability of chemical firms to move out of the low profit segments into high value production. Large chemical–related firms have also been among the most active in developing the use of interfirm co–operation agreements in R&D and in technology sharing. These include agreements among members of the world oligopoly as well as between these large firms and small R&D–intensive firms, universities or public laboratories.

The Alliance between Firms and Governments in the Advanced Countries

Within the pale of the broad "complex" of chemicals–related industries, competition in world markets is waged essentially by a very precise type of corporate organisation, namely the very large, diversified, strongly science–intensive and highly internationalised industrial groups discussed above. Collectively these groups form a very powerful global oligopoly, backed by the long experience they possess (often dating back to the 1920s) for allying competition and co–operation. They also enjoy the political backing and where necessary the financial support of their home country governments.

Both factors served them well in the late 1970s and early 1980s, when the maturing of petrochemical technology, the weakening of profitability and the change in the feedstock basis of competitiveness, as the Gulf countries began to use their natural gas, coupled with the opportunities and challenges created by the new technologies, led these MNEs to adopt a variety of redeployment strategies. Most of the world's most powerful chemical–related industrial groups devised long–term strategies permitting them to move out of petrochemicals into the new high value–added areas of the chemical–related complex of industries. Within this overall process the petrochemical industry has been particularly prone to large scale swaps of industrial assets between MNEs, in some cases "engineered" privately by oligopolists, in others supported or even conceived by governments.

In G–7 countries with relatively stronger industries and a weaker record of government action in industry, firms relied to a greater extent on their long experience of co–operation and competition and their mutual ties as oligopolists. They devised exchanges of assets and markets sometimes deemed by anti–trust authorities as possessing collusive aspects. In G–7 countries with somewhat weaker industries and a tradition of state intervention, firms enjoyed the help of their governments during this phase. Japan, France, and Italy all took steps to reorganise and restructure the chemical–related complex and assist their "national" champions in the world oligopoly to undertake appropriate restructuring. Yet today many would deny the right of newly industrialised countries to resort to similar policies, and would persuade their governments not to act in favour of the viability of an industry in which their countries have made heavy investments.

The Establishment of Petrochemicals in Korea and Brazil

In Brazil the history of the chemical industry dates back to before the Second World War. MNEs such as Rhodia and Solvay entered the Brazilian market in the late 1920s and were later followed by the large United States groups. Initially the requirements of the agricultural sector (fertilisers, agrochemicals) provided the main demand pull. This was later followed by pharmaceuticals and in the 1950s, MNEs built small capacities in synthetic rubber (for tyres) and synthetic fibres. In Korea, although the first modern chemical plant was not built until 1960, when the Chungju Fertiliser Company was established, development of the industry proceeded very rapidly thereafter. The Korean example thus becomes a good foil against which to compare the Brazilian experience.

Korea: Determined Government Action Backed by Strong Foreign Aid

Aided by the United States Agency for International Development and staffed by most of Korea's university–trained chemical engineers, the Chungju Fertiliser Company formed the nucleus of the modern chemical industry in Korea. In 1964 the first oil refinery was created as a joint venture by the Korean government and the Gulf Oil Co. and operated by the Korean Oil Corporation (KOCO) at Ulsan in south–east Korea. The Korean government then invited Arthur D. Little and the Fluor Corporation to do marketing and engineering feasibility studies for investment in petrochemicals. The first reports, submitted in 1966, indicated only a moderate increase in the demand for petrochemical products in the early 1970s and concluded that the domestic market was far too small to support plants capable of producing at low unit costs, relative to plants abroad (Enos and Park, 1988). Korean planners had however made different forecasts, yielding higher estimates of demand for petrochemicals, high enough to make new plants economically feasible. These demand estimates suggested that a petrochemical complex transforming 66 000 metric tons per year of ethylene would be appropriate (Enos and Park, 1988). To exploit economies of large–scale production, the Korean government chose an even more ambitious programme for inclusion in the Second Five–Year Economic Development Plan (1967–71), one which resulted in a petrochemical complex transforming 100 000 tpa (capable of expanding up to 150 000 tpa) of ethylene. This integrated complex was also to be located at Ulsan, adjacent to KOCO, so as to minimise the cost of transporting intermediates and provide a common source of inputs such as utilities and maintenance.

To fund the construction of this complex, the government, considering the limited financial capacity of domestic investors, took measures to encourage foreign investment. For petrochemicals it made exceptions to the laws concerning the entry of foreign capital and the acquisition of foreign technology. The industry started by being heavily dependent on foreign firms. It relied totally on their technology and know–how, but also received a significant amount of capital from them. All but one of the petrochemical plants at Ulsan (Hankook Caprolactam Co., which was wholly owned by the government) were built as joint ventures between a Korean firm and a major United States or Japanese petrochemical company. The pattern was that the foreign firm put up half of the equity capital and provided the technology, whereas the local partner, usually established as a state–owned enterprise, provided the other half of the equity capital, the site and most of the personnel. The bulk of the funds used in plant construction was secured from foreign investors in the form of long–term government loans. Consequently, 80 per cent of the total amount of the investment ($400 million) was in fact financed by foreign capital. All but one of the plants were designed by the foreign investor, utilising a modern process that had been well proven abroad. The choice of the technology was tied in with the choice of the foreign investor.

Representing the Korean government in the negotiations with foreign companies participating in the Ulsan petrochemical complex was the Chungju Fertiliser Company, which was then producing fertiliser in the country's two urea plants. Being the only modern chemical plant in the nation and employing the bulk of the nation's chemical engineers, the Chungju Fertiliser Co. was the only organisation capable of appreciating the technological complexities of the negotiations and of defending Korea's interests[8].

According to Enos and Park (1988), "[i]t took almost two years to complete the financial arrangements with foreign investors and international banks. During this period demand grew, justifying the ambitious programme. In 1970 the Korean government issued a Law for the Promotion of the Petrochemical Industry, which offered five years of full tax holiday. This incentive was supplemented by a guaranteed return on the invested capital". To seize this opportunity, many foreign investors competed in the bids prepared by the Korean government. Foreign partners in the joint ventures included Gulf Oil (for the core naphtha–cracking plant), Dow (for LDPE and VCM[9]), Skelly (for acrylonitrile), Mitsui (for ethanol, acetaldehyde and SBR), and Marubeni (for PP). The construction of the Ulsan complex was finally completed in October 1972. Continuous expansion of the existing plants and the construction of new plants in response to demand increases led to the rapid growth of production in terms of both scale and variety. By the end of 1976, at the Ulsan site, Korea had 25 affiliated plants alongside a 100 000 tpa core naphtha–cracking facility. In 1975 a second petrochemical complex at Yeocheon was launched without the need for special incentives (Enos and Park, 1988).

Brazil: Government Action as a Response to Reluctant Foreign Support

Brazil did not benefit to the same degree from co–operation with large foreign firms, although it had high expectations with respect to their involvement. Nor was the Brazilian government quite as convinced as the Koreans were that the industry should be built even if this required determined state action and an encroachment on the private sector's prerogatives. To the contrary, initially the state did not foresee any involvement in petrochemicals production. Petrobras, the state–owned petroleum firm established in 1953, was thus given a constitutional monopoly on oil exploration, production and refining, as well as a large say in oil imports. But petrochemicals had not been considered a sector of strategic importance for national sovereignty and its development was left to the private sector. As part of the general strategy of import substitution which all Brazilian governments espoused from the late 1950s onwards, Brazil hoped to build this industry through foreign investment in the same way as it had done in many other industries. While giving petrochemicals high priority in its economic development programme, the military regime confirmed this private–sector orientation after the 1964 coup. It still hoped that foreign investors would build Brazil's first full–scale petrochemical complex in São Paulo. Negotiations thus began with Union Carbide and Phillips Petroleum. The former, however, turned out only to be interested in building a small ethylene cracker (120 000 tpa) for its own downstream needs. The latter initially agreed to form a joint venture with a consortium of Brazilian private interests led by the Capuava group, but then decided that returns would be too low for a rapid recoup on its investment and withdrew in 1967. The government, which had given the building of the São Paulo complex high political visibility, now felt obliged to step in by instructing Petrobras to take the appropriate steps for entering the petrochemical industry[10]. Even then the government chose to adopt the strategy known as the "triple alliance"[11], namely the complicated association of three forms of capital — Brazilian private capital, Brazilian public capital and foreign capital — along with the offer of particularly favourable terms to the foreign partners. To comply with the 1953 law and other legal requirements, notably the prohibition against engaging in joint ventures with private companies, Petrobras set up a specialised subsidiary, Petrobras Quimica S.A., better known as Petroquisa, at the end of 1967.

Petroquisa immediately took an equity participation in Petroquimica Uniao (PqU), the firm which had been founded to build and run the core naphtha cracking plant (ethylene) at the São Paulo complex, joining two private Brazilian capital alliances: Unipar, which consisted of the Capuava group, the Moreiro Sales financial group and a mining company; and Ultra, headed by the Ultra group owned by the Igel family. A conglomerate of foreign financial institutions, notably the International Finance Corporation and a consortium of French banks prompted by Rhône–Poulenc, completed the investment package with long–term loans backed by the government. While there were thus three types of partners, this was not yet a "triple alliance". The loans by foreign interests were paid back, but lack of enthusiasm from the local private sector for this large investment soon forced Petroquisa to increase its equity share in PqU by progressively buying the shares of first the Moreiro Sales group and then of other interests until it finally became the majority shareholder (67.79 per cent) with the remaining members of Unipar and Ultra as minority shareholders. The capital was thus mainly public, while the necessary upstream process technology was obtained from large chemical engineering firms on the "open market" for technology. In 1972, the plant started operations, reaching full–scale production in 1974 with a 300 000 tpa naphtha–cracking capacity, later expanded to 360 000 tpa, nearly three times that of Ulsan's initial capacity.

In the downstream segments of the *filière*, where technology was still firmly appropriated by the MNEs, a different solution had to be found so as to secure their presence and obtain the required technology and know–how. The solution was the "triple alliance", accompanied by an offer of terms to foreign partners of a type Korea never made. The joint ventures set up first at São Paulo and later at Camaçari and Triunfo offer an early example of a particularly *rentier* variety of what were later to be called "new forms of investment" or NFI (Oman, 1982 and 1989). In contrast to the Korean joint ventures, foreign firms were not required to put up any capital at all in order to enter the Brazilian joint ventures: intangible assets sufficed. In exchange for technology, engineering skills and management know–how they were offered some 20 to 30 per cent of assets and voting rights in the firms that were set up. By virtue of a clause written into all the founding contracts, specifying the need for unanimity between shareholders on issues related to changes in the ownership of assets, mergers or new entry, they were even given a *de facto* right of veto over crucial aspects of corporate policy in the joint ventures. Certain regulations concerning profit remittance prevailing at the time were waived for joint venture partners. The conditions were sufficiently attractive to ensure the presence of foreign firms in the downstream capacities set up at the São Paulo complex and at the two subsequent sites in Camaçari and Triunfo. These firms had let Brazil assume the responsibility and risks of the large–scale upstream investments. Given the terms offered they showed a greater degree of interest in participating in downstream segments, but soon opted out and sold their voting rights back to their Brazilian partners (Roos, 1991).

The "triple alliance" was not simply a way of inducing foreign participation. It also represented a solution to the uneasy relationship between the Brazilian private sector and the state. The private sector lacked the capital and more seriously, barring a few exceptions, lacked the entrepreneurial capacity and the will to enter the petrochemical industry in a big way; but it was socially and politically powerful enough to stop the state from controlling and organising the industry rationally through Petrobras. This explains the rather baffling further division of ownership between Petrobras and Brazilian private capital, leading to a second set of domestic public–private joint ventures. As a result the overall outcome of the "triple alliance" in the petrochemical industry is incredibly complicated: at each site one finds a variable number of both types of joint ventures (domestic–foreign and public–private), along with a few firms under single ownership. At the time this seemed to be a clever way of combining the three forms of ownership, or as Fabio Erber put it, a kind of "Columbus' egg"[12] (Erber, 1995) to ensure that simultaneously there would always be a majority of Brazilian capital (private plus public), but also a majority of private interests (Brazilian private and foreign) thus ensuring that the state was never in full control. However the longer–term legacy of this solution has been extremely negative.

Structure of Ownership and Modes of Co–ordination in Korea and Brazil

As we saw above, one of the main sources of competitiveness in petrochemicals is the exploitation of economies of scale. This is a function of management as shaped by the pattern of capital ownership and is facilitated by vertical integration within a single hierarchy. Here is where a major difference between Korea and Brazil began to develop soon after the industry was set up.

In Korea upstream–downstream vertical integration emerged progressively, leading to integrated complexes under a single management as in the OECD countries. From the start operations were not simply concentrated on large sites, but were also organised within centralised corporate structures, commanded by a single management. Initially formed as joint ventures between the state and foreign capital, once foreign interests were bought out they were transformed into fairly large state–owned enterprises at different points along the value chain and subject to techno–economic co–ordination within a single hierarchical framework. Subsequently these fairly large state enterprises were transferred to the chaebols, which are of course even larger groups and were capable during the wave of investment that took place during the second half of the 1980s and early 1990s of achieving the same pattern of integration as the large OECD concerns.

In Brazil this has not been the case. The divided structure of ownership has impeded the industry from reaping the advantages of vertical integration[13]. For some 25 years, the main, indeed the sole, element of integration in the industry was the technical co–ordination provided by Petroquisa through the management of the naphtha cracking and aromatics production plants at the sites where it owned or controlled the core plant. This however did not ensure the kind of strategic planning that central management provides in vertically integrated companies. Nor could it compensate for the extremely fragmented nature of the industry situated downstream, where divided ownership has led to sub–optimal plant, extremely costly overhead expenditures and small cash flows even when profits are being made. At one point in the early 1980s, some 50 firms owned the 120 plants spread over the three sites. Most were, and still are, monoproduct firms in an industry where economies of scope call for the building of pluriproduct endeavours. The majority had divided ownership, with the exception of a few wholly foreign–owned "third level" plants. About 30 were joint ventures involving a quite large number of foreign firms (some 15 in all), implying that only a few had any individually significant stake in the Brazilian industry. Subsidised prices for naphtha and ethylene, high tariffs and low wages (by international standards) have kept the Brazilian firms in business until now. But the cost of this pattern of ownership has been very high with respect to the main long–term source of competitiveness in any industry, namely the building up of an endogenous technological capacity, in the course and as an outcome of the "catching up" process.

Phases in the Expansion of Capacity

Table 5.1 shows the expansion of capacity in Korea and Brazil. From 1970 to 1988 the pattern of growth is quite similar, with Brazil even slightly in the lead, but from then on the paths diverge brutally with a massive expansion of capacity by Korea. During most of the 1970s the demand for petrochemical products rose rapidly in both countries and outran the increase in supply. In Korea the government decided to construct a second complex at Yeocheon in order to improve the rate of national self–sufficiency (only 60 per cent in 1975). This investment was later included in the Fourth Five–Year Plan (1977–81) as one of its major programmes — the Heavy and Chemical Industries Promotion Plan, which organised the various government support measures to the sector. The new complex was considered essential for achieving the export goals set by the government of $10 billion in 1980. Construction started in November 1976 and ended three years later. The Yeocheon no. 2 petrochemical complex had a production capacity of 350 000 tpa in terms of ethylene and required total investment of $1.15 billion. Oil refining was entrusted to Honam Refinery, a joint venture between Lucky (50 per cent) and Caltex (50 per cent), while naphtha cracking and the production of olefins and BTX went to Honam Ethylene (then 100 per cent owned by the government). The production of second–tier intermediaries or derivatives was entrusted to Honam Petrochemical (government 50 per cent, Mitsui 50 per cent), Hanyang Chemical and other companies. Roughly 60 per cent of total investment was sourced from foreign capital (KPIA, 1977).

Table 5.1. **Growth of Naphtha Cracking Capacity in Korea and Brazil**
(in 1 000 tpa)

Year	Korea		Brazil	
	Site	Capacity*	Site	Capacity*
1972	Ulsan no. 1	155	São Paulo	360
1978	Ulsan no. 2	400	Camaçari no. 1	450
1979	Yeocheon no. 1	400		
1982			Triunfo	450
1989	Yeocheon no. 2	300	São Paulo	100 (expan.)
1991	Onsan	250	Triunfo	100 (expan.)
	Yeocheon no. 3	350		
	Daesan no. 1	350		
	Daesan no. 2	350		
1992	Yeocheon no. 4	350	Camaçari no. 2	500
	Yeocheon no. 5	350		
Total		3 255		1 960

* Capacities are so-called "nameplate capacities" and can rise a little at times of production peaks.

During roughly the same period, but starting somewhat earlier, Brazil launched the building of not one but two complexes. In 1972, the decision was taken to build a second large–scale petrochemical complex at Camaçari in Bahia, which reached full capacity in 1978. Before the Bahia site was even finished, the intention to build a third complex at Triumfo, near Porto Alegre in Rio Grande do Sul, was included in the Second Development Plan (1975–79).

The Camaçari complex was built near offshore oil and gas sources, where a large refinery (Conjunto Petroquimico da Bahia) existed. Environmental factors favoured the choice of the region, but there was also a desire to "decentralise" the petrochemical industry and to use the new complex as a tool of development in what had been an unindustrialised area. The core naphtha–cracking plant at Camaçari was built with a 450 000 tpa ethylene production capacity. The firm in charge, Copene, started out as a wholly owned subsidiary of Petroquisa, but this situation changed later as companies engaged in downstream activities acquired part of Copene's voting capital. The downstream segments of the complex represent the climax of the tripartite system, marked by Petroquisa's success in diversifying the origins of its foreign partners, notably through the participation of three Japanese groups, but also by the highly atomised nature of ownership and production with a large number of sub–optimal plants (Roos, 1991).

At Triumfo the ethylene producing firm Copesul was also set up as a wholly owned Petroquisa subsidiary, later joined by the state–owned investment bank BNDES. Copesul went on line in 1982 with a 450 000 tpa core ethylene capacity, but the tide had turned. Even before the onset of the crisis triggered by Brazil's foreign debt, which led to what became known as the "lost decade", the growth of the petrochemical industry had come up against the limits to Brazil's growth that were set by the size of its domestic market as shaped by income distribution (Erber and Verhulm, 1993). Investment in the downstream segments was both slow and weak (during the whole of the 1980s there were only 18 plants at Triumfo, while the São Paulo site had over 40 and Camaçari over 50), forcing the central unit to export as many products as possible to sites in nearby Uruguay and Argentina. This was part of a broader process. Until 1983, petrochemical production was aimed principally at meeting domestic needs. But the start of production at the Copesul complex, along with foreign debt payment imperatives, led to a strong increase in exports under the impulse of Interbras, the trading arm of Petrobras. Divestment by some of the foreign firms also started: out of the 24 initial joint ventures involving foreign firms, only 11 remained by the second half of the 1980s, the others having been sold to domestic groups (Bastos, 1989).

In Korea the completion of the Yeocheon complex in 1979 coincided with the second oil shock. The rise in costs along with a drop in the rate of operation drove the Korean petrochemical industry into recession until 1982. But after 1983 and as a result of the stabilisation of oil prices, falling rates of interest and drastic capacity reductions by OECD countries, including Korea's nearest competitor Japan, the balance of supply and demand of petrochemical products recovered, notably in East Asian markets. Since the end of 1985, the so–called "three lows" (the low price of the Korean won, the low interest rate, and low raw material prices including oil) brought about a domestic boom which led to a rapid increase in the demand for petrochemical products.

By the time the boom in domestic demand took place in the late 1980s, the industry had been transferred to the private sector and a totally new regulatory framework, discussed in the next section, was being put in place. The decision by firms not only to extend the existing petrochemical plants but also to construct new ones was made in this new context. The government authorised the building of new naphtha–cracking capacity and also announced that from January 1990, investment in petrochemicals would be completely deregulated as a final change in the regulatory framework. Two groups already engaged in naphtha cracking, Yukong and Daelim, moved downstream into "second" and "third generation" products. This provided Daelim with the opportunity to construct its second naphtha cracker at Yeocheon no. 2 and prompted four major producers of downstream products, Lucky, Hanyang, Honam and Korean Petrochemicals, to take classic oligopolistic reactive steps and build their own naphtha cracking facilities to secure their own upstream intermediates. The first three built crackers at the Yeocheon site (Yeocheon no. 3, 4 and 5), while Korean Petrochemicals built one at Onsan. Finally the two largest chaebols, Samsung and Hyundai, were authorised to construct integrated complexes (including 350 000 tpa crackers) at Daesan, the third major site established on the mid–western coast. As a result between 1988 and 1992, investment in basic petrochemicals reached 7.5 trillion Korean won (over $10 billion). This represented 11.4 per cent of total investment in fixed capital in manufacturing during the same period. The production capacity of Korea in petrochemicals leaped to 3 500 000 tpa in terms of ethylene output (the fifth in the world in 1993 after the United States, Japan, Russia, and Germany and a quantum jump indeed from a capacity of merely 500 000 tpa and the 18th position that Korea held in 1988).

In Brazil once the protracted process of political transition from the period of military regime was over, a new National Programme for Petrochemicals was established in 1987, based on a major new effort of government investment. The fiscal and political crisis of the state which developed soon after, high inflation and later world recession in the 1990s delayed several projects and curtailed others. At Camaçari Copene was able to expand existing capacity of its first plant slightly and then, with a three year delay, to duplicate its ethylene production capacity by building a second 500 000 tpa plant. An expansion of capacity in the existing plant of 100 000 tpa was carried out with some delay at the São Paulo complex and a greater one at Triunfo in Rio Grande del Sur. The building of a fourth site just north of Rio de Janeiro near Petrobras' main refinery, planned at the time of the 1987 programme, has not started due to the changes in the regulatory context and the private sector hesitations discussed in the next section. Total ethylene production capacity now stands at nearly 2 000 000 tpa. This is by far the largest capacity in the Americas outside the United States, but it is much lower than Korea's and more importantly it is organised within a very different structure of ownership and economic co–ordination.

Changes in Policy and in Government Instruments

In the early 1970s, the role of government in the petrochemical industry and the range of policy instruments used to enhance its development were largely the same in the two countries. Core firms in the petrochemical complexes were state–owned. In the case of Korea this feature was extended to all downstream firms requiring more than $20 million of investment, while in that of Brazil it was limited to joint venture participation within the tripartite system. In both countries, the range of government instruments was extremely broad. Capital was provided and/or borrowed abroad by the government, which also participated in negotiations with foreign firms on their participation in joint ventures and the acquisition of foreign technology. The Korean state was more consistent in its support. For Korea the policy of intervening in petrochemicals did not originate as a "second–best" choice as in Brazil, nor was it fenced in by hostile or at least jealous national and foreign private interests. The government had no qualms about having the industry closely controlled by the Ministry of Commerce and Industry under the Law for the Promotion of the Petrochemical Industry. Of course Korea enjoyed very different relations with the US government and private firms than Brazil. For a long time the government did not have to worry internally or externally about the extent to which its policies were orthodox and "legitimate" or not. For over 15 years there was virtually no competition in the Korean market. Imports were forbidden once local production of given petrochemical products started. The government also set the principle of "one product/one maker" to secure sufficient demand for each product in the domestic market. Firms thus enjoyed monopoly situations without domestic or foreign competition.

There were also other differences between the two countries, which influenced the subsequent development of this industry as of others[14]. Korea, for example, was careful to avoid an excessively large foreign debt. The government has always kept tight control over the domestic banking system, has had full capacity to tax and thus has never run into the major macroeconomic difficulties experienced by Brazil since the early 1980s. In addition, within the Korean private sector an endogenous process of capital accumulation by large industrial groups was taking place, along with a keen interest on their part in technological catching up and a continual consolidation of industrial entrepreneurship. This laid the foundations for subsequent privatisation. In contrast, at the height of Petrobras' leadership of the industry, the state–owned firm was able to alleviate some problems of management by seconding or permanently releasing highly trained senior staff to head private sector firms, but as we shall see below their capital continued to be held (and still is so today) by financial groups or loose conglomerates, thus impeding the process of technological and entrepreneurial accumulation. The consolidation of genuine corporate capacity permitted the Korean government to undertake a progressive transfer of the industry to the private sector, long before the start of neo–liberal noise and confusion about the illegitimacy of state ownership and its wastefulness, which may be true in some cases, but which does not bear hasty generalisation in the case of petrochemicals. This stands in sharp contrast to the way events unfolded in Brazil.

Differences in the Timing and Order of Changes in the Regulatory Framework

In Korea, by the early 1970s the capacity of the private sector to run plants and mobilise capital had become evident. Thus the industry was gradually handed over to the private sector. Between 1973 and 1987 all the major companies at the Ulsan and Yeocheon complexes (including KOCO, Korea General Chemical Co., and so on) were sold to Korean private firms (largely chaebols like Sunkyung, Daelim, Hanil and Dongbu). The state–owned petrochemical industry thus quickly became yet another chaebol–dominated industry. Initially there was little increase in the degree of competition. The new groups simply enjoyed the same monopolistic positions as their predecessors. Privatisation preceded liberalisation, but the ground had been prepared. Trade liberalisation started by the progressive lowering of quantitative barriers to imports. Confronted by external pressures to open Korea's booming domestic markets to foreign competitors, the government announced an "Import Liberalisation Plan" in 1984. It took care however to minimise the shocks to domestic firms by notifying them in advance of the items that were to be liberalised and by eliminating quantitative barriers over a four year period.

In 1986 all the industry–specific industrial development laws were abrogated including the one pertaining to petrochemicals. The government enacted an "Industry Development Law" (an "umbrella" law applying to manufacturing as a whole), stressing the autonomy of the private sector and the shift from direct to indirect promotion policies. At the end of 1988, following the suggestion of a private sector committee, an "Investment Guidance Scheme for the Petrochemical Industry" was published. It announced a complete liberalisation of new investment in petrochemicals from January 1990 and it authorised the new investments outlined above. The change this implied in the structure of supply can be read in Table 5.2.

Table 5.2. **Number of Producers in Selected Product Groups in the Korean Industry** (1980–92)

Products	1980	1990	1992
Ethylene	2	2	8
LDPE	1	3	5
HDPE	2	5	6
PP	2	4	7
PS	2	6	6
TPA	1	4	4
PA	1	2	3

Source: H.S. Kim.

With the entry of the large upstream firms, Yukong and Daelim, into the processing of downstream products and the building by major downstream producers (Lucky, Hanyang, Honam and Korea Petrochemical) of vertically integrated naphtha cracking plants, the demarcation between upstream and downstream business disappeared, along with the earlier "one product/one maker" principle. The new situation was completed by the entry of total outsiders in the form of Samsung and Hyundai. It was only once there had been this considerable increase in domestic competition, along with the enormous build–up of production capacity sufficient to meet the needs of the domestic market as well as those of export markets, that trade liberalisation was extended to tariffs thus achieving the complete modification of the regulatory framework. The change in the competitive regime preceded the opening of markets, and did not wait for or depend on this to occur as in Brazil. In January 1989, tariffs for petrochemical imports were cut gradually with the process ending in 1993: basic materials from 10 to 5 per cent; intermediate materials from 20 to 8 per cent and derivatives from 15–20 to 8 per cent.

In Brazil the corresponding changes in the regulatory system were begun much later, as a result of which they took place under severe financial constraints and strong external pressures. Few of the conditions that made for a sound and forward–looking transfer of responsibility to the private sector in Korea were to be found in Brazil and the changes were implemented far more quickly and without any of the careful transitional measures that existed in Korea.

The process started with the measure Korea had taken at the very end when everything had been done to prepare for it, namely trade liberalisation in the form of tariff cuts. Quantitative barriers had been somewhat less systematic in Brazil than in Korea, but the industry had extremely high tariffs with which the foreign firms had no quarrel since it allowed them to reap decent earnings with sub–optimal plant. Before the start of trade liberalisation in 1988 tariffs stood (in nominal figures) at 31.1 per cent in basic and intermediary products and at 50.7 per cent in downstream thermoplastics. By 1994 they had dropped respectively to 7.9 per cent and 15.0 per cent, with further reductions due in 1995 in the context of the Mercosur negotiations. This choice stems from international pressures of course, but it also reflects the complete dearth of an industrial policy geared to building competitiveness in the domestic industry through a range of measures, which can include progressive trade liberalisation but cannot limit itself to this step.

Starting with the elimination of tariffs might have been justified had it been part of an overall policy aimed at breaking with the past and restructuring the industry in a fundamental way. Privatisation represented another opportunity to restructure the industry for long–term competitiveness but this, too, depended upon the extent to which industrial objectives would prevail over ideological or short–term financial ones. This would not, however, be the case. To make sense of this outcome, we must take a further look at the industry's supply structure and some features of the firms operating in petrochemicals.

A Further Look at Corporate Ownership and Concentration in the Brazilian Private Sector

In Brazil the "one product/one maker" principle had never been an article of government policy in the same way as it was in Korea. But a similar result was attained nonetheless as a combined result of protection, oligopolistic behaviour on the part of the Brazilian firms, aided by lack of interest and weak competitive pressure by MNEs whose principal interests were in the fine chemicals and pharmaceutical parts of the chemical–related complex rather than in petrochemicals. In many segments of the Brazilian petrochemical industry, supply did and still does depend on a single producer (see Table 5.3). The presence of seven suppliers in polyethylenes does not imply a much higher degree of competition than in other product groups since there are several non–rival grades, notably between high–density and low–density polyethylenes (see the breakdown for Korea in Table 5.2). Competition is weak, indeed almost non–existent, within a broader manufacturing sector which is rife with monopolistic behaviour, in particular in raw materials, bulk intermediates such as cement and civil engineering (ECIB, 1993).

Table 5.3. **Number of Producers and Market Shares for Selected Product Groups in the Brazilian Industry** (end 1980s)

Ethylene	5	3 producers with 91%
Polyethylenes	7	1 producer with 27%
		2 producers with 13% each
		1 producer with 10%
		1 producer with 9.8%
		1 producer with 12.6%
		1 producer with 8.1%
PVC	2	1 producer with 64%
PP	4	1 producer with 47%
		1 producer with 24%
SBR	1	monopoly
DMT	1	monopoly
TPA	1	monopoly

Source: Oliveira (1990).

The other important point concerns the ownership structure of the firms operating in this industry. A recent study of the Brazilian petrochemical industry prepared for a major project on Brazilian competitiveness (ECIB, 1993) noted that "corporate strategies are strongly affected by capital ownership. The productive units have little autonomy to define their long term strategies because they are limited by the strategies of the groups that control them" (Guerra, 1993) and it stressed "the subordination of firms to holding companies that lay priority on the financial objectives of all their interests" (Guerra, 1993).

In the early 1980s, there were as many as 50 firms in the sector, owning the 120 odd plants at the three sites, São Paulo, Camaçari and Triunfo. Many of these companies were joint ventures. During the 1980s and early 1990s, a hesitant process of concentration took place as a number of smaller foreign firms exited the industry. Today there are only a limited number of MNEs left in Brazilian petrochemicals *stricto sensu*: Rhône–Poulenc (with its very Brazilianised affiliate Rhodia), Dow, Union Carbide, Monsanto, Azko, BASF, Hoechst, Shell and Mitsubishi. Their plants, however, are extremely small in comparison with those in home countries and their presence has not affected the competitive environment significantly.

Most Brazilian privately owned petrochemical firms are affiliates of larger groups, none of which have, at least until now, viewed the sector as a core business. With the partial exception of Unipar, which developed out of an alliance led by the Capuava group (now the Vila Velha holding) and helped to build the PqU plant at the São Paulo complex, no group has grown up in the industry or risked much money in it. Several of these groups are in fact conglomerates often built around a commercial bank (Banco Economico) or a financial institution (the Mariani Bittencourt investment bank), which are by nature particularly prone to take the view that the industrial assets they hold are basically little more than a given form of financial asset. Others belong to groups that have developed in another sector: civil engineering and construction in the case of Odebrecht; pulp and paper in the case of Suzano. A third type of group can be viewed as being "sector related" in a very broad sense of the term: Ipiranga, the country's fourth largest petrol distributor which is now one of the leading firms at the Triumfo complex in Rio Grande do Sul; the Ultra group, which had affiliates in fertilisers and natural gas before entering into petrochemicals at the São Paulo complex; the Cevekol–Rosenberg group which began as a user of petrochemicals in the plastic toy industry. But all three groups are in fact conglomerates quite as much as the others just mentioned. A major analyst of petrochemicals, who was also earlier in his life an important actor in the industry, has spelt out the implications of this state of things by defining the situation of the affiliated firms as "quasi–firms" on account of their total lack of financial, managerial and technological autonomy (Oliveira, 1994). The low priority given to the different facets of technological accumulation, discussed below, is a patent expression of the lack in the Brazilian industry of the managerial attitudes which are germane to genuine core businesses.

To date no Brazilian private petrochemical firm has the combined financial and technological capacity to offer the industry leadership and a sense of purpose. But several are strong enough financially and politically to prevent a rival firm from attaining this position. They are known to meet in secret, either among themselves or with senior politicians, to settle the industry's fate[15]. This is not unique to Brazil. In every country possessing a petrochemical industry, oligopoly prevails and secret meetings occur. What, however, are their objectives? In the Brazilian case, the domestic petrochemical oligopoly is finance–dominated, puny and conservative. The capacity to impede and to harm is probably the most widely distributed quality among its members. Thus stalemate solutions are often a "first best" for many, possibly all participants. This will become clearer when we consider the attitude towards R&D and innovation below. But it is also apparent in the nature of the options which the industry was able to impose on the weak and disoriented Brazilian administration when the decision to privatise was taken by the Collor government, and it is evident in the manoeuvres between uneasy alliances which have taken place since.

The Solution Adopted for the Privatisation of Petroquisa and Its Consequences

There were several ways in which the privatisation of Petroquisa, along with its fully–owned or majority affiliates and its minority holdings might have been organised. The most radical way of proceeding, which France and Japan, for example, applied in their own manner, would have been for the state, on the occasion of this shift of its assets to the private sector, to have planned administratively a full scale restructuring of the sector (to be subsequently ratified through a law), thus putting an end to the mix of sub–optimum plants, divided ownership and absence of domestic competition then prevailing in the industry. In the context of the early 1990s this may not have been politically possible.

Short of this, however, there were solutions which could have changed the organisation and working of the industry quite significantly. The government, or rather the BNDES to which it handed over the unpleasant task of dismantling an industry the bank had helped to build, had three alternatives from which to choose (Fundap, 1993 and Erber, 1995). The first was a solution put forward by Petroquisa's management. It consisted in privatising the state–owned firm and its affiliates as a single block, thereby creating the basis for a large and strong private corporation capable of becoming a pole for further restructuring of the atomised industry and so of competing in world markets. In the memorandum prepared by Petroquisa, one of the arguments concerned thresholds for R&D and the possibility of completing the construction of CENTEP, the state–owned firm's technical research and development centre. The memorandum also contained proposals for selling the stock of the future corporation in a way which would ensure a stable core ownership along with the floating of stock on the major world stock exchanges. By unifying management, building a solid research base and creating the kind of vertically integrated structure practised by other world class firms, this solution would have clearly improved the long–term competitiveness of the Brazilian industry. But it ran counter to the interests of the domestic financial groups and foreign MNEs engaged in the petrochemical sector.

A second solution which represented a variation on the first would have consisted in at least privatising Petroquisa's assets as a block at each of the three poles, thus forcing the private sector firms at each pole to undertake an accelerated process of restructuring and swaps. The third solution was that of the Brazilian private sector. It was tabled by ABEQIM, the industry's professional association, and consisted in privatising Petroquisa's assets bit by bit and organising sales in such a way as to respect the *status quo* within the private sector oligopoly as closely as possible. This was the solution which the BNDES was instructed by the Collor Administration to adopt. As the Brazilian competitiveness (ECIB) study concluded, this form of privatisation represented a "lost opportunity for concentration and integration", the "government having chosen a solution which did not give the priority to these objectives" (Teixera, 1993).

By privatising in this fashion, the sole element of integration in the industry, the technical co–ordination ensured by Petroquisa through the management of its naphtha cracking and aromatics production plant, was eliminated. In its place, at São Paulo and Triumfo where the firm possessing the core naphtha–cracking plant was transferred by the state at very low cost to the private sector, has come an industrial consortium owned jointly by the main users and the plant itself has been reconceptualised as a *"central de materia–prima"* or "raw materials production plant", a term generally reserved for electricity or urban gas. This of course is an unheard–of expression in integrated plants under single ownership in OECD countries. It does, however, reflect the way perhaps not all, but many, downstream private sector firms view a plant they did not build but received as a sort of "externality".

Among the Brazilian groups, privatisation led to the pursuit of a process of concentration guided more by financial objectives than industrial and technological ones through the early 1990s; no domestic group has taken the risk or been strong enough to upset the *status quo*. This could perhaps be ending. Vila Velha, one of the main owners of Unipar, recently declared war on Odebrecht, one of its main partners and rivals in PqU, the core firm at the São Paulo site (and indeed one of Vila Velha's own shareholders). Vila Velha has indicated that its aim is to break with the *central de materia–prima* approach and build a vertically integrated group at São Paulo. Petroquisa still owns 17.5 per cent of PqU and could help decide the outcome of this battle. As a counter move the Odebrecht group has proposed an alliance to the Suzano group which could lead to a major swap of plants scattered across the three sites. Likewise the bankruptcy in August 1995 of the Banco Economico of Bahia could force it to sell its assets in Copene which in turn might lead to changes of ownership of other firms and plants at Camaçari. It is hard to predict how far or how fast these processes, on which some observers and actors in the industry pin their hope, can go. Furthermore, in the absence of any group possessing a genuine "core competence" founded on an endogenous technological accumulation, apart from Petroquisa, it is difficult to say whether the outcome of a process of concentration could lead to a viable industry.

Exports, Imports and Competitiveness

Foreign trade is a reasonable indicator of short– and medium–term competitiveness. Korea has developed very strong exports despite its serious disadvantage in terms of the price of raw materials *vis–à–vis* oil–producing countries like the United States and the Middle East countries. With respect to non–price competitiveness, including quality and user service, Korea also still lags behind other countries. For instance, the number of grades in polyolefins produced in Korea is only 450, whereas it is 9 500 in Japan, 750 in the United States, and 1 150 in Europe. Japan is superior to Korea in user services such as technical service, claim handling and sales service. Yet over the past three years, Korea replaced Japan as the leading exporter of synthetic resins to South–East Asian markets and also succeeded in diversifying the destination of its exports to Europe, South America, Africa and even the United States. In 1993, Korea recorded for the first time a trade surplus for chemicals (exports: $2 880 million; imports: 2 669 million). The growth of exports has been particularly spectacular for resins and plastics as shown in Table 5. 5.

Table 5.4. **Korean Production, Exports and Domestic Demand for Resins and Plastics**
(in thousand tons and percentages)

Year	1985	1988	1989	1990	1991	1992	1993	93/85
Prod. (P)	1 278	1 993	2 241	2 689	3 395	4 792	5 351	27.0%
Exports (X)	253	191	345	446	960	1 912	2 272	44.2%
Dom. Dem. (D)	1 141	1 974	2 125	2 519	2 656	3 700	3 234	19.0%
X/P	19.8	9.6	15.4	16.6	28.3	39.9	42.5	-
P/D	112.0	101.0	105.5	106.7	127.8	159.4	165.5	-

Source: KPIA.

A part of the explanation for the surge of Korean exports in the Far East lies certainly in the appreciation of the Japanese yen, for reasons having now at least as much to do with the weakness of the dollar as with the inherent strength of the Japanese economy. As a result Japan has lost its price competitiveness, which has been further weakened by the low rate of operation (about 85 per cent) of its petrochemical plant. This is an external macroeconomic factor, favourable to Korea, and given the size of Japan's trade surplus, it is not simply a transitory phenomenon. But without several other factors specific to Korea, the export growth would not have been as remarkable. The first is Korea's geographical advantage, that is, its proximity to the rapidly growing Chinese market. Second and more importantly, the chaebols' particular capability to mobilise huge investments from a long–term perspective has allowed not only the full exploitation of scale economies, but also the introduction of state–of–the–art technology through massive acquisitions of plant. Third, Korea's successful export performance is also related to the process of innovation to be discussed more completely below. As a result of learning–by–doing and R&D, the productivity of Korean petrochemical firms in terms of output per man–day has reached the same level as that of Japanese firms, especially in the main items like LDPE, HDPE and PP (KIET, 1994). In Korea the trend in the rate of value–added is also interesting: between 1973 and 1988 it was stagnant and even declined slightly; but it has been steadily rising since 1989. This rise is all the more important because it occurred in a period not only of growing competition, but also of deep depression in petrochemicals.

The chaebols are now faced with the new challenge or indeed the new threat, which they have created for themselves as a result of their huge investments, namely the possession of production capacity well in excess of domestic demand (about 2.5 million tpa for synthetic resin). This challenge can only be met by dominating export markets in China and South–East Asia. To be competitive in these markets, firms have already sought to improve productivity, quality and product differentiation, notably by increasing the number of product grades (for LDPE, PP and PS, for instance, the number of grades increased from 87 in 1985 to 139 in 1992) and by reducing the time required for new product development.

Productivity, product quality and a respectable increase in the number of product grades also prevail in the core ethylene plant run by Petroquisa, but this is not true in the case of downstream products where the size of firms and plant and the lack of technology–related investment impede such developments. In spite of this Brazilian exports grew during the 1980s and firms made profits not only in the domestic market but also abroad. Research by Brazilian economists (see Erber and Verhulm, 1993, for an overview) suggests that this may be due essentially *i)* to the range of subsidies these companies (domestic and foreign alike) received during their initial investment (this was studied in particular at the Bahia pole) and *ii)* the relatively low price at which Petroquisa supplies these firms with ethylene/ethane intermediate inputs — a price which is derivative of the price at which Petrobas provides naphtha from the state–owned oil refineries. While Brazilian prices for naphtha and so for ethylene have evolved along the same lines as international prices, they have consistently been lower. Profit margins have oscillated around zero for oil refining (Petrobas), been somewhat higher for the products of the central cracking units (Petroquisa) and again higher for the *filière*'s downstream "final products". Exports of these products have thus been subsidised indirectly through the low price of basic inputs, as well as enjoying the export support measures provided to all industries (notably a special fiscal regime).

Exports levelled off in 1992–94 as a result of the difficult conditions for all firms in the international market for petrochemicals and grew again in 1994 as the world market for petrochemicals improved. A significant part of exports has been to other South American markets. But they have included sales to the United States of small quantities of quite sophisticated products for which there was no internal industrial demand. In 1995 exports were not expected to grow, since domestic capacity would be needed to supply the internal markets where a consumption boom has followed the success of President Cardoso's inflation stabilisation plan. Since 1990 the price differential for naphtha between Brazil and foreign competitors has narrowed considerably as a result of changes in government policy. The prospect of further changes in the price of naphtha "hangs like a sword of Damocles over the domestic industry" (Erber, 1995).

Table 5.5. **Brazilian Output, Imports and Exports for Resins and Plastics and Total Chemicals**
(in thousand dollars and percentages)

Resins and Plastics

Year	1991	1992	1993	1994	92/91	93/92	94/93
Total sales	1 900	2 086	2 309	2 638	8.7%	11.8%	14.2%
Exports	339.6	321.1	353.5	449.3	-5.4%	10.1%	27.0%
Imports	65.1	69.2	113.3	172.1	6.4%	63.7%	51.9%

Total chemicals

Year	1991	1992	1993	1994	92/91	93/92	94/93
Total sales	10.467	10.717	10.991	11.789	2.4%	2.6%	7.3%
Exports	1.089	1.086	1.051	1.225	-0.3%	-3.3%	16.8%
Imports	802	778	1.038	1.355	-3.0%	33.4%	30.5%

Source: ABIQUIM.

The most significant change during the 1990s has been the growth of imports which followed the liberalisation of trade. Since 1992 the rate of growth of imports in chemicals as a whole has been very rapid: a rise of 30 per cent over the previous year in 1993 and further growth of 19 per cent in 1994. The external deficit in chemicals has jumped from $992 million in 1991 to $2 716 million in 1994. Thermoplastics have fared significantly better and continue to show a fairly stable surplus of about $500 million. Despite a doubling of imports in thermoplastics in 1993 and a further 22 per cent increase in 1994, industrial leaders interpret the trade surplus as proof that this part of the industry has the capacity to face competition on its domestic market and continue a small but successful export activity. This is part of the same optimistic philosophy that sees the possibility for Brazilian firms to remain viable, while relying essentially on foreign sources for the acquisition of new technology. It is not certain however whether an approach simply in terms of follower strategies in technology and the search for limited or niche markets in trade (the Brazilian home market, Mercosur, and certain export markets for specialised products) will prove viable in the new competitive context of aggressive oligopolistic rivalry which is specific to liberalisation and the phase of globalisation.

Technology, Competitiveness and Viability in the Longer Term

Even quite critical reviews of the Brazilian situation (see ECIB, 1993, and Erber, 1995) refuse to contemplate the possibility that the petrochemical industry could disappear as a result of increased foreign competition through imports and the take–over of domestic firms by foreign MNEs. The only exception is Oliveira (1994), who recognises that this is something which could loom sooner or later on the horizon. Of course the destruction of the industry is not on the agenda in the same way as that of the electronics industry, once the "market reserve" policy broke down and the promotive legislation was reversed by the Collor government. Unlike electronics, petrochemicals are no longer a strategic sector and the MNEs can simply let market forces coupled with technological backwardness, lack of investment and complete dependence on foreign sources, do the work quietly. Here again the difference between Korea and Brazil has steadily grown.

Technological Acquisition and Learning Processes

Initially, in basic "upstream" petrochemicals the course of technological acquisition and accumulation was fairly similar in Korea and Brazil. Korea relied on technology provided by the large engineering companies, as well as by the US and Japanese joint venture partners when it built the first Ulsan and Yeocheon complexes. The new chaebols that entered the industry in the course of recent "investment liberalisation" have likewise relied heavily on foreign technology (see Figure 5.2). All along firms made strong efforts to absorb and adapt the imported technologies through the process of learning–by–doing. R&D investments however remained low until 1988–90 when the final set of changes in the regulatory regime, the lowering of trade barriers and the building by firms of capacities geared to exports strongly increased the pressure to innovate more significantly.

In Brazil learning–by–doing and an interest in maximising technology–pull effects in the capital equipment industry marked Petroquisa's role of leadership in the 1970s. The first São Paulo ethylene plant was built through a typical turnkey "package deal", with negligible domestic engineering inputs and a very low percentage of domestic procurement. The second plant, at Camaçari, involved increasing domestic participation for the provision of engineering services and capital equipment. This move was consolidated during the building of the third core naphtha cracking unit at the Rio Grande del Sul complex. Investment entailed not only a major effort to substitute domestic for foreign hardware and detail engineering services, and the maximum use of Brazilian technical skills, but also an attempt on the part of Petroquisa to appropriate as fully as possible, both in technical and legal terms, assets and skills related to state–of–the–art process know–how, process design engineering, and R&D in the ethylene field. The degree to which foreign firms tendering for the Copesul contract at Triunfo agreed to transfer effectively ethylene processing technology was one of the main criteria for their selection. Brazil's objective was to be able to build, if necessary, another identical plant without having to depend on imported know–how. The criteria for determining the effectiveness of technology transfer were the delivery of all appropriate engineering data, including the technology to obtain them, their updating, provision of technical assistance and training of technicians (Teixera, 1987). The choice of Technip (France) and KTI (Holland) was made on this basis. In the downstream segments where foreign firms were given shares in joint ventures in exchange for the technology they provided, the possibilities for Brazilian partners to assimilate and build on such technology appears to have been much more limited (Roos, 1991, and Bastos, 1989). Measures taken by foreign firms to preserve a hold over their technology, coupled with the lack of endogenous capacity by Brazilian partners, has meant that technological learning and accumulation have been significantly weaker than in arrangements where Petroquisa was involved.

The extent to which Korea and Brazil were at about the same point in the early 1980s is demonstrated by the fact that both were capable of exporting some technology to developing countries only then beginning a process of catching up. In the case of Brazil, Petrobras was able to provide technology for the production of ethylene from ethyl alcohol and MTBE from butanes. Korea recorded its first petrochemical technology export when Lucky exported PVC and VCM production technologies to Saudi Arabia in 1984. There was already one important difference in that in the former case the seller was a public firm, while in the latter, a private company. Then the process of technological accumulation started to diverge, before becoming a full–scale gap from the end of the decade onwards. Korea made no important technology exports between 1985 and 1990. Since then, however, they have steadily increased. The export of ABS technology by the Miwon Petrochemical Co. to China is particularly significant in that it was the first technology export on a turnkey basis by a Korean firm, and the tender was won through fierce competition with well–known US, Japanese and German firms. As a result of China's eagerness to build its own petrochemical industry, Korea has been able to sell its neighbour a substantial amount of technology. Indeed the largest part of Korea's technology exports are with China to which it also exports many petrochemical products, possibly heralding future problems of foreign markets for the country's huge output.

In explaining the Brazilian situation, the structure of the petrochemical industry is again an important factor. In the downstream segments, most Brazilian firms were too small to generate a sufficient cash flow to finance technology–related investments and those that did suffered from the nature of their ownership. They have rationalised dependency on outside technology as a permanent way of handling the upgrading of their plant. Yet much of the technology provided by MNEs in exchange for their shares in the "tripés"[16], has either been closely guarded or only provided when it was no longer at the technological frontier. Then technology–related investments came to a halt and even suffered a regression in the course of the 1980s. Initially this was a consequence of Brazil's debt–led crisis. It represents a key dimension of the "lost decade" in this industry as in several others. But the situation has continued into the 1990s and taken on a rather different and extremely serious turn, as the industry shed R&D personnel and lagged in the introduction of digital electronic control, equipment that could have direct effects on the industry's productivity (Teixera, 1993, 2.2).

Figure 5.2. **Technology Licensors of Major Petrochemical Processes**

	NCC	LDPE	LLDPE	HDPE	PP	Butadiene	BTX	SM	EO/EG
YuKong	Kellog (#1 70.12) (#2 87.6)	-	Du Pont (87.9)	Du Pont (87.9)	Himont (87.9)	Nippon Zeon (70.5) (87.10)	IFP/UOP/UOP (75.7) (88.1)	ARCO (87.11)	-
Daelim	Lummus (#1 76.6) (#2 86.3)	ICI (91.2)	Himont (92.3)	Phillips (87.1)	Himont (91.1)	Nippon Zeon (90.11)	(#1) LCI/UOP (86.11) (#2) IFP/UOP/APCI (90.10)	Badger (84.6)	-
Samsung	Lummus (89.12)	Mitsubishi Petrochemical (90.1)	BP (90.1)	Mitsui Petrochemical (90.1)	Mitsui Petrochemical (90.1)	Nippon Zeon (89.12)	IFP/KK/HRI (89.12)	Badger (89.1)	Scientific design (89.2)
Hyundai	Kellogg (89.12)	BASF (90.1)	Stami-carbon (90.1)	Phillips (90.1)	Himont (90.1)	Nippon Zeon (89.12)	IFP/ARCO/HRI (89.10)	Badger (89.5)	Scientific design (89.5)
Lucky	Lummus (87.9)	CdF (87.1)	-	Hoechst (90.8)	-	Nippon Zeon (89.4)	LCI/ARCO/HRI (90.11)	Lummus (87.11)	-
Hanyang	Stone & Webster (90.2)	Dow (70.6) (88.1)	UCC (84.6)	UCC (84.6)	-	-	IFP/HRI (90.6)	-	-
Honam	Lummus (89.4)	-	-	Mitsui Petrochemical (76.6) (81.2)	(#1) Mitsui Doatsu (76.6) (#2) Himont (86.12)	-	IFP/UOP/UOP (90.8)	-	Shell (76.6) (89.2)
KPIC	Lummus (88.12)	-	-	Chisso (70.11)	Chisso (70.11)	-	-	-	-

( ): Date of approval.

R&D Outlays

In Korea trade liberalisation and, more significantly yet, the building of huge new capacities geared to exports have gone hand in hand with rapid and substantial increases in the level of technology–related investments and the decision to make significant outlays on R&D. The increased competition from Middle East producers and Singapore and a much greater need to satisfy international regulations on environmental pollution than other developing countries (if only on account of Korea's candidacy to the OECD) have all acted to reinforce Korean technology–related investments. Innovation policy by Korean firms is no longer limited to learning–by–doing but also aimed at indigenous R&D capability–building. These are now considered by Korean firms as being complementary in enhancing innovation performance.

R&D is aimed at improving both price and non–price competitiveness. The main goals have been those of product differentiation as well as productivity and quality improvements. Until 1988 Korean private outlays for R&D in petrochemicals represented some 1 per cent of sales. But in 1990 it doubled to 2.1 per cent and has remained at that level since then. Of course, this is still much lower than those of developed countries like the United States or Japan, where in 1990 firms spent 4.5 and 4.0 per cent respectively. Nevertheless, it clearly implies a significant change in the innovation behaviour of Korean firms, enough to confirm their resolution to build up indigenous technological capabilities in the new competitive context.

Table 5.6. **R&D as a Percentage of Sales in Korea and Brazil**

	1988	1989	1990	Growth rate
Korea	1.17	2.14	2.09	37.5
Brazil	0.75	0.96	0.56	- 12.3

In Brazil the situation is dramatically different. Petroquisa was the only group for which petrochemicals has been a core business. As a result it is mainly in its plant that a genuine process of technological catching up and initial technological accumulation took place. However even in Petroquisa and its affiliates the level of expenditure on R&D remained low in the 1980s in comparison with Brazil. It represented between 0.3 and 0.9 per cent of sales during the 1985–90 period for petrochemicals as a whole and 0.4 to 1.5 per cent in the case of polymers. In the 1990s, the fiscal and political crisis of the state reached a point where the policy has been akin to "throwing the baby out with the bath water" in so far as Brazil's previous developmental objectives are concerned. This is reflected in the decision taken by the Collor Administration but maintained by the two subsequent governments to cancel the fairly large laboratory which Petroquisa had started to build at Rio de Janeiro. The skeleton of the building stands near the science departments of the Federal University and the Technical Centre which Petrobras was allowed to build in the 1970s. For the moment, Petroquisa has succeeded in keeping some of its research projects alive by lodging them at Petrobras's large Technical Research Centre located nearby which has a $160 million annual budget but they, too, are threatened.

The contrast with Korea in terms of the percentage of sales devoted to R&D shown in Table 5.6 is already striking. In absolute figures the gap is even more dramatic[17]. In 1989 at the highest point in R&D expenditure, Brazil only spent $53 million. The next year which was the start of a three year recession in petrochemicals, this amount fell to $38 million on R&D, while Korea despite the recession spent some $500 million. In an industry where thresholds in expenditures are significant for the very nature of the activity, this represents a quantum gap. At the Camaçari site, the Technical Research Centre of Copene (which is the largest firm in Brazilian petrochemicals in terms of cash flow and profit margins), only has a $2.5 million budget and a staff of 34 people, including 24 with university training, plus a few Ph.D. students. The scope of the Centre's work is limited and was cut down three years ago as a consequence of pressure by Norquisa (the consortium of private firms holding 47.2 per cent of assets). Previously the Centre did its own research on catalysts; now it is simply asked to scan the international market, advise on the licences to be bought and do minor adaptations. Its most important activity consists of simulation in the form of models and experiments in laboratory equipment for scaling up processes in the Copene plant. The personnel are concerned that the disappearance of Petroquisa as the majority capital owner on the board of Copene and the changes in management policy of the new owners may lead to more cuts yet. Their concern is not without foundation. In interviews held in 1995, influential leaders from private sector groups (including previous chairmen of ABIQUIM) were quite clear in indicating that their corporate technological policy does not go much beyond that of possessing the appropriate in–house expertise for choosing the right processes abroad and the skills for using them productively. They stated unambiguously that they considered R&D to be outside the scope of their groups as far as petrochemicals are concerned. Their aim is to remain competitive in the home market and for this the efficient use of the appropriate imported technology is enough. The last point about R&D is that the MNEs do very little work in this area in Brazil, for good reasons as far as they are concerned: scale economies in other laboratories in the groups, ease of transfer to affiliates, weakness of the indigenous Brazilian R&D system.

Sourcing of Intermediates and User–Producer Relationships

Korean firms have also begun to diversify into the area of the better known engineering plastics by developing products such as ABS, PC, PBT, PPS, etc. They do this by imitative R&D thus avoiding the high risks of developing innovative new materials. These are not totally "new" products in this sense, but they can be useful as a bargaining tool for future technological co–operation with firms from OECD countries[18]. As in other areas of high technology, collaboration is the main route for acquiring technology in advanced new materials, but it is one which can only be contemplated by firms having attained a respectable technological level. The opportunity given to the Korean firms to enter into the high–value new materials technology related to fibre–reinforced plastics and the new generations of polymers, e.g. engineering plastics, and special plastics, and start moving down the learning curves for such products, stems from the existence of thriving, dynamic firms in electronics and automobiles which are both Korean owned and often members of the same chaebol.

Here again the contrast between the two countries is worth highlighting. In Brazil the thermoplastics technical *"filière"* and value chain have received little horizontal support or stimulus to move downstream. The decisive user–producer relationships which have developed in the chemical–related MNEs in OECD countries and also in Korea are extremely weak in Brazil. Evidence regarding the sourcing of such materials by the mainly foreign–owned automobile companies suggests that they have made little call on Brazilian suppliers, relying instead on their relationships to suppliers outside Brazil either in their home bases or in other OECD countries. Trade liberalisation and deregulation (which put an end to government requirements regarding local sourcing) is likely to aggravate this situation by permitting a further increase in the imports of intermediary products and components by foreign firms in medium to high technology industries along with a further weakening of the demand addressed to local suppliers. This makes the future of building up user–producer relationships with domestic suppliers in engineering and special–purpose plastics increasingly unlikely[19].

Having noted the move by Korean petrochemical firms towards more sophisticated types of plastics, it is necessary to stress that the chaebols are otherwise weak in fine chemicals and pharmaceuticals, thus lacking the strengths of the principal OECD chemical–related groups. Most Korean firms operating in this sector today are small firms with fewer than 100 employees. There is a huge gap between these firms and world fine–chemical companies in terms of size and R&D capability. Chaebols operating in petrochemicals have indicated that potentially they are interested in fine chemicals. But none of them has yet dared to enter this part of the chemical–related complex on account of the magnitude of the technological barrier. Data on the Brazilian situation indicate that three–quarters of the market for fine chemicals and pharmaceuticals is controlled by foreign firms. Only one group operating in petrochemicals also possesses an affiliate in fine chemicals.

Some Conclusions with Broader Implications

Two conclusions appear to be of particular relevance. The first concerns the relationship between trade liberalisation and privatisation policies and the enhancement, in the industry targeted for privatisation, of medium– to long–term competitiveness, including the strengthening of technology–related strategies and outlays. Unless the objective is simply and solely to organise the state's exit from this industry, such policies can only be successful if they are part of a broader industrial strategy aimed at ensuring that the appropriate conditions exist in the private sector allowing it to take over the responsibilities previously held by the public sector in a way which guarantees the viability of the industry in the long term.

In OECD countries of course one meets both positions: in some countries privatisation policies are commanded by an "exit is our priority and let the industry sink or swim by itself" approach; in others restructuring and recapitalising take place prior to privatisation, while the state keeps a small but strategic stake (directly or through a closely held consortium of national firms that it can talk to) to ensure that the group is not dismantled by the new proprietors. Brazil comes closer to the first pattern and Korea to one in which the future of the industry continues to be of considerable concern to the government after privatisation, even if the balance of power in the relationship of industry to the state has changed considerably and the chaebols seem to call the tune on many issues. Our comparative case study also suggests that when the process of privatisation is part of a broader framework of industrial policy, it will be viewed by the authorities as requiring transition phases and so a certain period of time will be allotted to carry it through.

The second conclusion is addressed to industrial economists and academics in business schools, as well as to policy–makers. It concerns the nature of the factors accounting for the competitiveness of firms. Elsewhere we have defended the notion of "structural" or "systemic" competitiveness (Chesnais, 1986; OECD, 1992) and argued that the competitiveness of firms should be viewed as comprising two inter–related yet distinct ingredients, those pertaining to their endogenous management capacity and those stemming from their national macroeconomic and meso–systemic environments. This seems pertinent to the case in hand. When one considers the way divergence in competitiveness, and the capacity to invest in tangible and even more clearly in intangible capital, gradually grew between the Korean and Brazilian industries after a fairly similar start, it is clear that this process cannot be attributed simply to microeconomic phenomena as they are generally understood. Nor has it to do, as in telecommunications, with the advent of a qualitative change in technology which one industry was capable of negotiating and the other not. In petrochemicals change has been incremental. It has taken place along the same basic trajectory for over 30 years, even if productivity increases and a great improvement in the quality of products have occurred.

The divergence in the performance and capacity for long–term viability between the two industries is the outcome of a series of important, often decisive, macroeconomic and meso–systemic phenomena which have transcended a basically identical capacity of engineers in these countries to manage their plants or go about the process of technological catching up in petrochemicals. Consider the use of capacity and the cash flows of the two industries in the 1980s and so the possibility of making technology–related investments. The Korean petrochemical industry belonged to an economy where the state had paid back the greater part of its long–term debt before international macroeconomic instability resulted from the second "oil shock" in 1979, the 1980–81 US recession and the 1982 Mexican crisis which triggered a depression in Latin America. In contrast, the Brazilian petrochemical industry, like the rest of the economy, was severely affected by the long debt–led recession of the 1980s, along with the effects of a difficult political transition. Consider the timetable and approach to privatisation and liberalisation. Korea is of course a country on which some outside political pressure can be brought, but it is not as open to the immense pressure from Washington–based agencies that Brazil was subjected to as a result of the vulnerability created by its huge external debt and the fiscal crisis of the state.

Turning to corporate–organisational and meso–systemic phenomena, at least two of these appear to have played a major role. The first relates to the factors (discussed in the last part of the section "Exports, Imports and Competitiveness"), ensuring in one case a strong pressure from domestic demand for increasingly sophisticated intermediate products and leading, on the contrary, in the other to a sourcing of such products by foreign firms outside the host economy. The second pertains to the differences between the chaebols and the Brazilian finance–dominated groups in which the petrochemical industry is housed. The chaebols are industrial mammoths in many respects; they lack organisational flexibility but have considerable financial flexibility and cash reserves. Even if they are slow to change their course, they have shown themselves to be very active in diversifying. However conservative their reactions may look, the chaebols possess at least one great virtue — not of their own making perhaps (since the state has kept the financial system well in hand till now) but very important nonetheless — namely that of not being finance–dominated in their strategic management and hence not "short–termish" in their investment behaviour. In the case of petrochemicals, all these attributes gave the chaebols, first, the aptitude to take the industry over quite early, from the public sector of course but also from foreign firms, and to run large vertically integrated sites under a single hierarchy; second, the will subsequently to finance very large new investments (on favourable conditions made possible by the state's continued control over investment capital and interest rates despite growing financial globalisation, but with a capacity to risk large projects) and also to start financing R&D despite all the uncertainties such investment has even when it is not at the "frontier of science".

By contrast the Brazilian groups that own plants in the petrochemical poles are essentially finance–led banking, industrial and service conglomerates. They have always had their eyes riveted on the short–term balance sheet. In recent years their main object of attention has been the rate of return on capital in international short–term financial markets. There are no signs that they have ever demanded to take the petrochemical industry over from the state or severely complained about the state's role. They were certainly quite satisfied in the late 1980s and early 1990s with the particular structure of costs and profits generated at different points in the technical production process. No private group has lined up as a candidate to run a site on an integrated basis in the way the chaebols do in Korea. All these groups have done is to make quite sure a privatised Petroquisa would not be in a position to do so. The willingness of the Brazilian private groups to help their affiliates in petrochemicals make large investments with slow rates of return now that the state is moving out remains to be proved (witness their attitude to technology).

All the differences we have discussed fall well outside the scope of microeconomics as it now practised. While they are rooted in history and so possess undeniable sociological dimensions, it is not acceptable that they be evacuated from economic analysis (put into the *ceteris paribus* cupboard) on these grounds. They must be brought back into the theory of economic development and so conceptualised, as the fathers of this discipline — Lewis, Nurkse, Rostow and others — had sought to do, before the "new–style" development economics of the 1970s took over and sterilised many vital issues.

Notes

1. Subsequently oil was discovered in the Atlantic off the Brazilian mainland and has been exploited by Petrobras, covering about a third of domestic demand.
2. See Chesnais (1994 and 1995) for a discussion of globalisation and international oligopolistic rivalry; see also Oman (1994).
3. On the issues raised in this section see Guinet (1985), Chesnais (1989) and Bozdogan (1990). Concerning earlier phases in the growth of the industry see Spitz (1988).
4. See Chesnais (1989).
5. The NIH laboratories and the centres funded by the Department of Energy in the United States, or again INSERM and the Institut Français du Pétrole in France are examples.
6. Japan currently has the lead in these PAN–based fibres.
7. Polycarbonate is a basic component in compact disks, for example.
8. Under its subsequent name Korea General Chemical Corporation, Chungju also represented the government in some of the negotiations preceding the establishment of the second petrochemical complex at Yeocheon.
9. Low–density polyethylene (LDPE), vinylchloride monomer (VCM), synthetic butadiene rubber (SBR), polypropylene (PP).
10. In Chapter 4 a similar story is told about state involvement in the Brazilian telecommunications equipment industry.
11. Regarding this strategy and its problems see the seminar work by Evans (1979 and 1981) and the interesting research by Roos (1991).
12. Referring to the story concerning Christopher Columbus' clever move in cutting off the top of an egg so that it would stand upright on a table.
13. The case study of the Brazilian petrochemical industry prepared for the project on Brazilian competitiveness (ECIB, 1993) notes that "the capacity of firms to adjust is limited by the organisation of the industry. The firms are monoproducers, geographically dispersed, undersized and lacking productive integration. They cannot compete with the world leaders of the sector. The structure of the industry prevents it from achieving required levels of competitiveness, even if efficiency in production has been attained" (Guerra, 1993).

14. See Chapter 4 in this volume for a comparison of the development of the telecommunications industry in Brazil and Korea.

15. Roos (1991, pages 89–92) contains a fascinating section entitled "Relative Power between National Entrepreneurs", which quotes Suarez (1986) giving examples of such meetings. In private conversations economic journalists refer to the oligopoly today as "the petrochemical mafia" that "play their own game behind closed doors".

16. This is the familiar designation of the "triple alliance" joint ventures.

17. See the synthesis paper on the chemical industry by F. Teixera (1993) for the project on Brazilian competitivenes (ECIB), section 2.1.2.

18. A strategy similar to that practised by Telebras in the Brazilian telecommunications industry. See Chapter 4 for further details.

19. This is an often overlooked drawback of the presence of foreign capital on a large scale, within an industrial system attempting to engage in a process of technological catching up.

Bibliography

A. General

BOZDOGAN, K. (1990), "The Tranformation of the US Chemical Industry", in *The Working Papers of the MIT Commission on US Industrial Productivity*, MIT, Cambridge, Mass.

CHESNAIS, F. (1986), "Science, Technology and Competiveness", *STI Review*, No. 1, OECD, Paris.

CHESNAIS, F. (1989), "Chapter 3: Petrochemicals", in C. Oman, *et al., New Forms of Investment in Developing Country Industries: Mining, Petrochemicals, Automobiles, Textiles, Food,* OECD, Paris.

CHESNAIS, F. (1994), *La Mondialisation du capital*, Collection Alternatives Economiques, Editions Syros, Paris.

CHESNAIS, F. (1995), "World Oligopoly, Rivalry between 'Global Firms' and Global Corporate Competitiveness", in J. MOLERO (ed.), *Technological Innovation, Multinational Corporations and New International Competitiveness*, Harwood Academic Publishers, Reading.

CORTEZ, M. AND P. BOBOCK (1984), *North–South Technology Transfer; a Case Study of Latin America,* Johns Hopkins University Press, London.

GUINET, J. (1985), *The Petrochemical Industry: Energy Aspects of Structural Change*, OECD, Paris.

OECD (1992), *Technology and the Economy: The Key Relationships*, Final report of the TEP, OECD, Paris.

SPITZ, P.H. (1988), *Petrochemicals, the Rise of an Industry*, Peter Wiley, London.

OMAN, C. (1984), *New Forms of International Investment in Developing Countries*, OECD Development Centre, Paris.

OMAN, C., *et al.* (1989), *New Forms of Investment in Developing Country Industries*, OECD Development Centre, Paris.

OMAN, C. (1994), *Globalisation and Regionalisation: The Challenge for Developing Countries*, OECD Development Centre, Paris.

B. Korea

Asian Chemical News, 5 Dec. 1994, "Asia's Next Order".

ENOS, J. AND W.–H. PARK (1988), *The Adoption and Diffusion of Imported Technology: The Case of Korea,* Croom Helm, London.

Kim S.–S. (1993), "The Role of the State in the Petrochemical Industry", *Journal of Social Science,* Vol. 3, No. 2 (in Korean), University of Ulsan, Korea.

Korea Development Bank (KDB) (1993), *Korean Industry*, (in Korean), KDB, Seoul.

Korean Institute for Industrial Economics and Trade (KIET) (1994), *The Vision and Development Strategy of the Korean Industry toward the 21st Century* (in Korean), KIET, Seoul.

Korea Petrochemical Industry Association (KPIA) (1977), *10 Year History of the Petrochemical Industry*: *1967–76* (in Korean), KPIA, Seoul.

Korea Petrochemical Industry Association (KPIA) (1994), *Statistics for the Petrochemical Industry*, KPIA, Seoul.

Park D.–H. (1993), *The Strategy of Technological Innovation in the Korean Chemical Industry* (in Korean), Science and Technology Policy Institute, Seoul.

Park S.–S. (1990), "The Current Status and Problems of the Korean Petrochemical Industry", *Petrochemicals,* June (in Korean).

Samsung Economic Research Institute (SERI) (1988), *The Structure and Prospects of the Chemical and Materials Industry* (in Korean), SERI, Seoul.

C. Brazil

Abiquim (1992), Associação Brasileira da Industria Química e Produtos Derivados, *Relatório Anual do SDI — 1994,* ABIQUIM, São Paulo.

Bastos, V. (1989), *A Questão Tecnológica nas Joint–ventures Petroquímicas Brasileiras,* Tese de Mestrado, Instituto de Economica Industrial, Universidade Federal do Rio de Janeiro.

BNDES (1994), Industria Petrochimica: Minuta para Discussao, documento interno, mimeo.

Coutinho, L. and J. Ferraz (1993), *Estudo da Competitividade da Indústria Brasileira,* Editora da UNICAMP/Papirus, São Paulo.

ECIB (1993), see Coutinho and Ferraz (1993).

Erber, F. (1995), *A Industria Petrochimica Brasileira : Regulacion e Desempenho*, Instituto de Economica Industrial, Universidade Federal do Rio de Janeiro, mimeo.

Erber, F. and R. Verhulm (1993), *Ajuste Estrutural e Estratégias Empresariais,* Instituto de Pesquisa Econômica Aplicada, Rio de Janeiro.

Evans, P. (1979), *Dependent Development of Multinational, State and Local Capital in Brazil,* Princeton University Press, Princeton, NJ.

Evans, P. (1981), "Collectivized Capitalism: Integrated Petrochemical Complexes and Capital Accumulation in Brazil", in T.C. Bruneau and P. Faucher, *Authoritarian Capitalism,* Westview Press, Boulder, Colorado.

Guerra, O. (1993), "Competitividade da industria petroquimica", sector study for the *Estudo da Competitividade da Indústria Brasileira* (see above Coutinho and Ferraz)

Oliveira, J. (1994), *Firma e Quase–Firma no Setor Industrial — O Caso da Petroquímica Brasileira,* Tese de Doutorado, Instituto de Economia Industrial, Universidade Federal do Rio de Janeiro.

Oliveira, J. (1990), "Desenvolvimento Technológico da Indústria e a Constituição de um Sistema Nacional de Inovação : o Setor Petroquímico", Fundação Economia de Campinas, mimeo.

Quadros, R. (1992), "Why the Market Reserve Is not Enough: Lessons from the Diffusion of Industrial Automation Technology", in H. Schmitz and J. Cassiolato, *High–Tech for Industrial Development: Lessons from the Brazilian Experience in Electronics and Automation*, Routledge, London.

Roos, W. (1991), *Shaping Brazil's Petrochemical Industry: The Importance of Foreign Firm Origin in Tripartite Joint Ventures*, PhD Dissertation, Catholic University of Nijmegen, published as study No. 60 by the Centre for Latin American Research and Documentation (CEDLA), Amsterdam.

Silva Filho, A. (1990), "A Empresa Estatal no Desenvolvimento da Petroquímica Mundial", Petroquisa, Rio de Janeiro, mimeo.

Suarez, M.A. (1986), *Petroquímica e tecnoburocracia : capitulos do desenvolvimento capitalista no Brazil*, Editora Hucitec, São Paulo.

Teixera, F. (1985), *The Political Economy of Technological Learning in the Brazilian Petrochemical Industry,* PhD Dissertation, University of Sussex, Brighton, UK.

Teixera, F. (1987), "Dinâmica Empresarial e tecnológica das Empresa do Complexo Petroquímico de Camaçari", em Associação Nacional de Pós–Graduação em Economia, *Anais 1987,* Vol. 1.

Teixera, F. (1993), "Competitividade do complexo quimico", synthesis sector report for the *Estudo da Competitividade da Indústria Brasileira* (see above Coutinho and Ferraz).

World Bank (1989), "Industrial Regulatory Policy and Investment Incentives in Brazil", Washington, mimeo.

VI

Competition Policies and Innovation Practices: How the Two Relate

Lynn Krieger Mytelka

The main conclusion that follows from our study is that there are, unfortunately, no "quick fix" solutions to the problems of how to achieve and maintain international competitiveness. While in some cases (but not necessarily all) competitive conditions may be necessary for the achievement and maintenance of international competitiveness, they are often not sufficient.

Our studies have shown that an important "intervening variable" that often mediates the relationship between competition and international competitiveness is innovative capability, that is, the ability to bring about improvements in processes, products, management routines and/or organisational structures. Furthermore, in some cases an innovative capability can develop in the absence of fully competitive conditions and, where it is sufficiently strong, this capability can lead to the achievement and maintenance of international competitiveness, as in the Korean telecommunications and, to a certain extent, the Indian pharmaceutical industries. Clearly, therefore, the relationships between competition, innovation and competitiveness are complex, certainly far more complex than suggested by much of the traditional literature which proposes that competitive conditions are both a necessary and a sufficient condition for the attainment and maintenance of international competitiveness.

But where does this conclusion leave the policy–maker struggling with these relationships and their policy implications? In addition to attracting the attention of policy–makers to the importance of innovation for competitiveness, the case studies presented here provide some empirical support for the position that policy dynamics, that is the interaction between policies and the behaviour of actors they are designed to affect, are critical in shaping policy outcomes with respect to innovation and competitiveness. A better understanding of both the changing mode of competition within industrial sectors and the attitudes, habits and practices of firms in these sectors, notably with respect to competition and innovation, would thus appear to be essential first steps in the policy design phase.

Windows of Opportunity for Technological Catch–up

Although innovation was a critical element in the competitiveness of firms in each of the four industries covered here, three sets of factors shaped the mode of competition in these industries and hence the opportunities for catching up and for sustaining competitiveness over time. These are the nature and pace of technological change, industry structure, and capital requirements at various stages in the production process. Three of these industries, for example, experienced technological ruptures — the introduction of numerical controls in the machine tool industry, digital switching in telecommunications and genetic engineering in pharmaceuticals. In the first two, however, the pace of technological change subsequently slowed down and technological change became increasingly engineering–based, opening windows of opportunity for developing–country firms with strong engineering capabilities to catch up. In bio–pharmaceuticals, the slowness in developing and certifying new biotechnology–based products also opened opportunities for those developing countries in which a strong scientific capability had begun to emerge. In contrast, the petrochemical industry did not undergo a technological rupture but rather a shift from standard to speciality chemicals and an intensification in the process of R&D–based product differentiation. This was accompanied by changes in organisation and scale which had a major impact on the cost structure of standardised petrochemical products, making it more difficult for developing–country firms to keep up.

While capital requirements and concentration in the machine tool industry were thus relatively low, the petrochemical and telecommunications equipment industries were both highly capital–intensive and oligopolistic, making it more difficult for smaller developing–country firms to catch up and to compete in international markets without financial, R&D and other kinds of support from the state. In bio–pharmaceuticals, small dedicated biotechnology firms initially proliferated, but, more recently, these have become the object of takeovers by large, globalised pharmaceutical firms, in large part because of the high capital requirements for R&D, clinical testing and marketing.

Although windows of opportunity thus opened in all four industries during the 1970s, both the process of catching up and more importantly that of keeping up[1] have required a continuous process of innovation as competitive conditions changed. This applied as much to innovation in products and processes which gave Chinese Taipei machine tool makers and Indian pharmaceutical firms an edge in export markets, as to changes in organisational routines. Such changes, however, did not move in a uniform direction. The ability to manage decentralised production through sub–contracting networks, for example, by the early 1990s, had become a key competitive asset in the machine tool industry[2]. In petrochemicals, the reverse was true. There, price competitiveness and the resources needed to move into newer, more dynamic segments of the industry came to depend increasingly on vertical integration, a point which favoured the Korean petrochemical industry relative to petrochemical firms in Brazil.

Not only did the nature and pace of innovation differ in these industries over time, but the rules of competition and hence the meaning of competitiveness also varied across these globalised industries as we moved from the 1970s to the 1990s. Price competition remained important in the machine tool industry, but is less indicative of competitiveness in oligopolistic industries such as petrochemicals and telecommunications, where firm size and economies of scale permit the small number of giant firms that dominate these industries to cross–subsidise across product lines and markets. A healthy dose of scepticism with regard to this traditional indicator of competitiveness is also required because of the considerable evidence that cost and price are dissociated and that the latter is linked rather more closely to the firm's strategic objectives[3].

Whether one succeeds in marketing costly telecommunications systems abroad also has less to do with standard notions of competitiveness as indicated by global market shares than one might imagine. This is primarily due to the high cost of switching and transmission equipment which make international sales impossible without external financing, and this invariably implicates home governments as lenders or guarantors. Politics thus plays an important role, and political pressures and inducements have become the cement that binds many deals not only in telecommunications but in other industries where capital costs are high[4].

Through globalisation new rules of competition and new barriers to entry are thus continuously being set, giving rise to uncertainties that bedevil the best laid plans of industrial latecomers. Nevertheless, some firms in these industries have been able to compete abroad. Paradoxically, however, market opening policies did not always contribute to this process as theory might lead us to expect. In the case of petrochemicals, for example, domestic market liberalisation during the early 1990s produced significantly different results in Korea and Brazil, both of which had formerly protected and regulated this industry. In contrast to their Brazilian counterparts, which have encountered growing difficulties, Korean petrochemical firms widened their product range and increased exports. Several of Korea's telecommunications equipment suppliers also appear to have responded better to market opening policies than did similar firms in Brazil. But not all of them did.

Policy Dynamics

Much of this variance, our studies suggest, can be explained, not by simple dichotomies such as open vs. closed markets or market vs. state but by the interaction of many disparate factors of which four stand out in particular. These are *i)* the type of market opening policies, their timing and sequencing; *ii)* the traditional habits and practices of firms with respect to competition and innovation and hence the differing policy dynamics[5] which result from the interaction between policies and the actors whose behaviour they are designed to influence; *iii)* the extent to which firms have access, either in–house or through local networks of innovation, to the critical complementary assets — technological capabilities and financing — needed to respond to the new policy environment; and *iv)* changes in technology and in the rules of competition which alter the set of opportunities and constraints for latecomer firms at different points in time. Of critical importance is the contingent nature of these factors.

Here the within–country experience is particularly revealing. Chinese Taipei machine tool and pharmaceutical firms emerged within a similar competitive domestic policy environment, but they exhibited significant differences in competitiveness over time. Machine tool makers, aiming at the low end of the export market as a point of entry, pursued a strategy of innovation based on continuous cost reduction, product simplification and quality improvement which enabled them to capture export market share by moving rapidly in behind Japanese machine tool exporters as the latter moved upscale. Chinese Taipei pharmaceutical firms were far less innovative. They formed joint ventures with larger foreign companies, licensed technology from abroad, reformulated drugs for the local market and lagged behind machine tool producers in developing in–house R&D capabilities or in linking to public sector research institutions.

These differences in strategy, moreover, cannot be attributed solely to the specific characteristics of the pharmaceutical industry, as a comparison with India reveals. Given the degree of regulation in India's domestic market, we might have expected that both Indian machine tool makers and pharmaceutical firms would be less innovative than their Chinese Taipei counterparts. With regard to large machine tool firms, this was certainly the case. Interviews with Indian pharmaceutical firms, however, showed that through in–house R&D, these firms had built up their export capacity in generic drugs over the 1980s and were quicker to invest in bio–pharmaceutical research in the 1990s than Chinese Taipei pharmaceutical firms. The absence of competition in the domestic market thus did not lead inevitably to a lack of competitiveness in local firms, as the contrasting ability of Indian bio–pharmaceutical and machine tool producers to meet local needs at affordable prices and/or to export illustrates. Nor does an open market alone generate competitiveness, as the lack of innovation or exports by Chinese Taipei pharmaceutical firms illustrates.

While the examples of Chinese Taipei and India in the machine tool and bio–pharmaceutical sectors appear to suggest that competition in export markets provides a greater stimulus to innovation and competitiveness in latecomer firms than does competition in the domestic market, not all firms respond to these stimuli in the same way. Consider the response to market opening policies by two large machine tool companies in India, the state–owned Hindustani Machine Tool Company and the private sector Kirloskar Electric Company; or, to broaden the discussion to include other sectors, consider the response of Korea's pre–eminent telecommunications equipment suppliers, Samsung and Goldstar, relative to other firms in this sector.

In both Korea and India domestic markets for machine tools and telecommunications were highly protected. State procurement policies, moreover, provided a guaranteed market for domestic telecommunications equipment suppliers in the former and for HMT in the later. During the catch–up phase and into the keeping–up phase, Korean telecommunications firms were also the privileged recipients of digital switching technology developed by a public sector research institution. HMT licensed much of the technology needed for newer generations of machine tools, including numerically controlled machine tools (NCMTs) from abroad. In terms of global prices or product design and flexibility, the output of these companies at the end of the 1980s was not competitive. None of these firms exported at that time.

During the 1980s, however, these four firms slowly built up their technological capabilities. In the case of Korea this was primarily a result of government pressure to participate in joint research on digital switching. In India it was induced by the changing requirements for NCMTs in the Indian defence sector. Despite the availability of in–house technological capabilities, complacency rather than innovativeness characterised the traditional habits and practices of these firms. What broke these traditional habits and practices was the particular type and sequencing of policy reforms in each country and the growing conviction that policy reform would not be reversed. In both India and Korea, tariff reductions were introduced very slowly and only after considerable domestic restructuring of industry had taken place.

In the Indian case, the government first delicensed the machine tool industry, enabling dynamic Indian newcomers to enter the market more easily and stimulating a restructuring of the domestic industry as locally owned firms became more competitive by reducing their product range, concentrated production and began to make greater use of sub–contracting networks. Then, in 1992, the government abolished import licensing in industrial inputs. This enabled dynamic local firms with some in–house R&D and engineering capability to import inputs such as controllers, servomotors and drives used to manufacture numerical controls for the machine tool industry more cheaply. When surging domestic demand for vehicles created a boom in NCMTs and Fanuc, which dominates the world market for numerical controls, began to produce locally, HMT and Kirloskar Electric were thus ready to compete and did so by bringing out cheaper controls. Throughout this period, import duties remained high[6].

Similarly in Korea, reforms were first aimed at transforming both the ownership structure and the regulatory environment of the telecommunications and petrochemical industries. In both industries privatisation resulted in the strengthening of locally owned firms, and not until policy reforms had begun to stimulate these firms to look for new ways of competing was the market opened to foreign competition. Even then, trade liberalisation was a gradual process stretched over four years, with firms informed in advance of the products that would be liberalised. In the telecommunications industry where international competitiveness required the development of a vastly more elaborate marketing structure capable of working with a host of corporate and institutional users across a wide range of countries, sustained support in the form of public sector R&D and export marketing assistance was a major asset for Korean firms. In contrast, Brazil's large telecommunications equipment suppliers were buffeted by the global restructuring strategies of their parent firms and by the radical change in government policies which left little time to adjust and even fewer resources with which to do so.

Promoting Competitiveness: Policy Guidelines

In sum, one cannot assume linearity in the relationship between competition and competitiveness. Instead, as the above analysis illustrates, the link between these two processes is intermediated by other factors, notably those that impinge on the process of innovation. Nor, in light of continuously changing international competitive conditions, would it be wise to regard competitiveness as primarily a short–term phenomenon[7] or one measurable solely by international prices and market shares. Yet shifting to a longer term, non–linear perspective implies that policy analysts will be obliged to pay greater attention to the underlying processes that sustain competitiveness and this, we have argued, involves a view of policies and their diverse impacts that is more contextually embedded and interactive, a focus that we have captured in the concept of "policy dynamics".

Empirical evidence from these case studies suggests that policy dynamics, that is the interaction between policies and the behaviour of actors they are designed to affect, are critical factors in shaping policy outcomes with respect to innovation and competitiveness. In contrast to much of the literature which tends to treat processes and economic actors as homogeneous and to offer standardised policy prescriptions across all industries[8], therefore, a non–linear, innovation–based approach to policy–making would require policy–makers to take two factors into consideration in the design of policies aimed at the promotion of competitiveness at the enterprise level. These are competitive conditions across sectors and within sectors over time, and the habits and practices of economic actors within those sectors with respect to competition and innovation. From such a perspective, moreover, greater attention must also be paid to the sequencing and timing of policies and the complementarity between them.

Consider the impact of market opening policies. Where the international industry was oligopolistic and foreign firms were able to reproduce this pattern within domestic markets, market opening policies alone were ineffective in generating the kind of competition that led to innovation and competitiveness. Market opening policies were much better able to stimulate innovation in situations in which local firms had passed through a lengthy period of apprenticeship marked by the building of a broad range of technological capabilities[9] followed by policy changes which stimulated the development of habits and practices of innovation and permitted some degree of domestic restructuring to take place prior to trade liberalisation. In the Indian machine tool and the Korean petrochemical and telecommunications industries these policies included a gradual process of deregulation and/or privatisation coupled with a variety of complementary policies that altered the trade–off between change and non–change of behaviour[10] for the actors concerned.

Although there are no simple rules that a policy–maker can follow with confidence to achieve the objective of international competitiveness, it is, nonetheless, possible to draw up what can be regarded as "rough guidelines" that can fruitfully be followed by policy–makers attempting to grapple with the issue of improving international competitiveness. It is in this spirit that we wish to propose that policy–makers work through the following steps.

Step One: What Are the Main "Drivers" of Competitiveness?

One of the important conclusions to emerge from our study is that different causal factors can drive competitiveness in different industries and that these can change over time. Furthermore, competitive conditions in the domestic market are not necessarily the most important driver of competitiveness. Emulation of Japanese practices and interaction with foreign clients, for example, were more important inducements to innovation and competitiveness in the Chinese Taipei machine tool industry; government regulations that limited the domestic appropriation of rents from patenting at the same time as they forced prices lower on the domestic market were greater stimuli to innovation and exports in the Indian pharmaceutical industry.

It is necessary, therefore, for the policy–maker to try to establish from the outset what the main drivers of competitiveness are. This, however, will be no easy task. In countries like Japan, Korea and Chinese Taipei, the task has involved close co–operation between government bureaucrats and policy–makers and key representatives from the private sector through a variety of fora.

Step Two: To What Extent Is Innovation Necessary for Competitiveness?

Once again, this is a question that will require a detailed understanding of the specificities of the particular industry at a particular point in time. Close co–operation between government bureaucrats and private sector decision–makers may be necessary to answer the question. In answering the question it will be important to tackle two related questions: What kind of innovation is necessary? And, what else, apart from innovation, is also necessary for competitiveness? For example, are cost of production and selling price the main drivers of competitiveness (which suggests that process innovations are likely to be particularly important)? Or is product quality, customisation or product differentiation more important (which suggests that product innovations are key)? Other factors such as after–sales service or the ability to manage sub–contracting networks or R&D partnerships may also be critical competitive assets that firms must acquire.

Step Three: Are the Innovation Processes That Are Necessary Already Taking Place Effectively under Existing Circumstances?

If the answer to this question is "yes", then nothing more will be needed as far as innovation is concerned. However, if the answer is "no", then a further question must be tackled: What policies are needed to facilitate the necessary innovation processes?

In the light of the understanding that will by this stage have been acquired of the industry in question, it is at this point that policy–makers must consider the habits and practices of targeted actors in this industry with respect to competition and innovation since policy dynamics resulting from the interaction of policies and the behaviour of actors in the industry are critical in shaping policy outcomes with respect to innovation and competitiveness.

Step Four: Will Increased Competition Result in the Kind of Innovation That Is Necessary?

As we have repeatedly stressed, an important finding of our study is that increased competition does not necessarily produce the kind of innovation that is needed for competitiveness. In some cases competitive pressures may be so severe as to act as a disincentive for innovation. If the answer to the question in Step Four is that increased competition will have the effect of producing the innovation that is needed, then the next logical question is, how can this competition be created? If, however, the answer is that increased competition will not produce the needed innovation, then the question becomes, what conditions are needed to produce this innovation? It is this possibility that lies behind the attention paid above to the timing and sequencing of domestic deregulation and market opening policies and to the development of complementary policies.

By working through these four steps and the related questions, policy–makers will be able to develop a solid knowledge base for the formulation of policies to stimulate innovation and competitiveness in local firms. However, as the case studies presented here have shown, while firms in the developing world can learn to compete on the basis of a continuous process of innovation, becoming innovative takes time. At the level of the firm it requires considerable investment in building technological capabilities, a process stimulated by both government policies and intensive interaction with international suppliers and clients. But to sustain the competitiveness of individual firms, a wide array of domestic linkages between users and producers and between the knowledge–producing sector (universities and R&D institutions) and the goods– and services–producing sectors of an economy are also needed. Governments can play an important role in supporting the development of such linkages and the underlying infrastructure that makes them possible.

Notes

1. The capabilities, critical knowledge inputs, policy objectives and useful partnership linkages associated with catch–up and keep–up strategies are discussed in Chapter 1.

2. Chinese Taipei machine tool firms, with an eye to Japanese practices, had adopted this organisational structure early on, and more innovative Indian machine tool companies began to follow suit in the early 1990s as deregulation and liberalisation changed competitive conditions within the domestic market (see Chapter 2).

3. Consider the bids submitted in Brazilian, Indian and Korean telecommunications tenders over a two year period in the mid–1990s. In November 1993, AT&T, widely regarded as the world's least–cost supplier of digital switches, entered a bid of less than $120 in Brazil, where it had yet to sell its switches, while Alcatel, Siemens and other locally based contenders bid in the range of $220–230. Six months later, in a tender in India, AT&T's bid was 30 per cent higher than Alcatel's and 20 per cent higher than Siemens'. The average price of AT&T switches sold in Korea in 1993, the year that company was awarded a share of the Korean switching market, was $207.58, well below the price at which Alcatel, Samsung and Goldstar switches were being sold, but double the price at which it sells in its own home market and nearly 75 per cent over its bid in Brazil.

4. Petrochemicals, energy and construction are other examples.

5. For a more detailed discussion of "policy dynamics" see Chapter 1.

6. They did, however, fall from 170 per cent in 1992 to 50 per cent in 1995 though the impact of this decline was mitigated by a 50 per cent devaluation in 1991 (see Chapter 2).

7. A point that is also emphasised by McFetridge (1995) in his review of the diverse meanings and measurements of competitiveness that have emerged over the past decade.

8. See, for example, Porter's generalised opposition to mergers, acquisitions and alliances in the chapter on "Government Policy" (Porter, 1990, 662–669). A notable early exception to this tendency was Henry Ergas, who wrote with respect to the scope and limits of technology policy that "[t]he first and most fundamental is the dependence of technology policy outcomes on their economic and institutional environment" (Ergas, 1987, 232).

9. Following Ernst, Mytelka and Ganiatsos (1998) these are understood to include at a minimum, production, investment, minor change, strategic marketing and linkage capabilities.

10. These included a broad spectrum of policies such as threats to withhold credit for expansion into new areas desired by these firms, support for export marketing, removal of price controls and financial incentives for R&D.

Bibliography

ERGAS, H. (1987), "Does Technology Policy Matter?", in H. BROOKS AND B.R. GUILE (eds.), *Technology and Global Industry*, National Academy of Engineering Press, Washington, D.C.

ERNST, D., L. MYTELKA AND T. GANIATSOS (1998), "Technological Capabilities — A Conceptual Framework", in D. ERNST, T. GANIATSOS AND L. MYTELKA (eds.), *Technological Capabilities and Export Success: Cases from Asia*, Routledge, London.

MCFETRIDGE, D. (1995), "Competitiveness: Concepts and Measures", Industry Canada Occasional Paper Number 5, Ottawa, April.

NELSON, R. (1993), "A Retrospective", *in* R. NELSON, R. (ed.), *National Innovation Systems: A Comparative Analysis*, Oxford University Press, New York.

PORTER, M. (1990), *The Competitive Advantage of Nations*, Free Press, New York.

OECD PUBLICATIONS, 2, rue André-Pascal, 75775 PARIS CEDEX 16
PRINTED IN FRANCE
(41 1999 07 1 P) ISBN 92-64-17091-X – No. 50849 1999